To my wife, Peg, who has shared

a unique journey with me and shown me so

much about the shatterproofing elements

I wrote about in this book.

# CONTENTS

# ACKNOWLEDGMENTS

Several people helped me write this book, probably more than they know. Thanks to Tracy Todd, Ph.D., and my friend John Lane for their early suggestions and encouragement. Their understanding of the marketplace helped shape this work. I want to thank my former professor, Waymon Hinson, Ph.D., and colleague Karin Jordan, Ph.D., for reviewing an early rough draft and making suggestions.

I also want to thank Kirsten, whose story appears in this book more than once (under a pseudonym)—who is living proof that the ideas in this book are powerful and life-changing. And finally, thanks to my wife, Peg, for believing in me, believing in my work, and proofreading these pages countless times.

# INTRODUCTION

*W*hy another book on marriage? Bookstore shelves are full of them. But none of these books get to the real root of the divorce problem: people do not have the basic elements needed in their marriage to begin with. All marriages must have the right personal character, an understanding of what it is to love for better or for worse, and good habits for identifying problems and solving them effectively. It is ultimately a lack of one or more of these vital elements that creates marital problems and keeps people stuck in them. And all of that character starts with what you believe.

This is what makes or breaks the therapy process in my own secular counseling practice. We live in a society that craves quick fixes, but deep down, people want real answers that will make *the* difference. The available books simply aren't "difference-makers." My book is not a quick-fix book of "how-to's." Instead, it's a book full of "have-to's" with clear directions of *how* to do them. It's a book that exposes, in clear terms, the *internal* changes needed for a shatterproof marriage, then shares what those changes will *look* like when put into action. It's a book that shows the beliefs, attitudes, and actions required when the going gets tough in marriage. And it exposes the three key elements of a shatterproof marriage required to sustain you.

In my more than twenty years as a licensed marriage and family therapist and as an approved supervisor of marriage and family therapy with the American Association for Marriage and Family Therapy, I can safely say that I've seen it *all*. Day after day, I meet with people who have exaggerated expectations, a weak heart of character, and lives based on myths. Their marriages, at least on a bad day, can become a tangled mess. Outside my office are the majority of couples living with a false sense of security in their marriage. Things are relatively stable until life throws them a major curve ball. Most people do not understand the heart needed to rise above many of life's challenges, so they are unprepared when adversity hits.

Everyone wants to be "happy," but exactly what is happiness, and how can we find it and hold on to it? Professionals are recognizing what I am talking about here. In the November/December 2006 issue of *Family Therapy Magazine* (published by the American Association for Marriage and Family Therapy), the theme of the magazine was "Happiness." Of the five articles, four were wrestling with the above question, and the fifth addressed the importance of character as it related to being happy.

I could not find a self-help book *anywhere* to recommend to my clients that would really address what is going on within their hearts and, consequently, their marriages! So I decided to write one that cuts to the chase and touches the central nerve of the very problems I see: self-defeating beliefs leading to self-defeating attitudes and behaviors. The broad array of resources I use range from survivor personalities, to oncologists' experiences with patients, to psychological literature and the Bible—a unique and innovative blending of references. My more than twenty years of clinical experience and real stories of clients corroborate the ideas referenced from other sources. In the last several chapters, we follow one client's progress throughout as I describe specific tools used in marriage therapy. It is all integrated and woven into a single presentation of what it takes to shatterproof your marriage.

With all of the existing guidance out there, the divorce rate in the United States has been staggeringly high for years—by most estimates, at least 50 percent of first marriages end in divorce. The failure rate is still higher for second marriages, which post a 60 to 70 percent divorce rate. Here's another statistic: a 2003 Harris Poll found that fully 90 percent of Americans believe in God.[1] Worldwide, one estimate suggests that there are about 2.1 billion people who identify with Christianity, or 33 percent of people who claim any religious allegiance. This is nearly a billion people more than the next closest religion, which is Islam.[2] If that is really the case, and if all these books tell people what they need to know, how can we still be having so many failed marriages? Obviously, something is still seriously missing. The divorce problem has been an insidious epidemic for a long time now. It's past the time for treating symptoms and focusing on prevention—what we all need is an accurate diagnosis and a *cure* for what is really going wrong. I wrote this book with Christians in mind; however, I really wrote this book for those billions of people who claim allegiance to Christianity.

This book is the difference between a fad diet and a serious lifestyle change. It walks you, from start to end, through virtually all the *types* of issues I encounter in my clinical practice with typical couples. I give you real solutions to these issues by challenging you to work through the self-defeating attitudes, personality tendencies, past family influences, and expectations that contribute to any hint of vulnerability in your character. This book gives you specific therapy tools used in my clinical practice—the *best of the best*—after you wrestle with the challenge of changing your outlook. The primary point of the book is that techniques, a better sex life, new communication skills, enrichment ideas, fads, good research—and even the best "how-to's" in the world—do nothing if you do not have the right character to drive your efforts.

As a "brief therapist" trained to find concrete solutions as quickly as possible, I don't like to waste people's time with lofty platitudes or catchy quick-fix gimmicks. Therefore, I have designed a number of tools that I use daily and with great success in my clinical practice, and which I share with you. They reflect the sum of my clinical practice combined with all of my professional reading.

Many marital issues seem impossible. Either your spouse is unreasonable or you can't see how a solution can be anything outside of what you have visualized. Obviously, it takes two to tango, but you can dance for a long time even with a clumsy dance partner who steps all over your toes. If necessary, you can choose to be the lead dancer. Ultimately, a marriage is just that. It's the union of two people who care about each other enough to get involved in finding solutions and a meaningful connection. That, along with an open heart, is really all it takes if you have the right direction.

There are three primary elements every marriage must have to become shatterproof. Here are the three elements addressed in this book:

✓ **Element #1:** The right character
Build all personal character based on things you can count on.

✓ **Element #2:** The right kind of love
Truly love for better or for worse.

✓ **Element #3:** The right spirit
Always find a way to turn every problem into a solution.

As I said earlier, I'm not interested in a bunch of gimmicks and tips to make your marriage more interesting, exciting, or intimate. What I provide is a comprehensive guide to make your marriage virtually invincible. Whether you are having problems now or not, this book is for you. Most people give up on the process long before they should. I urge you to open your mind and heart like never before. Decide you are willing to venture out and consider a new way of being. Start *right now*.

# The Right Character

*Build all personal character
based on things you can count on.*

he difference between carbon dioxide and carbon monoxide is actually very small—one atom. One gives life and the other kills. The extra atom of oxygen is what makes the carbon dioxide compound essential for our blood to function properly. There are a total of 117 chemical elements, such as oxygen and hydrogen; various combinations of these basic elements make up our planet. These elements cannot be broken down into other chemical substances and maintain their properties. There are lots of chemical compounds in the universe, but a relatively limited number of elements. Some elements are far more common and vital than others, like oxygen, hydrogen, and iron, for example. Without these more common elements, our survival would be in immediate jeopardy. Radium is an element that is not nearly so critical. It was used in the mid-1900s as paint for clocks and watches.

What in the world does this have to do with marriage, you say? A lasting marriage is the same. After decades of being married myself and working as a marriage therapist, I have discovered three vital elements that have the properties necessary to create a shatterproof marriage. The first element, which we explore in the next several chapters, is personal character. The character you bring into your marriage sets you up to succeed or fail before you even get started. It is common for married couples to come into my counseling office and expect me to dive right in and fix things right away: give them a couple of tools, tell them what the problem is, and how to go home and make things better. Blaming and finger-pointing is also something I have to contend with, day in and day out.

By far, the vast majority of people have not examined themselves well enough to see how their personal character impacts everything that goes on in their marriage. Rachel was just such a person. Just twenty-five, she had already been married several years and had a young daughter. Her husband, Jack, not unlike so many men these days, had become addicted to pornography. In his case, however, he would even injure himself with self-stimulation. This had a terrible effect on their physical intimacy, as she felt like he was always thinking of someone else. He also had a lot of unresolved issues from his childhood that he brought into their marriage. He shut down if there was conflict, did not help around the house, spent most of his free time on the computer, and tended to have explosive outbursts when he got angry.

Both were regular churchgoers, although Jack was on the fringes of what church was all about. Rachel had good intentions and was reluctant to admit she wanted a divorce, but she was ready to walk out of the marriage by the time she made it into my office. Hurt, angry, dejected, and hopeless, all she could do was focus on how bad things had gotten between them. She had tried yelling, taking all the initiative in the marriage herself, biting her tongue. Nothing seemed to make any difference. Rachel was not smart enough or powerful enough to control the situation and get the result she so desperately wanted.

Then a friend gave her a copy of this book. Within just the first few chapters, she realized that her own character was being put to the test. Instead of leaving, she decided she had to stay and fight for the marriage. She became quick to look first at herself before seeing Jack's faults. This one significant change was so noticeable it paved the way for Jack to start owning up to his own problems, which he did.

Real change was now possible and beginning to happen.

# 1

# See Opportunity
# in Adversity

*Whenever I feel the urge to exercise
I lie down until it goes away.*

Mark Twain

our life is now.

Every moment of your life is a new opportunity to be better than you were. Your attitude, outlook, and the way you relate to everything around you defines who you are. Some of these moments are big ones; most are small and happen often, even minute to minute. What you do with these moments speaks volumes about you. They say who you really are and how much strength of character you have. In other words, the way you respond to life's defining moments tells the rest of the world, and more importantly you, what kind of character you have.

Marriage tests your character every day. Your marriage could be unhappy and full of problems, or it might be sailing along smoothly. Your contribution might be highly noticeable, or the routine of life may cover up how you are living your married life. But I guarantee you, even a quiet *lack* of action speaks volumes about your personal character. Element #1 is about having

3

the right personal character. That starts long before you are married and is not confined just to your marriage once you are.

Stan and Marsha can tell you all about how important this first element is in marriage. Both in their second marriages, they had been married for eleven years and raised the young children from their previous marriages together. It was not without an occasional bump, but overall life had gone along very well. They became empty nesters at a relatively young age and decided it was time to have some real fun together. They planned trips, had cocktails in the hot tub, and basically did whatever they felt like doing whenever they wanted to do it. Every weekend they looked forward to drinking beers and getting pretty tipsy, since they never drank during the child-rearing years. One night Marsha had perhaps one too many, and she unleashed an explosive fit on Stan. This was highly uncharacteristic for her. Then it happened the next week, and then again the next. Marsha insisted she had no idea why she would do such a thing, alcohol or not.

After several counseling visits, she discovered that she was angry and resentful at Stan over the way he overlooked some outrageous behaviors of his twenty-year-old daughter. Among other things, she lied and stole money from them. Upon further exploration, it turned out that Stan had a horrible childhood. The family moved an average of four times a year all through elementary school. He wanted so badly for his daughter to have everything he did not have, he raised her to be spoiled and unprepared to have to work for things. Marsha did not agree with this approach, but her earlier experiences with conflict made her shy away from any big disagreement. She became convinced that Stan, being so sensitive about his daughter, would blow up at her if she even voiced honest feelings.

You see, both of these partners shied away from uncomfortable situations for years, and it was finally catching up with them. Their avoidance turned into a unique kind of dance in their marriage, producing some habits that were very destructive and hard to break. What was needed was for both to step up and bring a stronger character to their marriage. Stan had to face the anxiety of letting his daughter fall on her face since she would not listen to him. Marsha had to face her fear of Stan and speak with honesty to him. They had reached a huge defining moment in their marriage. It could have been avoided if they had responded to all the small, daily, defining moments during all those child-rearing years.

There are tons of real-life marriage examples in this book. Before we get too deep into them, this chapter challenges you to start looking at *you*. What kind of person are you bringing to the marriage? Are you tough, or would you just rather avoid adversity? At the end of the chapter, you will have an opportunity to take inventory of your own personal character within your marriage. If you don't start there, all the "get well quick" ideas in other marriage books don't mean a thing.

## KEY ATTITUDE:
**See opportunity in adversity and expect positive things.**

Some people call life's defining moments "growth opportunities." We find them in every part of life, not just in marriage. To bring the right character into your marriage, you have to be facing adversity in every other part of your life—your job, friendships, driving on the highway, in the retail store. We all know people who are a breath of fresh air everywhere they go. Maybe you're one of them. But I haven't met anyone yet who doesn't have some areas of personal weakness, and that's where strength of character becomes most important.

There are all kinds of techniques, gimmicks, tools, therapy, and self-help materials to make you a better person, marriage partner, public speaker, employee, parent, and so on. You might even get pretty good at building your skills and this may serve you quite well. But how many stories have we heard of accomplished doctors who see their patients only in scientific terms, and the cures involved something deeper and more intangible? There is more to you than just the sum of your abilities.

Back in 1991, I was working in central Florida and worked twenty hours a week on the cancer ward of a general hospital. My job was to offer support and counseling to any cancer patient who was interested. I also visited a couple of outpatient oncology offices daily, making my "rounds" for support counseling. One day a patient who had advanced bone cancer wanted to see me. She suffered from chronic pain, all day, every day. She wanted help coping with her pain. Up to this point, her doctor had been prescribing pain medication but it was not working as well as she wished. I spent some time getting to know Martha, especially some of the biggest disappointments and stresses in her life. One thing became clear in talking with her: she had been used to being self-sufficient and highly independent. Her illness and pain was an enormous barrier to this. That day I asked Martha to focus on some of the strengths she already had. We spent a lot of time talking about the power of her subconscious mind, and I told her she had more control than she gave herself credit for. I shared with her a story of how a woman named Wanda had similar pain and she had learned that no one could be perfectly self-sufficient. So Martha was receiving two messages—she could feel reassured things were okay despite the pain, and absolute self-sufficiency was impossible so don't want it so badly. This was all communicated in a hypnosis session, which enabled us to access her subconscious thoughts.

Our session ended, she thanked me, and we went about our days. The next week I saw her in the office again, and she reported to me that she had no pain for a week! None at all! She had confirmed bone cancer throughout her body. Well, I didn't see her for three or four months, so when I did I was interested to see how long this lasted before the pain returned. The pain never did return! Was it really my incredible talent? No, not at all. Martha's cancer was a major defining moment in her life and she had become stuck. With some help, she was able to adopt a new, healthier view of herself and life that even eliminated physical pain. Before that, she and everyone around her was blind to what the real problem was. She had a heart that was open to new ideas, changed her view of life, and began to *live differently*.

A similar thing happened to the apostle Paul when he converted to Christianity, only this involved God moving directly in his life. He was threatening and murdering Christians after the rulers of the day ordered Jesus crucified. As he was traveling and gathering up Christians, a bright light flashed around him and God asked him why he was persecuting Him. Paul was then literally blind for three days until Ananias laid his hands on him. God filled him with his spirit that day and the Bible says that something like scales fell from his eyes. Paul could finally see clearly—not only physical things but also who God was and what life was really about. God will enable you to navigate through life's defining moments too, but you have to want it.

These examples reveal one simple truth. It's your *attitude*, as seen in your actions—or lack of them—that make you and your marriage what they are. The only way to have a shatterproof marriage is to consider a major attitude adjustment and put it into action. The fact is, if you believe in God and get to know Him, your overall view of life comes into focus. You realize that giving more than you receive in life *always* results in something greater than you.

> There is one primary thing that enables people to overcome any marital challenge: the amount of "heart" they have based on their strength of character.

## YOUR HEART IS THE TRUEST MEASURE OF WHO YOU REALLY ARE

Years of doing marriage therapy with a variety of people has shown me without any doubt that we are all basically the same despite some obvious differences. You are unique yet you are no different from me. You are unique in your life experiences, cultural values, ethnic background, skin color, financial status, religious beliefs, and political views. Those things are important for us to consider when working out differences. Yet there is one primary thing that enables people to overcome any marital challenge: the amount of "heart" they have based on their strength of character. You could be Hispanic, African American, or Caucasian, but how you respond to problems is the key no matter who you are.[1] I'll share some valuable marriage tools later, but they just don't work without this ingredient. I have had numerous marriage-counseling clients who became quite skilled with some communication tools and anger-management techniques. But when their defining moments come up at home, the skills don't get applied. Their view of life is wrong. Sometimes paying therapy clients do not do homework assignments even when they agree it would make a huge difference. There's an attitude there that is sometimes hard to get to and is hard to quantify, but it makes all the difference.

## Key Attitude:
### All things are possible.

I am a big Saturday afternoon college-football fan. Have you ever wondered how teams with great talent get beat by teams that are obviously weaker? I have! Don't they want to win? I've wondered this for years and have had discussions about it with lots of people. Finally I asked a friend of mine who played football at Auburn University back in the early seventies. I asked him why he thought this was such a common thing in football. His answer is the only answer that has ever made sense: "What sets one team apart from another is how much heart they have. They are comprised of individual players with all kinds of heart." He should know. He is only about 5'11" and had to play against much bigger players as a lineman! To this day, he holds some athletic records in Alabama. When things get tough, you can give in or refuse to give in.

Later in the book I'll share some valuable tools for your marriage, but without heart they won't go very far. Proverbs 4:23 says to "Watch over your heart with all diligence, for from it flow the springs of life." If you and your spouse work at growing a big heart patterned after the character of God, your marriage will endure anything.

## DEFINING MOMENTS ALWAYS
## INVOLVE SOME KIND OF CHOICE

Sometimes it's the choice to learn a lesson or it could be a choice about what to do next. These choices often come up when we are faced with some kind of adversity. But even your successes are defining moments, for it's also what you do with success that reveals your true character. If you don't develop strong character out of your successes, how can you hope to be prepared when bad things happen? Some people gloat, get cocky, or don't remember where blessings really come from. The fact is, any earthly blessing can be taken away in an instant. There are thousands of hurricane victims from New Orleans who can testify to that. If you don't acknowledge where your blessings come from, you may not have the heart to "answer the bell" when those tough times come. The Bible tells us that every good thing bestowed and every perfect gift is from God.[2]

Christopher Reeve (the actor who played Superman) was on top of his acting career when he suffered a life-changing horse-riding accident. He was strong, good-looking, athletic, and popular as an actor. The accident paralyzed him and he never did regain his ability to move. This whole period in his life became one big, defining moment. There were also a bunch of small moments daily. Like it or not, he had to make a choice, then keep making that choice every day. He could choose either to become a cripple and approach each day like one, or choose to use this situation as an opportunity for another day of life fully lived. He not only maintained his marriage with a beautiful wife, but he even continued doing some work in the movie industry! He became an inspiration to people with all sorts of debilitating conditions. One thing is sure—Reeve did not live a life without character before the accident and his earlier movie success did not go to his head. Otherwise he would have been unprepared to rise above his situation once his big moment of truth arrived.

Dr. Bernie Siegel, a well-known surgeon and author who gave hope to his patients in addition to medical treatment, puts it this way in reference to terminal cancer patients: "Even if what you most hope for—a complete cure—

doesn't come to pass, the hope itself can sustain you to accomplish many things in the meantime. Refusal to hope is nothing more than a decision to die."[3] Is this just another appeal to think positive, or does a big heart—proven character—make a measurable difference in your life? It has actually been shown that positive and negative expectations have opposite effects on the amounts of cortisol and prolactin in your blood. These are the hormones most important for activating your immune system.[4] That can and often does fight off cancer cells!

What do you suppose might happen if you applied this attitude to your marriage? Don't you think marriages develop cancers too? By believing some incredible things might be possible, you are strengthening the immune system of your marriage.

## KEY ATTITUDE:
### Be willing to face the pain.

Children who are resilient under adverse conditions come from families that define expectations clearly about life and go after them in positive ways.[5] In fact, the reason these children are studied in the first place is that their resiliency flies in the face of what we would expect—a lifetime of problems due to their adverse conditions. Positive expectation is the result of character strength. Your character grows one choice at a time with all the opportunities life gives you. Just think what is possible if you apply this to every area of your life!

This may sound inspirational, and it should, but most of us are tempted to take the easy road when life wants a piece of us. Oftentimes, we'd rather avoid the issue, give in to our impatience, rationalize why something isn't fair, allow a situation to stay mediocre, insist on life meeting our rigid expectations, get carried away with our egos, not allow our comfort zone to be stretched. But if you want true character, you must be ready to face some pain. The key point here?

Don't run from uncomfortable things. Instead, face them with courage and address them openly. Think about the things in your marriage that cause the most pain. Write them down, then talk openly with your partner about them. Listen to your partner about his or her pain. This might be painful, but it's like cleaning a wound. Take the pain!

**KEY ATTITUDE: It's important to look at yourself honestly.**

If someone asked you to describe your comfort zone honestly in every major part of your life, could you do it? When do your responses start to become less consistent and predictable—and helpful—in your job? When the company pressures you for results despite what it does to you and other people, do you give in to the pressure instead of doing what your heart tells you is right? If your marriage partner is too confrontational for you to be comfortable, do you just retreat into yourself? Life is just full of encounters that test us for who we are. A later chapter will explore how we develop some of our attitude and behavioral habits so you can see more specifically what your comfort zones are. Once you're more aware of them you will be better able to let them stretch in defining moments.

There are two roads to building character. There are shortcuts and there are established, reliable routes. Shortcuts are great, but when they backfire it can create a real mess. The shortcut is actually easy at first and gives the illusion you are getting somewhere fast, but it isn't long before people sometimes realize it was a mistake. It's full of bumps and curves and often gets you lost. Sometimes you might even get lucky and get where you want to go. But in the case of character development, shortcuts *always* end up a dead end.

Avoiding pain and discomfort simply postpones the inevitable. An athlete who doesn't train enough eventually has to face the consequences of his inaction. Then when it's time to compete, he stands no chance against his opponent. A football team that loses the first couple of games due to poor conditioning has dug itself into a hole. So just doing the necessary work ahead of time makes more sense and in the long run leads to maximum success.

Every time you miss an opportunity to let a situation build up your character, your character begins to atrophy. God wants you to have character that you pattern after him. He created you this way, and if you live selfishly and only for the moment, it damages your ability to think with a godly perspective. If this goes on long enough your heart turns selfish. Selfishness gets us nowhere, then we begin to lose hope. Once hope is lost, there won't be any positive expectation when adversity comes. It really comes down to knowing the right thing but not doing it.

Instinctively, we know whether something is right or wrong, constructive or destructive. The Bible says that some unbelievers knew instinctively what God said was the right thing to do, that it was written in their hearts. Furthermore, their own conscience confirmed this to them and the thoughts that filled their minds showed where their hearts really were.[6] If you choose to respond to small adversities by serving primarily yourself, they add up. You develop mental, behavioral, and even emotional habits based on this kind of heart.

## IF ONLY WE WOULD BELIEVE THAT GREAT AND "IMPOSSIBLE" THINGS ARE POSSIBLE!

History is full of one example after another that should convince us to pursue character with every fiber of our being. Facing our biggest fears and pains leads to great things! People have survived incredibly threatening situations by keeping their wits about them *and believing they could survive*. They faced their own fears, self-doubts, and tendency to get tired and give up.

In 1992, Colby Coombs was on vacation with friends in Alaska. At twenty-five, he was a highly experienced climber. They were trying to establish a new route up Mount Foraker, a 17,400-foot mountain. A storm moved in, creating an avalanche. Knocked unconscious, Colby woke up six hours later to find both his friends dead. He broke his shoulder, ankle, and two vertebrae in his neck. It took him four days just to work his way back down the mountain. He reported that the only way he could do this was to ignore the pain. Then he had to hike five miles to find help.[7]

History is also full of examples illustrating how many people don't rise to the occasion when faced with challenges. How many of those people can you name? Who has written a book about medical patients who give up, die prematurely, and become famous for it? No one. Thousands of years ago, God's people continued in their unbelief despite all kinds of signs God had done in their midst.[8] We've all heard of Solomon, King David, and Samson—but no one knows the names of any of those other people. History is overflowing with examples of the power of belief. Jesus was talking with a family who had an epileptic boy (or perhaps he was troubled by an evil spirit). The family asked Jesus to please help them if He *could*. This floored Jesus, who told them, "All things are possible to him who believes." If you believe, and if you believe in the power of God, there just isn't anything in the universe that can stand in your way.[9]

I blew out my knee several years ago and had to have knee ligament surgery. Like any major surgery, the pain afterward is pretty unbelievable. But the doctors wanted me rehabbing within the first twenty-four hours, starting with the smallest of tasks. During several months of this process I encountered many other people going through the same rehabilitation. It was amazing to me how many people refused to face the pain and consequently did not make much progress. I met people who had been rehabbing for a year who could only bend their knee halfway!

Don't let that happen to your marriage. Rise above the culture of mediocrity. If I have convinced you that you want to be more than you have been in your marriage, the first step to take is to assess just how big the job is going to be. If it's a big job, don't lose heart! The rest of this book will show you how to change all that. Take the following inventory, answering the questions with as much honesty as you can. If you have a good score, this book will be a refresher and an encouragement. If your score is not so good, prepare yourself for an exciting journey of growth and blessing that will come out of some important changes in your life.

# Marital Heart Meter

Think about how consistently you live with the following attitudes in your marriage. Answer each question with a 1, 2, 3, or 4. Your answers *should* be the same as if you included situations outside your marriage (such as work relationships and friendships). If they are different, ask yourself why (this could be important). Be as honest as you can with yourself.

### HOW MUCH I THINK AND ACT THIS WAY

| 1 | 2 | 3 | 4 |
|---|---|---|---|
| Usually like me | Somewhat like me | Somewhat unlike me | Usually unlike me |

_____ 1. I think there is opportunity in adversity and positive things can come from it.

_____ 2. I look at myself honestly on a daily basis to consider any changes I need to make.

_____ 3. I am good at knowing what my emotions are and am in control of them at all times.

_____ 4. I love with little thought to what I am going to get out of it.

_____ 5. I think of others before myself as a matter of habit in any kind of situation.

_____ 6. I make a conscious effort to consider the thoughts and feelings of others in all my interactions.

_____ 7. Having put thought into it, I know the difference between my wants and needs in my relationships.

_____ 8. When it really comes down to it, life owes me very little and I am truly entitled to very few things.

_____ 9. I am comfortable admitting when I am wrong and apologize.

_____ 10. I accept my partner fully, faults and all.

_____ 11. I am quick to compromise when it will solve a problem.

_____ 12. I take the time to do the things most people would rather not have to do, even if I get no recognition for it.

_____ 13. I am open and honest at all times with my partner, including my thoughts, intentions, and feelings.

_____ 14. I want to know the truth about myself, measuring that against what God expects of me.

_____ 15. I have taken time out to learn how God thinks and have worked at making that the way I think.

_____ 16. My life clearly reflects lots of time and energy invested in making my marriage everything it can be.

_____ 17. I know what it would take to make me want to give up in my marriage and have found ways to keep making positive efforts anyway.

_____ 18. I have learned to accept the things in life that I cannot change, and apply this in my marriage.

_____ 19. I give my partner the benefit of the doubt, even during the hardest of times.

_____ 20. Setbacks and failures in my marriage relationship do not alter my behavior significantly.

_____ **TOTAL SCORE**

# Scoring

Add up your score for all the questions and put your total score above.

**20–25**  **Exceptionally Tough Heart.** Though not many, some situations will still be challenging. Those should be your focus. Few people have hearts this tough.

**26–32**  **Strong Heart.** You have mostly strengths. You could have one or two major weaknesses that lead to big relationship problems. You have a very good foundation from which to build. A minority of people have hearts this strong.

**33–39**  **Average Heart.** You have many definite strengths, but your heart needs to be strengthened considerably in key areas. Under the best of circumstances, you could go for a long time without serious problems. But with adversity, you will likely have a tough time navigating through it without contributing to the problem yourself. Your marriage has definite chinks in its armor and could be uprooted with certain challenges of life. The majority of people have these hearts.

**40–48**  **Unconditioned Heart.** Your heart has atrophied in at least a couple of very important ways, leaving you with clear weaknesses that could result in disaster. You are not able to withstand the rigors of any major tests to the heart of your marriage. Your condition is urgent.

**49–80**  **High-Risk Heart.** This range represents a serious condition that requires immediate, emergency attention. There are a large number of habits and attitudes that must change for your marriage to have much chance of long-term success.

I know what you are thinking. The "grading scale" is too tough, you say. But think about it. Which one of these characteristics could you be weak in during a major life crisis and still be okay? Jerry and Liz can certainly relate. They were a very well-educated couple who were considering marriage. They were caring, considerate, and mature people in their early thirties. But they kept having arguments over what they called silly things, and just could not understand why. Rightly so, they were concerned that maybe marriage would not be a good idea. It turned out that one of the biggest bones of contention was that Jerry, who was very sociable and outgoing, became frustrated with Liz because she did not act like the life of the party at social gatherings. Liz was actually very charming and warm, just not particularly outgoing. They were stuck on #10 of the Marital Heart Meter! After lots of work, Jerry just could not accept Liz for who she was. She finally got tired of it and took a job transfer out of state. That's the end of their story. Just think if they had gotten married and Jerry would not accept her for who she is! It was a huge character weakness on his part.

And remember, the bigger the crisis, the bigger your strengths have to be. Did you know that there is an annual marathon run at Mount Everest? The start of the race is at 17,000 feet! Even well-conditioned athletes begin to stagger at 14,000 feet because of the thin air—and that is just from walking! Marriage can be and often is a tough thing. It's for life. Don't be fooled into thinking you can make it to the finish line without lots of serious preparation. You will find yourself "dropping out" of the race well before it's over. No one wants to start something they can't finish. With adequate preparation, however, others have shown us we are capable of some incredible things.

Simply put, it's the size of your heart that counts. You have to believe that defining moments come your way every day and that rising to the occasion each and every time does make a difference. Admit the fact that you really do have choices every day. Be honest about what those choices are. As we were raising our kids, my wife constantly asked our children what kind of people they wanted to be. Not what kind of work they wanted to do, but what kind of people they wanted to be. I saw a couple on the verge of divorce because the stepdaughter was becoming too frustrating for Joan, the stepmother. Joan was becoming mean and it was breaking up the marriage. Then one day she came in and all was good again. I couldn't believe it! So I asked her what in the world happened. Her answer? "John, I realized I didn't want to be that kind of person, so I stopped behaving that way." It was just that simple!

I hope that by now you are encouraged to "sign up for the race" and begin training no matter what your score is. If your score was above average, it is still important to examine every last aspect of yourself and eliminate any possible weakness. If your score was below average, begin with those areas that seem to cause the most distress. Even a small improvement in just one area can set in motion a series of very positive changes. After completing the book, answer these questions again to see if you have made some changes. Use these questions to set some long-range goals for yourself.

There are many more attitudes shared in this book. A summary of them can be found in the Summary and Conclusion at the end of the book. This vital first element—personal character—must *never* be taken too lightly. Don't give in to the doldrums of habit. Decide today to do whatever it takes to "be all you can be." Then, and only then, will you begin the journey toward having the heart of a shatterproof marriage.

## Main Chapter Attitudes

✓ See opportunity in adversity and expect positive things.
✓ All things are possible.
✓ Be willing to face the pain.
✓ It's important to look at yourself honestly.

# ATTITUDES IN ACTION

**1. Attitude: See opportunity in adversity and expect positive things.**

What are the biggest defining moments that you still encounter in your life? What about in your marriage? Identify at least three of each and discuss them as a couple. Include in your discussion how you need to handle these defining moments, for your marriage to be at its strongest.

**2. Attitude: All things are possible.**

What kinds of things in your life discourage you and challenge your belief that things can be better? In your marriage? What do *you* need to do to have a different attitude? How can you act on this change? Share your answers with your partner.

**3. Attitude: Be willing to face the pain.**

What kinds of painful experiences do you avoid the most in life and in marriage? Discuss with your partner what you can *both* do differently to help face these situations when they come up.

**4. Attitude: It's important to look at yourself honestly.**

a) Talk to your partner about your score on the Marital Heart Meter. Commit to him or her to make daily efforts on strengthening your heart in marriage. If you dare, ask your partner if he or she would give you a different score on any of the items. Listen with an open mind and use this feedback to give you more direction as you work through the material of this book.

b) What would others say is your biggest character strength, and your biggest character weakness? (You can use the Marital Heart Meter if necessary to give you ideas.) How do you see them getting expressed in your marriage? Discuss these with your partner, committing to specific action steps for any improvements needed.

# 2

# Value the Things
# That Matter

*Wherever you go, go with all your heart.*

Confucius, 551–479 BC

Most "messy" marriage problems are not complicated at all. Contrary to popular belief, it's not a matter of learning some better "how-to's" of marriage. Bookstores line their shelves with books teaching various skills and formulas for success that win only style points. People come in for therapy every day asking for help with their communication skills. Within minutes of talking with them, it's clear that the real problem is really something much different. They are preoccupied with their feelings, have bad attitudes, or have developed behavioral habits that make it impossible to have the kind of relationship they want. Element #1 is about personal character. What you value says a lot about your character.

## YOUR ATTITUDE, EMOTIONAL, AND BEHAVIORAL HABITS TELL THE WORLD WHAT IS MOST IMPORTANT TO YOU

You just can't hide what you really value in life. Ultimately, this determines how you deal with the defining moments in your life. Do the things you value enable you to face life's challenges with absolute confidence? What you value either helps or hurts the strength of your heart. Marriage is one of the biggest arenas where your heart shows what it can do.

## Your Attitudes Reflect What Matters to You

Your attitudes are the sum total of all of your daily thinking habits. They are pretty reliable predictors of how you will respond to most of the things that happen to you. At the end of a typical day in your life, what are the true desires and intentions of your heart? As you go through life, what does your mind always come back to? This is your primary focus. Some people focus on money. Others are planning for some day in the future when they can retire a certain way or be in some ideal financial position. Most of their life and thinking is centered around this.

Lots of people put their focus on "personal happiness" and go after it in an infinite number of ways. If you examined what consumes most of your time, effort, and attention, that is what you value the most. Jesus said that wherever your treasure is that's where your heart is.[1] What occupies us forms our attitudes and thought habits. It reflects how we view the world, God, and ourselves. How many times have you heard someone say, "I deserve to be happy, so I'm going to do this or that to make sure I have it"? Many people believe that life, and marriage, owes them certain things to make them happy. This is often not even a conscious thing, and sometimes people don't get in touch with this part of themselves until they are in marriage therapy.

When faced with adversity, our default reaction is to protect what we really value and think we should have. One couple in therapy was having conflict over money all the time. She wanted to live for today and he wanted to plan for any and all possibilities. If terrorism or hurricanes affected the price of gasoline he wanted to be in the best possible financial position. Both approaches certainly have merit, but either extreme creates problems. His agenda in life, and in marriage, was to take maximum precautions at all times. His family constantly felt pressured to forgo enjoying life in the here and now. His wife and kids were walking on eggshells whenever something came up involving money. It really put a wedge between them and Dad. Dad had to reevaluate what was most important to him—material security or the feelings of his family.

The Bible says that what you think is who you are.[2] Years of research have shown that your thoughts are what produce depression and anxiety.[3] They also produce joy, contentment, and love. A lot of self-help books and seminars teach people how to develop attitudes that enable them to accomplish great things. Tony Robbins teaches people to walk on hot coals. You can go to a ropes course and learn to overcome your fears by walking on tightropes high above the ground. What fills your mind is powerful! The good news is that we can all harness our minds to do unbelievable things. We were *created* that way.

> *When faced with adversity, our default reaction is to protect what we really value and think we should have.*

## KEY ATTITUDE:
**Giving to others is more important than serving yourself.**

Most people say it's how much mental toughness we have that shows our character. It does, but there is one attitude that puts all character-building efforts in the right perspective. It's the one attitude that empowers your marriage to work through virtually anything. This attitude is a perfect reflection of a strong character, which believes that giving more than you receive in life *always* results in something greater than yourself.

Here it is. Your treasure—what you value the most—must be to let go of yourself and be focused on God and others.[4] This must be your value every day if you want to begin experiencing the fruit of powerful attitudes. This attitude can be mimicked and still get results. If you just decide to put your marriage partner first, this will solve lots of problems all by itself. But if this is truly how you *think*, it means you are already predisposed to facing marital adversity with the heart of a lion! Even then, if your power and motivation do not come from a relationship with God, you might be like most people and cave in when the situation gets tough enough. The attitude of a big heart puts others first and the motivation comes from a strong relationship with God.

We will explore what this looks like in practice later, but this attitude says you are willing to make personal sacrifice in your marriage as a matter of habit. Positive outcomes are expected and, if your partner does not respond in like manner, you realize there is a higher motivation than just his or her response. You do it because Jesus sacrificed his life for you, because God calls you to die to yourself,[5] and because it's the right thing to do. You do it because that is what you value most. Your world is oriented around it. Your thought patterns and expectations are focused in this direction. If they are not, you are building your marriage on a shaky foundation no matter how compatible the two of you are. If you're lucky, you'll cruise through life without too many challenges to your marriage. But statistics indicate most people aren't that lucky, with half the marriages in the United States failing *despite* the fact that 90 percent of Americans say they believe in God, 82 percent believe in heaven, and 69 percent believe in hell.[6]

An attitude that places God and others before your concerns can accept whatever life has to dish out. You will refuse to be defeated because you understand that nothing can defeat you. The Bible says that love never ends[7] and that nothing can separate us from the love of God.[8] When you take this attitude, suddenly the tools available to build good marriages become effective and work.

> If your main focus and motivation is God and others before yourself, your marriage will flourish! That's the attitude of true character, which will overcome virtually any marital problem.

I find after doing more than twenty years of marriage counseling, if I had to pick just one attitude habit, this is the one attitude separating the successes from the failures. In a nutshell, if your orientation is selfish, you are much more likely to fail. If it is outside yourself, you are much more likely to succeed.

## Your Emotions Expose Your Values

The way you handle your emotions becomes a habit that reveals what you value the most. Let me tell you the story of Tom. He is like so many people who end up with failed marriages, male and female alike. When Tom and Beth met, both were heavily involved in Christian ministry. They were very caring to each other, had children together, and spent many busy years raising them in their Christian faith. They had the model family of the neighborhood.

But Tom repressed his feelings on most big issues that came up. Either he didn't know how to resolve something with Beth, she didn't respond the way he wanted, or he thought there was no solution for things that disappointed him. This worked for a long time. After all, no conflict means no problems, right? He was so good at ignoring his feelings that much of the time he didn't even know what his feelings were. He valued the ease of ignoring unpleasant feelings more than he valued resolving problems (or even admitting there were any).

The fun had left the marriage. Life became a chore as he had ignored his true feelings for too long. Beth did not make him feel the way he wanted to feel, she was moody and did not follow through with household tasks consistently. After years of allowing these resentments to build up, Tom couldn't keep his feelings in anymore. They began to control everything he did. He had an affair, thinking his wife was the problem.

Tom finally realized that he had not addressed his emotions all those years, but unfortunately the neglect of the marriage proved too devastating and his feelings were still seething under the surface. He left his wife for the other woman, only admitting afterward that the problem was within himself. He was miserable, confused, and had lost his life as he had known it. Years of unresolved emotions had taken a toll on him, not the least of which was living with the consequences of his inaction.

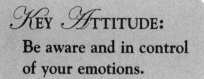

**KEY ATTITUDE:**
**Be aware and in control of your emotions.**

Feelings can make us crazy. They tend to be unreliable, unpredictable, and can get us into all kinds of trouble. Feelings can be unbelievably powerful and even convince us something is real when it is nothing more than something we created in our heads. They really go haywire if we ignore them. All too often we can't count on them to lead us in the right direction, despite clichés such as "Follow your heart." I tend to be a romantic myself and believe in being true to my heart. But this is not the same as being true to your feelings. They are two different things.

Feelings should never be the guiding force for how we manage ourselves in relationships. But God gave us emotions for a good purpose. We are feeling beings—just as God is. To ignore or suppress our feelings betrays us and those around us. An old proverb tells us that we are liars if we conceal hatred.[9] If we have feelings about something and keep it to ourselves, we are setting ourselves up for major problems later. Likewise, fooling ourselves about what we really feel—ignoring our real feelings—does not work. Learn to listen to your feelings for what they can tell you, but then consider all the other information available to you. Your feelings may be telling you there is something wrong with how *you* are approaching a situation.

*To ignore or suppress our feelings betrays us and those around us.*

♥ Spend a few minutes reflecting on how you really feel deep down about your marriage. Is there something that is eating away at you in some way? If there is, don't run from it or stuff it. Admit it to yourself and begin exploring what your true thoughts and feelings are. Are they just feelings or does all available information validate them? If not, get your feelings under control. If the information does validate them, talk to your partner about it. Develop a plan to make necessary changes.

Remember, what you feel is mostly the result of what you tell yourself. Sometimes you are telling yourself the wrong things. In Tom's case, as is the case with so many, he had formed this picture in his mind about how his wife should be and how his life should go. Reality was different from his picture, so it was inevitable that he would realize his desires would never come true. Then, disenchantment set in and he was bound to be unhappy. If he wanted to feel better, he had to alter his view of things. Once he accomplished this, his feelings would eventually change. This process takes time and feelings are always slow to catch up. Be patient and give it time.

What if your view is reality-based and you still have some negative feelings? This points to an issue that might be eluding you. Just what the issue is is often somewhere under the surface. In this case, work backward, paying attention to the feeling and what thoughts you connect to it. It is not uncommon for people to have trouble knowing right away what is eating at them. If this describes you, stop blaming your partner and take some time figuring out what the real problem is. Then you can communicate it more clearly to your partner.

Let me illustrate. Years ago a family came to therapy who had a depressed fourteen-year-old girl. Since teenagers often do not understand their own feelings, it was not surprising she and the family were baffled about why she was depressed. There was no traumatic event that would clearly explain the situation. However, her parents had divorced a few years earlier and Mom had remarried twice after that. The girl got along fine with her stepfather but was in conflict with her mother. She rarely saw her biological father. The family had also moved to another school district during all this upheaval.

What happened here? This girl was going through puberty and was naturally off balance about herself. Her social support changed due to having moved. Mom had "caused" uncertainty in her life with some of her personal decisions. In talking with the daughter, I discovered that she did not have a clear idea who she was, even more so than your typical teenager. She had concluded that she was alone in the world and didn't even have a legitimate place in the family anymore. As a result, she felt lonely, discouraged, and depressed. By addressingthis openly within the family, she was able to receive emotional support and develop a new understanding with her mother. This resolved her depression.

Janine wasn't so lucky. She didn't resolve some things from her childhood and kept reacting in her marriage based on these ancient issues. Her parents had been verbally abusive to her and everyone in her family. She learned to clam up, avoiding conflict at all cost. Her husband, Paul, was not without his hang-ups. Unfortunately, despite being mild-mannered (which is why Janine was so attracted to him), he could become extremely jealous. Janine was exceptionally attractive and received lots of attention from men. If she so much as looked at one, Paul would go into a rage. This couple came to me completely unable to talk about their real issues. Literally, they would look at each other in discomfort and say nothing, even under my direction! With time and courage, Janine was able to take small risks and begin talking. This couple made great progress, but not without a lot of hard work. Both partners had to know what was really eating away at them, and that took time to uncover.

The point is that the emotions of a big heart are well managed but they are not ignored either. You must learn to allow emotions to help you uncover the real problem and provide the energy needed to find solutions. Just because facing certain feelings may be painful, avoiding them is not the answer and just makes matters worse. True character recognizes that emotions—all emotions (not mood swings)—can be useful and that facing them openly and honestly makes you a stronger person.

## THE WAY YOU MANAGE EMOTIONS ALSO REVEALS HOW SELF-CENTERED YOU ARE

This is really an attitude, but if you are self-centered, a telltale sign of it shows up emotionally. If whatever you value centers mostly around you and your desires, this part of your life is self-centered. There is nothing wrong with this as long as you stand ready to give this up for "the greater good." Giving of yourself to others is the telltale sign of being *others*-centered. Living for your pleasure works only when it is subject to caring first about what those around you might need.

The Bible says to do nothing from selfishness or empty conceit.[10] Don't get puffed up and think too highly of yourself, even with pursuing the things you like. Even a hobby can become selfish when it interferes with being available to your spouse. You are thinking too much of yourself. If you tend to be selfish, your preoccupation with yourself has the effect of isolating you. It's you and, well, you. Isolation can be addictive. Once you're hooked on something selfish, situations that challenge your isolation make you uncomfortable and "antsy."

> *If you tend to be selfish, your preoccupation with yourself has the effect of isolating you.*

A few quick examples should be sufficient here. If you are a cheapskate and are always hoarding every penny, getting a fast-food burger with your family makes you anxious. I know someone like this—you probably do too. If you are a "private person" and get into a routine of spending most of your time with your mate and no one else, asking you to begin spending a lot of time with others will make you very uncomfortable. It will be an invasion of your space and interfere with things you're used to doing just for your own comfort and enjoyment. Or maybe you have been "trained" by your spouse to be waited on hand and foot. When it comes time for you to do the serving, it feels strangely uncomfortable. You actually have to give of yourself and you just aren't used to it. When do you want to be selfish? Does it interfere with being giving to others?

**KEY ATTITUDE:**
**Do the helpful thing even if you don't feel like it.**

Feeling like it is not a prerequisite. Being self-centered simply means you value *you* more than everything else. Your focus is to protect the things that are important to you. When a defining moment provides the opportunity to forgo your selfish desire and be more concerned with others, what do you do with it? Do you listen to your uncomfortable feelings and back off the opportunity? If there are already some difficulties in the marriage relationship, this is where most people lick their wounds and take the self-centered route. Then when presented with solutions to their problems, their selfishness prevents the solutions from working. Marital solutions usually involve having to give something of yourself to the situation.

> Consider the situations in your marriage in which you have the most difficulty being completely giving of yourself. Consciously and deliberately make a point this week to give yourself completely in one specific way. Decide to make that a new habit in that one area from now on.

A lifestyle that makes a habit of following your feelings can easily become your primary approach to life. And this is a *huge* problem, folks. The Bible says that we become slaves of what we obey—either our own desires or God's.[11] That's just the way it works. If you want to have a heart that is a master of emotions, you must learn what they really mean when you feel them and be ready to face some discomfort.

If you practice healthy emotional management, your emotional life will actually change to conform to your decision to place others before yourself. That becomes your comfort zone and it becomes more natural to you.

**NOTE:** *Some people's emotional development has the appearance of being stunted. The depth and range of feelings they have is limited. They are very uncomfortable discussing feelings at all. Others have spent their lives with emotions out of control much of the time. It is either their emotional style or they have unresolved personal issues. All of these situations may require personal attention before it is possible to apply all the ideas in this section.*

## Behavioral Habits
## Come from What You Want

*Keep yourself under subjection to what you really value in the emotional life of a big heart by consciously managing your feelings.*

There are times when behaving right is all you have in you. Your behavior shows true character when it is consistently doing the constructive thing. You won't always have a great attitude and feel great. Being human, your walk with God does not always seem like this awesome experience despite the reality that heaven awaits true believers. Many people do not pursue a daily walk with God because it does not always feel inspirational. Likewise, your marriage partner isn't always attractive or particularly inspiring, even when his or her commitment to you hasn't changed. A strong character is "on good behavior" no matter what is going on around him or her. This is because a strong character knows what is true no matter what it feels like.

Sometimes a wife or husband will say the other partner's efforts aren't valid because they're forced. I say nonsense to that! That's actually the test—no, the measure—of someone's commitment to you! What good is someone's affection if it only comes when he feels like it? Don't you value your partner getting you a soft drink more when you know he is not feeling well? In all enduring relationships, it is sometimes necessary to *act as if* you feel like doing the right thing even when you don't.[12] Research clearly shows that if you behave the way you want to be, attitudes and feelings will eventually follow.

If it only meant something when we felt like it, our heroes would have been average people. Sacrificial single mothers would not qualify to be everyday heroes. Other people became heroes through personal sacrifice. People like Martin Luther King Jr., Mother Teresa, Abraham Lincoln, soldiers who gave their lives for freedom, and thousands of others whose stories were never made famous. Behaviors of a big heart come from a decision to do the noble thing regardless of feelings. The feelings will follow.

If you are learning to relax by listening to New Age music, it will not happen if you don't sit down and turn on the music. Likewise, you can't develop a godly attitude by meditating on God's word if you don't make the time to sit down and read it. Making a decision to do the right thing always involves acting on it. You have to *want* what is right. Pursue the right attitudes and a healthy emotional life, then put them into action. Oftentimes, putting them into action *is* the way to pursue them!

A good example of behaviors working with attitude and emotion is dieting. There is a new fad diet coming out every week it seems. People rave about how much success they had losing thirty pounds on this diet or that. Then you see them six months later and they gained all the weight back. Everyone knows that most of the dieting U.S. population experiences this. They start out with an attitude of sticking to the diet plan until the weight is lost. They fight the urges to cheat, whipping their emotions in line. Then the weight is lost, they let down their guard, and go right back to the old eating and exercise habits from before. If you talk to people who keep their weight off, they tell you it's because they made a lifestyle change. They developed new and better eating habits, which involved a whole different attitude and new long-term behaviors. Their feelings about it followed these important changes. The behavior has to be there, but it can only be sustained when the right attitude is in place. This keeps the right behavior going, which helps you keep the right attitude going.

The Bible puts it this way—be a doer of the right thing and not just a hearer who fools himself.[13] Sometimes we like to fill our heads up with lots of good advice but we never act on it. Why exercise now when we can do it tomorrow? If you want to change your habits, you have to start small and just get through today. Start by putting your shoes away every day if you are always messy. Adopt the right attitude, then do something about it.

How you spend your time—minute to minute as well as weekly prioritizing—is an easy test to see what your behavior patterns are all about. Spending every chance you get to read a book or going golfing may be an indicator you are more concerned with self. It all comes back to what is most important to you, what takes up your time, and what you are preoccupied with.

A classic example of this is two couples that came to me for marriage counseling with almost identical problems. Both wives were upset that their husbands spent an inordinate amount of time doing what they liked to do. Both husbands thought their wives were being unreasonable.

Betty was pregnant and having some difficulties with her pregnancy. She also had another young child at home who required her attention. Bob was either late coming home or gone quite often, plus he regularly played golf on weekends. Betty pleaded with him to stay home, help her with their child, and spend time with her. At one point, Bob said, "If I want to be selfish with my life I deserve to be. It's my life." This put Betty in an impossible bind. She married someone who proclaimed with pride he was living only for himself. Most people are not this obvious, yet the result is the same. Betty's response was to become angry and demanding, which drove Bob further into his selfish mode. I urged both to get back to focusing on being good marriage partners.

Patti and Paul worked opposite shifts. He worked regular day hours and she worked second shift, including weekends. Paul spent his whole life being footloose and fancy free, having raised himself from a young age since his mother was so busy with her own life. He spent more time at the houses of his friends as a kid than he did his own house. Parents of his friends were just as important to him as his own mother. He learned complete self-sufficiency and coped with stress by learning not to get upset about anything. Worrying and answering to anyone were foreign ideas to him. He still had lots of male friends and wanted to spend several evenings a week with them, even if it cut into the little time he could have with Patti. Patti was a beautiful young wife and Paul genuinely enjoyed spending time with her. But she had become a nag over this issue because she felt such deep hurt by his perceived neglect. The more she nagged, the deeper he dug in his heels about going out.

One of these couples worked things out and the other did not. You can probably tell already which one worked things out. Paul was truly not aware that his habits came across as selfish; that's just how he lived. Once the couple was able to discuss it calmly, he began to see that his approach to life was the problem. He still wanted to be with his friends as much as always, but

Patti was more important to him than hanging out with friends. Because he wanted *more* to be sensitive and giving to her, he changed his routine for her. His urge to go out with friends didn't disappear, but he chose the behavior that was more consistent with what he valued the most. With time, his view changed, and so did his feelings. Friends became much less important than they had been.

Bob, on the other hand, had made his bed and he was determined to lay in it. He made some accommodating behavioral changes, but they were the minimum to be able to say he did it. His attitude was no different and there were still times he just did whatever he wanted. Betty acknowledged the improvements, but the efforts were too little too late. She stayed miserable.

♥ *As an experiment, choose one day to cater to your partner's desires (this won't kill you!). Then consider what you have learned about yourself and your partner from this experience.*

**KEY ATTITUDE:**
**Do whatever it takes to address issues, challenging yourself to behave differently if needed.**

Doing what is right is only right if it comes from sincerity (which is not an emotion). We can all find loopholes in order to get by with the minimum. If we are trying to exercise regularly, it's easy to cut the workout short or skip one in the name of busyness. No one ever became a world-class pianist by practicing once a week. It's the same thing in relationships. Getting by with minimum effort always results in minimum relationship quality.

Developing the behaviors of a big heart often involves stepping out and taking risk. It could be a risk of rejection or maybe the risk of others learning to expect certain things of you. It might just be the risk of your partner not responding to your efforts, resulting in disappointment and hurt.

## What You Value
## and Your Biggest Weakness

The things you value most are often exposed when your biggest weakness is tested. Your biggest weakness has a negative impact on your marriage relationship no matter what it is; I guarantee it. If eating chocolate under stress is honestly your biggest weakness, you will undoubtedly resort to it at times when you should be managing your feelings better. This in turn spills over to the way you relate to your spouse. Perhaps you become more irritable, or maybe you just withdraw into yourself so that it's just you and your friend Mr. Chocolate. When our weakness kicks in, that's when we start isolating—it's just us and whatever it is that's our focus. Do not make the mistake of understating the importance of this. Think of all the little ways your weakness interferes with your approach to life's stresses. Then consider how this affects the kind of marriage partner you are at those times.

> *The behaviors of a big heart result from having the attitude of sincerely wanting to do the right thing for others and putting that want into action.*

**KEY ATTITUDE:**
**Admit your weaknesses as a matter of habit. Choose to make this your value!**

People tend to have a small handful of weaknesses that stand out more than all the others. If you aren't sure what yours are, ask a couple of people that are around you a lot on a personal level. Most of the time, they know!

Your weakness might be to get easily discouraged and therefore drag other people down. You might be a procrastinator, be too introverted or too extroverted, make careless remarks too often, let the opinions of others control you, force your opinions on others, have trouble with sexual temptation, lack discipline with keeping your word, are quick to become defensive, and the list goes on.

Your biggest weaknesses tempt you to indulge yourself enough to stay comfortable. The Bible tells us that our human weaknesses are waging war with our minds and that we find ourselves giving in to these weaknesses even when we don't want to.[14] Why do some people get so carried away with their weaknesses? Mostly because they indulge them. We are tempted because we allow our desires to grow by catering to them. This is preventable by changing your desires—the things that you really want deep down.[15]

Over time, everyone develops favorite self-indulgences. Some are innocent, like rewarding yourself with a favorite dessert for working hard. The kind that cause trouble are the ones that end up controlling you more than you control them.

We'll explore this more later, but some kind of self-indulgence can develop when someone has hurt you. You could struggle with trusting others, you could get stuck with feeling demoralized for a long time, or you may become vengeful. In our Hollywood culture of "Let's get revenge," taking out feelings of anger and revenge on the perpetrator has become commonly accepted. Being tempted to pay back our partner when we have been wronged is normal—especially if you have been hurt in the past. But it is never okay.

One such couple, Jim and Bobbi, had been married for almost forty years. They raised highly successful children and everyone who knew them saw nothing but success. He had spent a long career building a nice pension and was able to retire early, while she was a career woman; she was also known as a wonderful hostess among their friends. He was so good at his career that she ran the household—and very well—by herself for the most part. Bobbi gave of herself in this way to everyone. Sure, she had some emotional needs that Jim was not meeting. But things ran smoothly for decades like this. Jim was able to take early retirement because he was so good at his career.

After he retired and the kids left home, Bobbi realized she was lonely. Her way of coping with this was to become angry at Jim for all those years of "wasted time." He couldn't do anything right now. She could not, and would not, forgive him. Jim realized how he had neglected her in many ways and wanted to make things right. But Bobbi allowed her anger to consume her, stopped going to church with Jim, and berated him daily for all the injustice he had done to her.

Bobbi's biggest weakness was a tendency to give herself completely to others, forgo her needs for the moment, then become highly judgmental when others didn't measure up to her expectations. Feelings were building up inside her that became her downfall. She allowed this to turn to bitterness, which slowly consumed her every day. Although Jim recognized he needed to be a better marriage partner, Bobbi was determined to keep him down as payback. She indulged her unforgiving attitude quietly for years until she could no longer control it. This is *always* the result of giving in to your temptations and avoiding the pain of doing the right thing instead of the easy thing.

A final thought about this: when counseling clients have reached their goals and are convinced they are ready to stop therapy, I always discuss relapse prevention with them. Usually they think this is repetitive and kind of boring. We discuss in detail what it would take to fall back into old habits. The reason is that unless you plant positive change deep into your mind and heart, you will be tempted to indulge those old weaknesses.

If you are serious about being a good marriage partner you must identify your biggest weaknesses and wage war on them. You must be proactive, making it a daily habit to think about how you are using every moment to be the person you know you want and need to be. We will look at what this looks like in specific terms in pages to follow. We'll also take a closer look at how strong your character is now and how you became the person you are today.

## Will You Value What Counts?

Struggles in the marriage relationship expose us for who we are more than a lot of things in life. Marriage without conflict is lacking some of the intimacy it could have and is a sign that the partners are likely just postponing major problems. Healthy conflict will help expose your true values.

Most people end up valuing things that don't last, like leisure, material things, vacations, hobbies, or personal pleasure. None of these things will serve you well when you are challenged in marriage.

*Unless you plant positive change deep into your mind and heart, you will be tempted to indulge those old weaknesses.*

**KEY ATTITUDE:
Value the things that will last beyond your lifetime.**

You can make a conscious choice to value those things that last beyond your lifetime—real love, strength of character, holding true to your commitments, to name a few. Either your life needs some adjustment to be consistent with lasting values, or you need to change your values. The price to be paid for not doing this is a marriage unprepared to weather anything that could come along.

In Colorado where I'm from, there are people who love to climb "fourteeners." These are the mountains that are 14,000 feet high or more. They pride themselves on climbing all of them. Each mountain presents unique challenges, such as narrow paths with 500-foot drops, serious weather changes during the climb, thin oxygen toward the top, and sometimes loose rock that makes footing pretty shaky. Unfortunately, it isn't uncommon to hear on the local news of someone who died for his or her efforts with this popular "hobby." Sometimes people reach the summit only to get blown off the edge by the wind and fall several hundred feet to their death! The exceptional few who reach the summit love the feeling it gives them, and all the challenges along the way help make the satisfaction complete.

Life is a lot like climbing fourteeners. Some people set out to climb them and turn back early. Others go about halfway and realize the wise thing to do is turn back, either due to their lack of preparation or weather conditions. They just aren't up to the challenge. Then some make it all the way to the top. Being prepared, accepting the challenge, and facing adversity is the only way to make progress at times. Likewise, marriage is full of challenges, big and small, and what you do with them is what counts.

The apostle James from the Bible tells us that we should "consider it all joy" when we encounter life's challenges because it tests our faith, producing endurance.[16] It's worth paying the price for a strong character. It's what God wants of you, and through it you will become an exceptional marriage partner. Notice I said you will become, not be, an exceptional marriage partner. It is a lifelong process that only starts when you decide to start it. If you believe in God, you place a high value on giving more than you receive in life. You know that it *always* results in something greater than yourself. That is worth the pain of change.

If I haven't fully convinced you to face your troubles with courage and do what's right, consider what a child wrote while she was in family therapy with me many years ago. Chelsea had been deeply hurt at a young age by an abusive father. In a poem she wrote about memories, she said that ". . . while saving our memories may hurt, and some may pass over a thin line, we move on and we move up. But still I know I'll keep saving mine." She was twelve when she wrote this.

Chelsea showed more character than most adults have! Having character that is selfless enough to face discomforts and pain of all sorts is a key ingredient to an enduring marriage. What things in life are really important to you? Those are some things that reveal part of your personal character. They affect your marriage, to be sure.

> Having character that is selfless enough to face discomforts and pain of all sorts is a key ingredient to an enduring marriage.

Later in the book we will explore some important areas of character application in marriage. Some tools, skills, and activities will be shared that have been very effective with marriage counseling clients for more than twenty years. They *do* work, but only when participants bring a heart of giving, forgiving, and caring to the process. No matter what the hurt, you have to want solutions more than you want to keep pointing fingers or dwelling on your feelings.

Next, we'll be looking more closely at what kind of personal attributes you bring into your marriage and how you became who you are. Self-awareness is the beginning of change. We all have blind spots about ourselves that keep us from being at our best. Once it becomes clear what it is about us that needs to change, making the change becomes much more possible.

But before you go further, a few questions are in order. Are you going to approach the defining moments of your life, and your marriage, with a big heart, or will you *choose* to live with pain and failure? In the movie *A Few Good Men*, Jack Nicholson's character said, "You can't *handle* the truth!" Are you willing to face *yourself*, warts and all?

I implore you to examine yourself closely enough to see the full truth about yourself. At times it will be confusing, and at other times painful. Slow down if you have to, but don't stop now.

## MAIN CHAPTER ATTITUDES

✓ Giving to others is more important than serving yourself.

✓ Be aware and in control of your emotions.

✓ Do the helpful thing even if you don't feel like it.

✓ Do whatever it takes to address issues, challenging yourself to behave differently if needed.

✓ Admit your weaknesses as a matter of habit. Choose to make this your value!

✓ Value the things that will last beyond your lifetime.

## ATTITUDES IN ACTION

**1. Attitude: Giving to others is more important than serving yourself.**

When do you tend to be the most selfish? What about in your marriage? Pick one area that needs improvement and train yourself to be more giving every time that one area presents itself. Remember: change happens one minute at a time. Tell your partner what you are working on.

**2. Attitude: Be aware and in control of your emotions.**

What are some times or situations in which you could improve the way you manage your emotions in your relationships with people, especially in your marriage? Come up with three specific things you can do about this and start making changes this week. Don't keep reading this book until you have started doing these things.

**3. Attitude: Do the helpful thing even if you don't feel like it.**

Do you have the discipline and habit of doing what will be constructive in your marriage, even if you don't feel like it? Ask your partner to tell you one way you could contribute to your relationship being better.

**4. Attitude: Do whatever it takes to address issues, challenging yourself to behave differently if needed.**

Are there any issues in your marriage at all that you have not fully faced? Discuss this with your partner and decide together to face them with an honest desire for solutions. Stay with it until you reach some kind of agreement about the change(s) needed and progress is made.

**5. Attitude: Admit your weaknesses as a matter of habit, choose to make this your value!**

What is your biggest single weakness, and how does it show up in your marriage? Discuss this with your partner and brainstorm together how you can begin making positive changes.

**6. Attitude: Value the things that will last beyond your lifetime.**

Name ten things you value, as seen in your daily life. They could range anywhere from work to TV to being left alone. Then name ten things you think your partner values based on what you see every day. Share your lists and discuss whether any of these things make a strong marriage more difficult. Are there enough things on your lists that will last beyond your lifetime?

# 3

# Have the Personality
# of a Survivor

*You know what makes a good loser?
Practice.*

Ernest Hemingway

Without the ability to focus, we may as well be blind.

Imagine trying to fight off an invading enemy blindfolded. Or reading a book in the dark. Proper focus in life is a lot like looking at an optical illusion. Those are the pictures that don't look like anything unless you stare at it. If you focus as if you're looking beyond the picture, images begin to get clear. The fun is not knowing just what you will see and being surprised when you can finally see it.

Seeing ourselves honestly works pretty much the same way. We need to look intently at ourselves, seeing beyond the present to what the future will be like if we continue being exactly the way we are right now. If we don't, our picture of life is blurred and is just not accurate. And doing this once every ten years is not enough—it needs to be a daily habit. Your personal attributes may contribute to a failed marriage. Being blind to them until it is too late is obviously foolish. So why aren't more people taking the time to examine themselves? Part of addressing your personal character, which is Element #1, is developing a "survivor personality."

Don't you just hate it when you keep doing something over and over and you know it isn't helping the situation? Doing the same thing again and again and expecting different results—that's one definition of insanity! We do that because we aren't seeing the real picture clearly. Then there are times your behavior helps shape problems in your relationship and you don't fully understand how it does. We know what many of our shortcomings are, but that's only the tip of the iceberg! The *Titanic* hit the iceberg tip, but it's what the captain couldn't see that was so destructive. We also have blind spots about our surroundings and ourselves, those areas we don't see so clearly.

The way we interact with our marriage partner is a dance that looks fairly simple and straightforward to an outsider, but in actuality it's a sophisticated dance. There are hundreds of books available that talk about personality differences, temperament types, and theories about why certain types of people clash with other types. They can be very helpful, but they also tend to catalog people by saying, "You're an XYZ type personality," or, "Opposites attract, so it's no wonder you are having issues." Sometimes this is true, and sometimes it isn't. What we want to do is examine our personal attributes honestly and objectively, then make the changes needed so that we can be the best marriage partner we can be.

This chapter is about finding a good target and shooting for it with accuracy. It will challenge you to look at developing some personal attributes beyond what you find "comfortable." Element #1 says that you need the right character for a shatterproof marriage. If this means you change some things about yourself, the impact on your marriage will be powerful.

## PAY THE PRICE TO BE A GOOD PARTNER

**KEY ATTITUDE:**
**Work on personality growth whenever and wherever needed.**

The kind of person you have become does not—should not—have to stay the same. We all have shortcomings and we should be a "work in progress" for as long as we live. Certainly, the more we know about ourselves the better off we are. But the *type* of personality or temperament you have is not *you*. Knowing what kind of *heart* you have—and have had—is what really opens the door for you to grow and change for the better. Your heart is the fingerprint of your soul. You can have all kinds of ugly shortcomings, but you can always be better today than you were yesterday. So can your marriage. It is your heart that holds your true thoughts and intentions[1] and it is with your heart that you believe in God. Some people believe in what is *possible* while others focus on why something is *not possible*. Adolf Hitler almost broke the spirit and hope of the free world. But some courageous leaders like Winston Churchill believed in their hearts that Hitler was someone the world could defeat. Despite huge losses against seemingly hopeless odds, the free world won the fight for freedom.

Ultimately, it comes down to what kind of heart you bring to any situation. You could have been a victim of physical or sexual abuse as a child, come from a broken home, had your emotional development derailed by family conflicts, dealt with an alcoholic parent, had harsh or perfectionist parents, never learned how to be intimate

*Your heart is the fingerprint of your soul.*

with another person, developed any number of possible addictions of your own, have a big anger problem, avoid conflict at all costs, be overly controlling because of past experiences, get your feelings hurt too easily, don't trust anyone, can't manage stress, have poor impulse control, or struggle with mood problems. The fact is, we are all sinners and fall way short of God's glory.[2] Jesus came to this earth to save sinners, not hang out with the "beautiful people."[3]

A question I often ask clients in marriage counseling is, "What kind of marriage partner are you?" They usually come in all set to give me the lowdown on their spouse, so this question stops people dead in their tracks. Surprisingly, most people know when they have become poor partners, reacting out of their own unhappiness. They usually confess they need to improve their efforts. Once they start looking first at themselves, progress is possible. Jesus said it best some 2,000 years ago when he said to first take the log out of your own eye before you try to take the speck out of someone else's.[4]

My own parents split up when I was in fifth grade, largely because of my father's alcoholism. We went from an upper middle-class neighborhood to living above some stores in an old apartment building. There were rats in the garage and a gang hung out right outside the front door to the building. Every day I left the apartment I had to go past this gang. Being a timid kid, it terrified me and I had to learn to be tough quickly.

By the time I reached eighth grade I was vandalizing and shoplifting. By the time I started high school I had a huge temper, felt like the whole world was a hostile place, and had all kinds of emotional hang-ups. When I was in my early twenties I was looking for a potential marriage partner out of emotional need instead of a well-adjusted attitude. I went to Kent State University during the Vietnam War protests (at the same time as the shootings of the students in 1970). By this time my views of life and myself were radical, confused, and distrustful. My emotional development stopped in my teen years, so being a giving partner in a loving relationship without overreacting to situations was foreign to me.

Now does that sound like the catch of a lifetime for a future wife? Fortunately for me, I became a Christian the year before I married my wife. She was a well-grounded Christian with a deep character rooted in values based on following God. A happy ending, right?

Well, not so fast! Character growth can and often does take a lifetime. We have spent years, even decades, working through one painful experience after another. We're both stubborn to begin with, and adding my background to the mix has been a real challenge at times. Those who knew us at certain

points throughout the years surely had impressions
we didn't have a chance! There were periods—
times of normal stress—in which my stunted
development as a kid turned into times of abnor-
mal stress for both of us.

We have had to learn over the years to recognize how those early years still "reared their ugly
heads" at times. When past weaknesses do crop up,
they can bring out the worst in me, which then brings
out the worst in my wife. It still amazes me how much of
those early years can haunt us at times. Through the grace of
God and my wife's unwavering character, we have been able to beat the odds
of such a rough history. We will continue to be a work in progress as long as we
live. Recognizing who we are at all times arms us with the information we need
to choose to respond out of character instead of reacting selfishly.

> *Recognizing who we are at all times arms us with the information we need to choose to respond out of character instead of reacting selfishly.*

It simply doesn't matter how "messed up" you or your partner is—a big
heart *can and will* carry you through anything. God can and does forgive anything you've ever done if you ask and repent. Jesus said to build your house
on solid rock. If you do, all the pressures and problems of life *cannot* destroy
you.[5] It doesn't guarantee a smooth ride by any stretch of the imagination,
but you *will* be able to finish the ride.

## KEY ATTITUDE:
### Invest the effort to learn from past experiences.

The family environment you came
from is supposed to equip you to live
in healthy adult relationships.
Attitudes, behavior habits, values, life priorities, and emotional development all happen within the family context. Most of it is automatic—it's
unspoken. Patterns of relating to others and how you think about yourself
emerge from this. If you do not know much about your family history and
how it has influenced who you are today, you are missing out on some

important insights. Gaining this kind of insight makes it much easier to make personal changes if they are needed.

Let me illustrate by examining a couple of famous families whose stories may be pretty dramatic but show us how powerful family influences are. Four of the nine Kennedy children died before middle age. Everyone thought John was dead on at least three different occasions before his assassination. Rosemary was lobotomized. Kathleen died in a plane crash right after cutting ties with her mother. Ted broke his back in a plane crash less than a year after John was killed. He was then involved in a traumatic accident at Chappaquiddick a year after Robert was killed. Pat separated from her husband the day of John's assassination. One grandchild died of a drug overdose, another lost a leg from cancer, and at least four others had problems from drug overdoses or psychiatric hospitalizations. This is only a partial list of this family's difficulties.

This whole family had its share of defining moments! Maybe all these life events have nothing to do with this family's resolve and determination, but the coincidence would be pretty big.[6] How many people do you know who have suffered a tragedy or even fell on some rough times? Is it in you to rise to the occasion or shrink back when life gets really tough? Some studies have shown we are more susceptible to accidents after stressful life events.[7] The impact of various family members on each other is far-reaching, even passing down for generations. Your family experiences while growing up gave you a unique set of strengths and weaknesses that either help or hinder you when marital difficulties arise. Make it your business to know what those things are from your history.

Eleanor Roosevelt's family is another example of the way our unique family histories contribute to our character.[8] Her paternal grandmother died a few months before her birth. In her early years, her father had a drinking problem and had to receive inpatient treatment. Her brother died when she was five and her mother died when she was eight. Then her father died when she was ten.

Instead of falling apart, these experiences seem to have built Eleanor's character from an early age. She later married Franklin Roosevelt and became known throughout the world for her caring and sensitivity to the tragedy of others. Folks, my point is this: you don't live triumphantly by accident. Even if you're famous. There has to be something within you that takes problems and turns them into character-builders. Don't let marital disappointments defeat you! A founding theorist in the field of family therapy has noticed that two-person relationships are not nearly as stable as three-person relationships.[9]

Even if you are married with no children, your past and present relationships with your growing-up family have an effect on you now. We can all look at our growing-up families and see these three-person dynamics. These dynamics are more *stable*, but not necessarily in a good way. Bad family patterns while we are growing up have a tendency to keep repeating themselves, don't they?

A classic example of this is when parents bring in their eight-year-old son because they believe he has ADHD (attention deficit/hyperactivity disorder) and they cannot manage his behavior. Everyone at home is angry. A closer examination of the situation reveals the parents do not agree on how to parent the child. They have grown resentful of each other and have become quite unhappy in the marriage. An emotional triangle that is not healthy for the son begins.

Just think of how this plays out beyond one generation. The son grows up feeling persecuted by his parents for his behavior and criticized for things he does that he is not even able to control. He might get married to a woman who feels a need to be in control (from her own history), especially since he is used to having people try to control him and may ironically find this to be somehow comfortable. All the while, this could be triggering his memories of not being allowed to be himself. By this time, he has emotional, behavioral, and attitude habits that cause him to be reactive under certain conditions. If left unchecked, the original emotional triangle has a ripple effect that can, and often does, reach many generations. It evolves over time, taking on many different faces.

Chances are, you were influenced *somehow* growing up as a result of this kind of interaction at home. What is your story? Understanding where you got some of your comfort and not so comfortable zones can help you see things about yourself that are helpful and things that are not so helpful. Then you can see what needs to change. There are tools in the appendices designed to help you explore this.

## SURVIVORS IN LIFE MOTIVATE US TO STRETCH

You may be asking, *So if I know some of these things about myself, what difference does it really make? I can't change my past.* No, but you *can* change your future. Research shows that survivors of life-threatening situations and of family trauma have several things in common. Developing these qualities, even starting now, will enable you to respond with true character when tough times come. You can't change your past, but you can change what happens today and tomorrow. This might mean doing a "180°" on some of your personal attributes.

A review of these qualities will help you see areas in your life that need some attention. It gives us all a good target to aim for, a clear target we can focus on. This will help your marriage immensely. Bringing strength of character to your marriage is the highest gift you can give your spouse. You may be weak, afraid, domineering, or a poor communicator. But a heart of courage acknowledges personal shortcomings you have and empowers you to become a great marriage partner.

### One characteristic of survivors is having insight about the realities of their situation.

A survivor senses when a situation may be harmful or dangerous, sees the danger for what it is, and understands well enough what is going on to take precautions.[10] So awareness—of yourself and your surroundings—is the beginning of understanding. The book of Proverbs tells us to acquire wisdom, which leads to understanding. "Prize her, and she will exalt you."[11]

♥ Take one concern in your marriage and learn everything
possible about the realities of it. Become the "resident expert"
on it, including how, when, and where you and your partner
behave in the ways you do when this concern is happening.
Discuss how this new insight helps your marriage to be stronger.

## Survivors in life also have a consistent curiosity about why something in life seems to work well or doesn't.[12]

They are like a next-door neighbor who is always tinkering in his garage on an old car. To many people this is a complete waste of time, but some people just love to see how things work. I've had friends like this who fixed my car for free just for fun! The same is true with life. Survivors just want to know what makes life go smoothly, especially in the face of adversity. So the point here is that if things are not clicking on all cylinders at home, work on being curious about why they aren't. Not to blame, but to understand.

♥ Pick one thing about your partner that confuses or
intrigues you. Find out what it is that makes him or her
tick with that one thing. Play detective and experiment with curiosity. How and when can this be helpful in your marriage?

Viktor Frankl experienced this firsthand when he was a prisoner in Auschwitz during World War II. In the middle of horrifying conditions that threatened prisoners daily, he describes developing an unusual curiosity in response to the constant crisis. He says, "Cold curiosity predominated even in Auschwitz, somehow detaching the mind from its surroundings, which came to be regarded with a kind of objectivity. At that time one cultivated this state of mind as a means of protection. We were anxious to know what would happen next . . . "[13]

*Behaving with a knee-jerk reaction is usually not prudent. Instead, commit to being more aware of yourself and your surroundings.*

When you're in the heat of the moment, the middle of marital stress, do you find yourself acting like a reactionary or someone more deliberate in working for solutions? Behaving with a knee-jerk reaction is usually not prudent. Instead, commit to being more aware of yourself and your surroundings. Become genuinely curious about your spouse's behavior with objectivity. This will change your attitude from one based on past conditioning to one of "stepping outside yourself." You will think more clearly and your partner will not feel threatened because your approach will not focus just on you.

Let's look at several other personality qualities that are typical of survivors. Think about your attitudes, emotional style, and the way you tend to behave under stress, as these aspects have evolved since childhood. Ask yourself honestly if these survivor qualities describe you. If they don't, write down the areas needing improvement and commit to working on them every day. Get feedback from those who know you for suggestions you can work on.

## Survivors have a healthy sense of "independence."

Survivors have developed the ability to distance themselves—rise above—the pain of difficult situations. They have a sort of emotional "insulation" based on what they tell themselves about a given problem. They have even learned the art of physical distance to keep themselves from being overly affected by a problem.[14] To the surprise of many, a problem that goes on long enough without a solution needs a healthy dose of apathy about it to keep someone from being overwhelmed.[15] This helps you keep the problem in perspective without making it bigger than it is.

Sometimes we just get too wrapped up in a problem. A typical characteristic of many domestic violence cases, for instance, is that the partners are often together in a limited physical space (cabin fever) too much. We can do the same thing to ourselves mentally. Our thinking can become so narrow

that we are unable to separate the problem from the
bigger picture of life.

This calls to mind one of my all-time favorite
phrases, which is actually the title to an interna-
tionally bestselling book by Paul Watzlawick
called *The Situation Is Hopeless, but Not Serious.*
This follows closely along with one of my favorite
interventions to a variety of problems. I sometimes
tell people to end the problem by *proclaiming* it's no
longer a problem, and it often works!

> *A problem that goes on long enough without a solution needs a healthy dose of apathy about it to keep someone from being overwhelmed.*

Let me illustrate. When my kids were little, we would
take them to church. I knew little at that time about what to expect from
young children. I wanted them to be well-behaved and not be a disturbance,
so I tried to make them be absolutely quiet at all times. When they didn't
always conform to this, I would worry about it and get all upset. This made
me parent harder and harder, making matters worse. One day some people
pulled me aside and told me the kids' behavior, while it could be a little disruptive, was actually normal.

That day I proclaimed the situation no longer a problem. The behavior
didn't change much, but my *view* of it did. And trust me, there was less conflict in my marriage after that! Most of the things that tend to upset us are
really not as critical as we've made them. Ask yourself, what's the worst that
can happen even if the situation doesn't change? Find ways to get emotional
and physical distance from problems so that you can be more objective and
less emotional. Ask others how they do it. You can learn a lot by doing this.

> Choose a problem—any problem—in your marriage and
> act like it isn't a problem for one day. Just one day! What
> happened? If you could not do it, the bigger problem may be your
> inability to back away for a while.

## Life's survivors have meaningful relationship connections.

While it's good to know how to distance ourselves from problems, resilient people who survive difficult experiences also become skilled at connecting with others.[16] This tends to fly in the face of what most of us want to do during bad times. After all, it's risky getting close to others. Why in the world should we risk anything if things are already rough? If you or your partner tend to isolate yourselves, you need to challenge this part of your comfort zone.

Reaching out and having relationships with others when there are problems shows a bit of defiance for the issues at hand. This quality—being defiant—serves us quite well and we will talk about this shortly. The main effect of connecting with others is that it forces you to have more of a balance in your life. It puts focus outside of you and onto others. Being "others-centered" is one of the central themes to having a strong character, remember? Relationships with others also keep us honest. It makes us accountable to good behavior and quickly shows us when we slip into a self-centered rut. Good friends make each other better, just as one piece of iron sharpens another piece.[17]

*Being "others-centered" is one of the central themes to having a strong character.*

When people come in and tell me horrible stories of things that happened to them in childhood, I tell them there is good news. They don't have to repeat the pattern in their lives! They have the power to choose a different way of living, and this happens in the context of present relationships.

Another reason for having relationships is what I call "spreading the need." When you live this way, you are patterning your relationships the way God wants, for it "fulfills the law of Christ" when we bear each other's burdens.[18] It is unhealthy to look to one person to satisfy all your relationship needs. This is particularly a problem in marriage, because our daily routine revolves around living with our spouse. It's easy to get into a rut of doing the same thing every day, coming home and crashing on the couch in front of the TV. The net effect sometimes is unintentionally looking to your partner to meet all your personal relationship needs. If you ask a marriage therapist to look at his or her active caseload of clients, he or she will tell you that many of them have this very problem.

People with survivor personalities have learned to tap into a kind of synergy in relating to others.[19] They have discovered that being giving to others actually ends up being in their own best interest. Jesus said it best, telling the crowd, "For whatever measure you deal out to others, it will be dealt to you in return."[20] There is a dynamic created when we give to others that adds up to more than just the sum of the parts. Our perspective is right, our focus is right, and the response we get from others becomes a blessing.

## A critical byproduct of meaningful relationships is the development of empathy, and this is a quality that survivors have.[21]

Has your marriage partner ever been frustrated with you because "you just don't seem to understand"? When you think about it, being able to understand another person's world requires you to experience what he or she is going through. Obviously, it isn't possible to experience everything that everyone has or is going through. Sometimes we have to look for something similar we went through, and sometimes we just have to care enough and listen closely to something that is new to us. That requires genuine effort.

> The point is, the human condition provides every one of us with experiences that make it possible to show caring and empathy.

Simply reduce it down if you want to be more empathetic. Empathy does not mean we have to fully understand everything a person is experiencing. I've never lost a child to cancer. There is no way I can pretend to know what that is like. But I know what it is to love my children and I also know what it is to feel pain and loss. Being empathetic may mean I know what it's like to feel alone and like no one else understands. The point is, the human condition provides every one of us with experiences that make it possible to show caring and empathy. Anyone can learn to be empathetic. If you have trouble showing or feeling empathy, just ask yourself what life experiences you've had to help you understand any part of the situation.

♥ If you have good personal relationships, plan a new way to call on these relationships the next time a problem comes up without necessarily discussing the problem. If you do not have other relationships, plan a strategy to start pursuing them beginning this week.

## Survivors are creative and even playful.

Many years ago, I saw a couple in marriage counseling who were simply too serious. On a personality profile they both scored in the 90th percentile on the scale of being overly serious. The other end of this scale was to be extremely lighthearted and happy-go-lucky. Without even knowing anything else, it was clear this was an important problem in their relationship. Everything remotely bad that happened to either one of them became a big problem. Any sign of disagreement or conflict led to a crisis.

My homework assignment for them was to go home and list out all their problems on paper. Then, going down the list one by one, they were both to make jokes about each problem. I knew they weren't going to be able to do it, and I was right. Upon returning, they said they tried but just couldn't do it. After getting them to laugh a little about this (a good trick, right?), I sent them home with the same assignment and told them it was a big problem if they couldn't do it. Of course they didn't want another serious problem! Sure enough, they came back and said they had the time of their lives poking fun at themselves.

Before counseling was all over, they established an extremely strong relationship that was still going strong even years later when I ran into them. They consciously used humor to keep from becoming too upset when things didn't go right. Now I work at getting people to laugh in counseling! If they can't, I know we have serious issues in this area.

People who can bounce back during stressful situations have learned how to be playful and laugh *despite* their circumstances.[22] It's just one way we show that we follow the Bible's encouragement to be content in all our circumstances, showing we trust God to be in control.[23]

Think about it. What happens when your emotions run high? They crowd out rational thinking. Your first love, anger at someone who cheated you, fear that grips you as you look over the ledge of a fifty-story building, are all strong emotions making rational thinking difficult. Humor keeps your emotions in check so you can continue to think clearly. It's powerful!

Survivors are more playful than others, also using humor, and they use it to get through tough times. If a problem or situation amuses you, this has the effect of saying, *This isn't such a big deal, I can play with this thing.* Both humor and being playful enables you to keep your head, have some confidence, think clearly, not blow something out of proportion, and essentially get out of your own way.

A modest example of this principle is a case cited by a therapist who trained with the guru of modern clinical hypnosis, Milton Erickson, M.D. This protégé, later to become an outstanding therapist in his own right, met with a thirty-three-year-old woman named Katherine who had been in one of his seminars. She had severe anxiety attacks in any situation requiring her to perform in some way. She knew on a conscious level there was no good reason to be anxious, but her emotions would overwhelm her ability to think rationally about it anyway. She would run out of routine business meetings if she was supposed to provide a report.[24]

Katherine admitted to having low self-esteem due to being overweight. She had been sexually abused by her father at age eleven, and described her mother as rigid, uptight, and hypercritical. During her hypnotic state, indirectly the therapist made references to things important to her to tap into her subconscious strengths.

She heard stories that even included her childhood stuffed panda while she was under hypnosis. The stories had events and endings that she could apply to her situation. Using playful memories became useful even as an adult.

Katherine returned the next day to the seminar and, as assigned, presented a 15-minute report to a group of sixty professionals! Several months later, she was continuing to make improvements in several areas. The point here is that conquering strong emotion is important, and sometimes you achieve that with humor and playfulness. Think of how that could make you a better marriage partner.

*Intuition is a key ingredient to creativity.*

## Survivors learn to trust and use their intuition about problems.[25]

Intuition is the key ingredient to creativity. This is the flip side of conquering strong emotion with play and humor. Ask any logical person if it's hard to think with true creativity about something he or she knows a lot about. Instead of emotions being the problem, sometimes overthinking is. Some people can't stop thinking about a problem, becoming obsessive and making themselves sick. For this kind of person to rely on intuition can feel next to impossible. But once the paralysis of analysis stops, creativity can begin. Just be careful to rely on more than intuition alone.

Whatever your tendency, if it blocks your ability to be playful, humorous, and be intuitive with problems, it isn't helpful. This represents another opportunity to strengthen your character. The first step is to recognize and admit it. Then develop some kind of plan to get control of that part of your personality. It will add a great deal to your character. If you are unable to do this, realize this may be preventing growth in your relationship. Don't keep blaming your partner for something that *you* need to change.

♥   Sit down with your partner and agree to make jokes with
    each other about some of your most sensitive issues. Don't
stop trying until you are able to do this successfully.

## Survivors initiate efforts to solve problems.

There are frogs everywhere in Florida. After a heavy night rain, frogs can be so thick on the street you can't walk across without stepping on them. In the morning, frog pancakes are all over the street from the cars. They aren't the brightest creatures on the planet and don't do much to ensure their own survival. You've probably heard that if you put a live frog in a skillet and slowly turn up the heat, it will sit there and fry until it is dead. Only if you toss it into an already-hot pan will it jump out due to the heat. This may be a myth, but it does make a point.

Amazingly, many people are married to frogs. They do nothing about issues in their marriage, often not even noticing there are issues. When told there is an issue, they act like they don't believe it. Only a crisis gets their attention, then after the crisis is over, it's back to life as usual—whether the problem has been fixed or not. It's one thing to be laid-back and relaxed, but it's another to sit back and provide no energy to your marriage.

People who stand up well to life's challenges have a keen eye about what is good and what is not, and then they take the bull by the horns and dive into finding solutions.[26] If you want to be this kind of person, you have to get up each day and be focused, organized, and goal-oriented about your life and especially your marriage. If your circumstances or even your partner make this difficult, you don't back off the challenge. This does not mean you become oppositional or combative, but you should be stubborn about having high standards for your marriage.

In the previous chapter you heard the story of Jim and Bobbi. You may recall they had been married forty years and she had become bitter and full of anger from years of unexpressed disappointment. Jim could do nothing to make things right. All he knew to do was keep trying to do the right thing, correcting prior mistakes one day at a time. He continued to appeal to Bobbi to let go of the past and make today count. Finally, after three years of daily badgering Jim, she finally announced she wanted to let go of her anger. Jim was a frog for years by neglecting the marriage. But he decided to stop being one no matter what it took. It finally paid off in a big way. He is one of the lucky ones—many spouses end up leaving a frog.

## Survivors have a "stubborn expectation" that things can and will turn out well.[27]

There is an optimistic spirit about them, which leads them to keep trying. There is even a defiant quality to this outlook. Persistent patience instead of knee-jerk reactions is part of this trait. Many of us often misunderstand these people because they tend to test the rules and even break some of them. Al Siebert tells of an ex-POW of the Korean War who witnessed an example of this controlled defiance. He witnessed a prisoner who was told "by a guard to sit at one end of a four-foot long bench without moving and how, with the guard watching him, he moved very, very slowly until he was eventually sitting on the other end."[28]

If you want your marriage to be the best it can be, don't be a frog that does nothing. Don't be afraid to challenge the status quo. Don't just "settle" because a situation seems impossible! Learn what a good relationship looks like, then don't settle for less. Accept the challenge, even welcoming it as something you know you can conquer. Survivors do not shrink back at these defining moments—they roll up their sleeves and immediately start focusing on solutions.[29]

Pick an area in your marriage relationship that you know could be better. Without being controlling or aggressive, bring this up to your partner and concentrate on it all week. Don't settle for mediocrity. Do your part to make things better. Then discuss whether the benefits outweighed the disadvantages of doing this.

## Survivors know when to do nothing.

There are situations all around us that are best handled by doing nothing. Our very efforts to solve a problem have often become part of the problem. Remember the old Chinese finger trap made out of straw? You insert each index finger at opposite ends and pull from both ends. The result is a tightening of the trap and neither finger comes out. It's only when you pull gently that it is no longer a trap. This comes up all the time in relationships. The more you try the worse a situation gets.

*Our very efforts to solve a problem have often become part of the problem.*

A stepmother came in concerned that her eighteen-year-old stepson, Paul, was becoming more and more disrespectful to her. She and the father had been at odds for years about how to parent the boy. The father insisted he was the primary person responsible for parenting, a message Paul picked up on at an early age. She wanted to micromanage Paul's behavior and the dad wanted to overlook some behaviors until they became part of a bigger pattern. During arguments, Paul would tell his stepmother he did not need a third parent, but then later he wanted her to do things for him. What always triggered this disrespect was the stepmother trying to enforce her expectations of Paul.

Well, Paul was getting mostly As and Bs in school, had a job, and was preparing to graduate from high school in a few months. Then he was going away to college. What would you do? Stepmom did not want to back down from her stance that he *did* need another parent figure, that his behavior was unacceptable, and he should let her give him direct guidance as a parent figure.

My advice to her was to consider doing nothing. Redefine what her role was and save herself the grief. Paul had made it clear for years that he cared about the stepmother but viewed her as an extra parent figure. Dad had reinforced that idea for years. Paul was leaving home in just a few months *and* was performing his responsibilities at a high level. Dad still had expectations that he was willing to enforce. In a case like this, it makes more sense to do nothing and change the way you think about the situation.

An old friend told me something a long time ago that has always served me well. We were discussing the challenges of being the parents of teenagers and he said, "John, I decided to stop giving my son things to resist, and now he cooperates." This doesn't mean you roll over and accept a bad situation. Instead, it suggests we need to get out of the way sometimes so solutions can work themselves out. Sometimes fewer words are more and reduced efforts are better.

This rings true in all relationships, especially marriage. The rule here is this: keep your efforts to control the behavior of your partner to a minimum. It's great to ask for what you want, but then you have to be able to let your partner show some effort. We'll talk more about how this works in a later chapter. But if you find your marital conflicts are always charged with high emotions, this is a red flag suggesting it's time to back off a bit. Many people find this hard to do because they lock themselves in with one way of thinking. It's okay—no, it's preferred—not to control everything or know exactly how everything will turn out. Jesus said to be concerned only with today because God even takes care of the birds of the air. Focus instead on what is truly lasting in life.[30]

> With an issue that you have been actively trying to "fix," do absolutely nothing for a couple of weeks. While this may have some negative results, determine ways this helped and incorporate those things into all of your future efforts.

## Survivors have a clear sense of morality.

Regardless of your spiritual orientation, it has been found that those who are strongest in the midst of problems are those who actively serve others.[31] Having a sense of right and wrong where others are concerned has helped people through the toughest of times. Christians have known this for a long time, since the coming of Jesus had been prophesied for centuries before his birth. He sacrificed his own life for others, encouraging us to follow his example. We'll cover this much more in a later chapter, but what better place to serve than with your marriage partner?

This is one of the great paradoxes of life. By giving of yourself to others, you get more in return. This works even if your motives are selfish, but the danger of that is that your love is conditional. Give to your partner because you love him or her *and* because it is the right thing to do. This motivation will never fail you. This kind of love never fails, regardless of what your partner does. It carries you through anything. And if your partner is also living this way, nothing can tear you apart.

Unfortunately, this ideal is sometimes not what we find ourselves experiencing. Let's take a look at a few situations that are too common in our society.

## ATTRIBUTES OF "UGLY" MARRIAGES

Since each marriage *partner* has a distinct personality, merging the two results in a unique *marriage* personality. Sometimes the net result can look pretty ugly. Character strengths and weaknesses play off each other and, over time, produce some predictable patterns of interaction. Some are good and some are not so good.

> Understanding the personality of your marriage helps you see if there are some character attributes needing attention by either partner.

The personality of your marriage influences the way you do everything as a couple. Looking at the attributes of your marriage can help you pinpoint what drives it to have the personality it does, including some clues about what it will take from individual partners to make it stronger. Understanding the personality of your marriage helps you see if there are some character attributes needing attention by either partner.

We will explore how to get out of destructive patterns later in the book, but there are a few common "marriage personalities" worth a quick mention.

## The Never-Good-Enough Marriage

This marriage personality has frequent issues around measuring up to a high standard. Criticism is common at home. One or both partners feel like married life is performance-based. You often feel under pressure, as if you are expected to be perfect. This theme is usually traceable to childhood experiences, although it can certainly develop later in life. Interactions usually become defensive with a lot of finger-pointing. If one partner already has a low self-esteem, this way of interacting will create a polarity between partners. One will often feel attacked while the other is frustrated that the progress he expects is slow or nonexistent.

The never-good-enough marriage often becomes shame-based if the issues do not get resolved early in the relationship. Shame, if allowed to blossom, becomes an extremely negative energy force. It overshadows everything like an overcast day. Marriages with a lot of shame tend to have a lot of denial and inflexibility going on within them, for example, "There is only one way of doing things and I'm the one to tell you what that way is."

A young unmarried couple came in for counseling and one of the main issues was that he would not settle for "average" in any area of his life. She was perfectly okay with average. Not below average, just average. Sometimes that works just fine for us. As a result of this pressure, she felt talked down to, lectured, and even parented by him. After a while, she began to doubt herself and question her own intelligence.

If this describes your marriage in any way, what is needed most is a calm discussion about how measuring up seems to be too high on the priority list. Regardless of specific issues or complaints, there is a *way* of approaching these things that comes across as inflexible, demanding, and accusing. The question should be asked, *Is there really only one standard or one way of doing something?* And, *How could I make requests with a spirit of acceptance and an appreciation for differences?*

A final thought: if your standards seem too high for your partner, you need to be humble enough to ask yourself if your expectations should change. Who made you the boss of expectations? On the other hand, if your self-esteem is low and you struggle with feeling good enough on any given day, don't put that onto your partner. Take responsibility to address your own insecurities and learn to be assertive in communicating your personal struggles. Otherwise, your partner will stay confused about why you react the way you do. It is common for both extremes to be going on at once. Then, both partners need to meet in the middle someplace. These situations are important defining moments. Ask yourselves, *Who needs to do what for this marriage personality to change?*

## The Pain-Avoidant Marriage

Some marriages evolve to a point where one or both partners would rather just avoid important issues. They have given themselves permission to develop a comfort zone in which nothing negative exists. Partners become resident experts at predicting the response of their counterpart and base their behavior on this fantasy response. What develops then is a mountain of misconceptions about each other.

One woman in marriage counseling was so convinced she knew what her partner *really* thought that there was nothing he could say to convince her otherwise. She was guilty of mind reading and refused to consider other possibilities.

People with this kind of marriage tend to argue very little, if at all. Conversations about important issues often trail off with no resolution. Some conversations can take several months to finish because people are so busy avoiding anything painful. Meaningful connection with each other suffers since your relationship is so limited. The danger of growing apart is huge.

If one partner operates this way and the other partner wants to address whatever he or she thinks is important, overall marital discontent sets in for the "working" partner. The avoiding partner puts a wall up, keeps his thoughts and feelings to himself, thus preventing intimacy. He may even become passive-aggressive in response to pressures to address things directly. He'll say he agrees and then turn around and do the opposite.

If this is the personality of your marriage, whoever has a habit of avoiding pain needs to discuss—with complete honesty—what that is all about. Most of us are experts at "training" our partner to interact with us a certain way. If my wife knows I go crazy if she spends any extra money, either she will not spend it or she will hide the fact she did. Rather than continuing to hide her behavior, the healthy thing to do is to tell me honestly she doesn't agree with me about being able to spend money once in a while. And if your partner approaches you with something like this, the worst thing you can do is tell her it's all her problem. She is who she is, and you need to learn how to "work" with the situation in a way that encourages her to grow and face the issue.

Your marriage has everything to gain by being forthright and honest, even if temporary pain results. The Bible tells us that the wounds of a friend are faithful[32] and that it's a blessing when we are corrected by the righteous.[33] Harboring bad feelings does not work. Face yourself if this is a problem for you. Develop the strength of character to leave your comfort zone for the sake of your marriage.

## The Selfish Marriage

This marriage type consists of one or both partners who focus mostly on their own wants and needs: a husband who wants to go out with his buddies all the time; a wife who has an elaborate agenda about how home life should run. Partners in this kind of marriage typically show little understanding or empathy for the other. They are only concerned with how day-to-day life serves them.

Interactions often lead to power struggles and hard feelings. Partners do not feel listened to because they aren't! The selfish partner has a hard time being anything but preoccupied with his world. His goals, thought life, priorities, communication style, marriage expectations, and response patterns are all filtered through what he is going to get out of a situation. When he does thoughtful things it's because somehow he will benefit. Of course, the nature of human interaction is such that we relate to others based on getting something out of it. But the selfish partner rarely gives unconditionally and selflessly. How you give of yourself to casual acquaintances or strangers is a quick acid test of how giving you really are. Agreed-upon solutions in this kind of marriage are often short-lived. Selfishness creeps back in and the other partner feels like he is doing all the giving.

If you are in a relationship like this, the problem is frankly a deep one and will take time to fix. The prognosis for this problem depends on how indulged the self-centered partner was growing up and whether he can point to experiences or times of selfless behavior. Did he learn a value of giving unconditionally even if he was overindulged? If the answer is no, he has to be willing to admit this is not an admirable trait and that it needs to change. A "values overhaul" is needed.

Sometimes people become selfish in marriage over time because they have been unsuccessful resolving issues in the marriage. Focusing on themselves is how they cope with the disappointment. Of course, this does not make it right, but it is a whole different problem. Uncover the source of this and deal with it. And by all means—do not hide behind blaming the other person to justify selfish behavior. Regardless of the reason, it is never helpful nor justifiable. Identify the specific situations that often lead to selfish behavior. Then decide on specific new behaviors that you need.

## The Emotionally Charged Marriage

These marriages feel like a roller coaster because at least one partner is an "emotional thinker," or else issues have escalated to an all-time emotional high. A course of action is right only if it *feels* right. Conflicts almost always have lots of negative emotion. Moods rule the day. Sometimes it's calm or happy at home, and sometimes it's anxious, angry, or depressed.

Emotions carry with them a sort of electrical charge. Have you ever stood outside before an electrical storm and felt your hair stand up? Or gone to bed, turned out the lights, and seen flashes of electricity on a wool blanket when you pull the covers down? Emotions tend to work the same way. After a while, they just seem to fill the air and have a similar effect on all the people in the room. If your partner worries all the time, you eventually tense up. If depressed, you find it hard not to get gloomy yourself.

Unfortunately, emotions are unreliable decision-makers because they can go up and down so much. If you follow your emotions you are subjecting your thoughts to them. Your thoughts will just keep reinforcing the feeling. You'll stay confused and feel at the mercy of whatever feelings you have.

If this describes your marriage, each partner must take personal responsibility for his emotions. It is a myth to believe that if it feels right it must be right. Identify the source of the emotion. If it is a relational issue then you have something meaningful to talk about. Unresolved issues from the past could be driving the negative energy, in which case you must address them. Some people have learned destructive emotional habits and simply need to re-pattern their emotional responses. Some need to change their thinking and make their feelings take a backseat. If there is no logical explanation for the feelings there is always the possibility of a mood disorder. A true mood disorder results from a chemical imbalance and is not the "fault" of anyone. You should consult a physician if this seems to be the case.

I have found that one primary issue usually drives a relationship in which there is a lot of negative emotional energy. Day-to-day bickering can be about any number of things and camouflage the real problem. It is often helpful to ask what the real problem is, assuming it is under the surface of recent arguments. Spend some personal time in reflection until you sort out what it is that the emotion is really about.

## The Control-Based Marriage

These relationships are all about controlling things. It may be the result of one partner who is like this and forces the other partner to choose how he will adapt. He may give in, ignoring his own needs. Occasional efforts to break out of this result in running into a brick wall. Or he may refuse to give in and then the relationship starts to look like both partners have to be in control. One-upsmanship is where most disagreements end up. Compromise does not

happen easily at all. One person is likely to get the short
end of the stick more often than the other unless both
partners are stubbornly vying for position.

Power struggles and vicious cycles set in when the
need to control typifies your relationship. You reject
reasonable options for solutions and it sounds like
you are always making excuses for why a solution
won't work. Rational attempts at being reasonable seem
to get nowhere for some unidentifiable reason. Thinking outside the box and being creative with solutions rarely occur. Venturing into
unfamiliar waters in the relationship is prevented by black- and-white, one-
sided thinking.

> *Marriage partners that jockey for position need to air out all their fears of losing the control.*

Marriage partners that jockey for position need to air out all their fears of
losing the control. It could be the definition of your role at home, a certain task
you perform, or just the way you do certain things. If you relaxed, what do you
think would happen? Whatever you think would happen, even if it did would
it be so bad? Does your partner really understand what your concern is? If your
partner understands, says he will change and doesn't, you should both be honest enough to address this openly. There is some reason he is not changing. If
he does not understand, there is no way he can do what you want until he does.

Remember: you can't force anyone to do anything. Any two-year-old will
tell you that! If stepping up your efforts to get control has not worked up to this
point, it probably won't work to keep doing that. A horse won't drink the water
you put in front of him until he's thirsty. Find out what gets the horse thirsty.

## The Smothering Marriage

Too much pressure on the marriage to meet all of your needs smothers the
relationship and both partners. This happens when one or both partners iso-
lates themselves from much of the outside world, centering everything on
their spouse. You keep friends, if there are any, at a distance. Individual
hobbies are few. The couple is rarely apart from each other and individual
sense of identity becomes blurred.

In smothering marriages, roles get skewed over time. Early on in the relationship, isolating as a couple serves to help meet some perceived personal needs of each person. One such couple came for therapy after living together for fifteen years. When they met, Linda was twenty and Joel was twenty-six. She found the relationship offered the security she was seeking, and he was comfortable taking on a paternal role. She always looked to him for his opinions and preferences, altering her behavior to please him. They spent a lot of time alone together. After years of this (and sometimes this worked well), Linda had grown and matured. She no longer needed nor wanted a paternal relationship. Joel isolated himself and didn't have his own friends and interests, relying solely on her, which made her feel smothered.

When I met them they had separated over the stress of this. They fought constantly and bitterly. Joel had learned to become anxious about Linda's newfound liberation. He misinterpreted it as wanting to cut him out of her life and even became jealous, thinking she wanted to have an affair whenever she went out without him. Once they were able to see what was really going on, they were able to legitimize Linda's perspective and help Joel readjust his focus in his life.

People in smothered marriages first need to understand how and when they got that way. There may have been a perfectly understandable reason that served a purpose for a while. Additionally, you may now see some personal insecurities that need to be addressed some other way. Breaking out of the isolation will evoke some anxiety, so be prepared for that. Work on having a healthier balance between couple time and individual time. Learn to appreciate and encourage your partner's individuality. After all, that's what makes them special, and that's what they alone can give to you.

## The Cynical Marriage

Computer programs have certain properties that behave in a predictable, unique way and that limit what is possible. Whenever you try to do something outside the program, it just defaults to what it can do. Cynical relationships are a lot like this. One or both partners has a natural tendency to be negative and expect the worst. Interactions have an overall lack of joy and the mood of the relationship is one of discouragement. Marital goals either do not exist or they are filtered through the hope of things being less bad instead of good. You see life and/or marital issues like a glass that's half empty instead of half full. Even positive partners have a hard time staying that way in this kind of relationship. Sooner or later, the cynical marriage always brings the positive aspects of the relationship down into this negative perspective.

Routine day-to-day interactions appear as if someone is depressed. People start changing their behavior in anticipation of this, resulting in such things as avoiding their partner, staying away from certain topics, escaping through other outlets, becoming self-absorbed, and finding excuses to come home late, to name a few. Discussions that are goal-focused and successful at resolving issues rarely occur.

If you are in this kind of relationship, ask yourself some honest questions about how much of the negativity you bring to it. Be watchful of how positive you are even with day-to-day things. Does your conversation tend to be critical, do you make fun of others too much, or find fault? Is it just not positive? If so, start by watching how positive your normal conversation is (don't overlook nonverbal communication).

When you are involved with a problem issue, do you spend any meaningful time talking about how you could solve it? Many people say "yes" here but focus mostly on their complaint. Be sure to include "solution talk" in the things you discuss.

If your partner is being cynical much of the time, try to get him or her to see that. Be honest. Share how it affects you. Look at how the cynicism has modified your behavior and refuse to let that continue.

## The Carry-on Baggage Marriage

Don't you love it when someone gets on the plane with two suitcases that are supposed to be carry-on luggage? They hold up the line trying to fit them in the overhead bins, and they certainly won't fit under the seat. Some marriages are like this in that they have partners who bring lots of unresolved personal issues with them. These issues clearly get in the way of a healthy marriage and seem to come up at all the worst times.

Sometimes these issues are concrete and easy to spot, like being a neat freak or an uncontrollable penny-pincher. These kinds of unresolved issues can be difficult to change, but at least they are not confusing to identify for what they are. Then there are those hang-ups that have evolved so much over time it's hard to know exactly what they are. One reason they can be so confusing is they take on the form of a chameleon. Today the marriage has a cynical personality and tomorrow it has a control-based one. To further the confusion, there is often more than one major issue from the past interfering with the present.

This is often the most difficult marriage personality because it takes the most effort to get to what is really going on. It requires people to be willing to look at themselves with painful honesty. Denial is common, making insight limited. The simplest way to uncover these issues is to work backward from a problem. What is the problem behavior or interaction? Then explore what makes it so important for the person to respond the way he does. This step may take some time and reflection to complete. If he just cannot answer this, try a different angle. What would be so bad about doing things differently? If there is still no answer, the solution may simply require the person to behave differently despite the anxiety it produces. However, if he can identify what the hang-up is, trace it back to the last time in his life it was *not* an issue. This will get you to the source of the problem and give you enough information to begin working on it.

If you have brought too much carry-on baggage into your marriage, have the courage to look at yourself honestly. Identify the ways it alters your behavior. Watch for situations that trigger these responses and commit to a response showing strength of character. That is how you know you are bringing the right kind of heart to the situation.

♥ Discuss with your partner what personality your marriage has (it may not be one of the ones described here). Include how it influences your behavior and how you contribute to this personality. If this isn't the kind of personality you want, come up with ways to change it for the better.

## YOU TOO CAN BEAT THE ODDS

Divorce is all around us. Your personal attributes will either help lead to divorce or they will help shatterproof your marriage. Anything in between will not serve you well if the stress becomes severe enough. To believe that giving more than you receive in life always leads to something greater than you, you must look at your own personal attributes. What you may need to "give" is the sacrifice of changing something about yourself. If your personal attributes are not serving to shatterproof your marriage, make the decision to change them. If you do, you can beat the odds and have a lasting marriage.

You may be thinking you are too weak or too messed up to change anything significant about your situation. Or perhaps there have already been a lot of really bad things happen in your marriage and it just feels hopeless. Right now could be the biggest defining moment you have faced yet. If so, your situation also invites the biggest question you have ever faced so far. What are you basing your life on? The Bible tells us that *nothing* can separate us from God's love[34] and that love *never* fails.[35] No matter how dark it looks there is always hope. Even if things are terrible, you can *choose* to face it like a true survivor.

Let us continue learning from the survivors of Nazi prison camps for as long as we live. Despite certain predictable responses, "it becomes clear that the sort of person the prisoner became was the result of an inner decision and not the result of camp influences alone. Fundamentally, therefore, any man can, even under such circumstances, decide what shall become of him—mentally and spiritually."[36] Every single day is a new opportunity in your marriage by making an inner decision to be the kind of person you need to be.

Don't allow the problems in your marriage to determine your behavior. Decide today to put an end to destructive patterns in your marriage and fight the battle one minute at a time. Stretch yourself. Take some discomfort. It is well worth the price! You can refuse to keep contributing to the bad things that happen with your own behavior. This can, and often does, make enough difference for both of you. Remember: Element #1, personal character, requires some distinct personality strengths.

Keep reading, and we will take a closer look at how you can fight this battle.

## Main Chapter Attitudes

✓ Work on personality growth whenever and wherever needed.
✓ Invest the effort to learn from past experiences.

### Attitudes in Action

1. **Attitude: Work on personality growth whenever and wherever needed.**
   What survivor personality trait(s) do you need to work on the most? How can you start developing it, then applying it in your marriage?

2. **Attitude: Invest the effort to learn from past experiences.**
   How did your childhood family make it easier or more difficult to be married? With your partner, identify specific situations that bring this out in you. Determine how both of you can communicate better at those times instead of being reactive.

**3. Attitude: Contribute your best to the marriage.**

Are you a good marriage partner right now? If not, what specific changes do you need to make immediately to be one? After you answer these questions for yourself, ask your partner to answer the same questions about you. Discuss what you are going to work on changing.

# 4

# Be Intelligent with Expectations

*The game isn't over till it's over.*

Yogi Berra

More often than not, what you expect in life is a self-fulfilling prophecy.

If you want something bad enough, you are more likely to get your wish. Anticipating a certain outcome contributes to its happening. If you expect your day to go slowly, your whole outlook becomes one of watching the clock. It *does* go slowly. When you expect to reach certain goals, you have already increased your chances of reaching them. What you expect out of life—and your marriage—says a lot about your personal character. To have the right personal character for a shatterproof marriage, it's critical you review your expectations regularly.

Years ago I had to move away from my dream spot (Colorado) and move to the East Coast for a job. The local economy was in trouble and I had little choice. After a couple of years, I still had frequent dreams of returning. Believe it or not, I would dream of the sound of the wind going through the trees up in the mountains. There is no other sound like it. Finally one day I called an old work acquaintance and asked him how good he thought the chances were that I might be able to return. Had the economy improved enough? He told me something that jarred me and has stuck with me to this day. He said, "John, if you really want to come back, you will." I thought, *How could this be? Is he right?* A year later and I was back! I became passionate about returning and did a lot of things to make it possible. Now I do believe that God is ultimately in control, as you might, but I learned a valuable lesson that day. Our expectation about something has more power than I ever realized before.

*If the expectations you have about your marriage are actually part of the problem, you have the power to change them.*

This principle is at work even when you are not aware of it. Thinking you will do well at a job interview before you get there usually results in a good interview. Expecting your child to fail often leads to exactly that. There is an "air" about you that shows what kind of expectations you have. If the expectations you have about your marriage are actually part of the problem, you have the power to change them. Richard Stuart, a contemporary pioneer of social learning theory, says, "The individual is thus seen as the partial cause and the partial result" of the interaction between his behaviors and those of his partner.[1] He goes on to say that this is the result of "expectancies that each person has learned from experience."[2] We all do it. What you expect in your marriage has a direct bearing on what is happening in your marriage. Your life experiences and the way you have responded to them have played a major role in determining your expectations.

A great example of this is a couple that came in for help because the wife did not seem to be able to get through to her husband. She had a picture in her mind of what the intimacy in their marriage should look like, and he just didn't get it. So I asked them both to tell me what a good marriage looks like. She articulately went into detail about the kinds of affection they would express, how they would work well together, and even how they would approach conflict constructively. Then it was his turn. His answer was this: "I like it when my partner doesn't hit me or call me names." I said, "Now Bob, are you sure you understand the question? The question was, what does a good marriage look like?" He affirmed his understanding of the question and stuck by his answer.

Holy smokes!

This was honestly how he gauged whether things *were* ideal at home! It turned out he got hit and was called names a lot in his first marriage, so he became "trained" to expect very little. Consequently, he gave little and couldn't even understand requests for anything positive. Needless to say, the rest of this couple's therapy focused on helping him explore and modify these expectations. Once his expectations were raised, marital interactions improved dramatically.

## KEY ATTITUDE:
**Be open to changing your expectations.**

We all have expectations of the world around us that determines how we behave. This trickles down to the most routine of situations. Asking yourself a few questions can help you identify some of your expectations. Is the world basically a friendly or a hostile place? Safe or unsafe? How do you determine if you are an "acceptable" person? What is the right response to injustice in your life? Is showing any kind of personal weakness an okay thing to do? These are just a few of the philosophical questions that you answer every day, even when you don't realize it. For example, if you think the world is basically a hard, hostile place, you are likely to brace yourself for a fight when conflict arises at home. You communicate your "readiness" nonverbally and this naturally produces a reaction from others.

What kinds of situations trigger the biggest reaction from you? What set of expectations trigger it? Your personality, life experiences, and the people in your life have shaped this view. Chances are there is *some* part of it that is not consistent with reality. By examining your expectations more closely, you will then be able to modify them as needed. Then your reactions to life will be more in your control.

This is a big part of Element #1. Having the right character in marriage requires you to challenge your most basic expectations in life. This may not be easy, but is part of the shatterproofing process in marriage. It *always* results in something greater than you, and is well worth the effort. If you would like to explore your own expectations more thoroughly, refer to the Common Reactions inventory in Appendix D.

## DARE TO EXPECT SOMETHING DIFFERENT

Most everyone knows the divorce rate in America has been on the rise for a long time. We are in a time of incredible change and have been since the Industrial Revolution. There was a lull in the fifties, but since then the change has been rapid and dramatic. Morality has evolved, too. The traditional model of marriage in the fifties has been challenged by attitudes that promoted "love-ins," open marriages, increased drug usage, the "Me Generation," the "Generation X-ers," and on and on.

*Key Attitude:*
**Develop a clear sense of your obligations to your marriage and live up to them.**

Once you do, this will filter any self-defeating expectations you might have. Frankly, the American culture has become a permissive one where the freedom to divorce is more accepted than ever. David Brenner, associate director of the Institute for American Values, sent an editorial to the *New York Times* in 1999 addressing this. He said, "Society's greater acceptance of divorce may itself be contributing to the decline in marital happiness. A study published in the *Journal of Family Issues* recently concluded that 'by adopting attitudes that provide greater freedom to leave unsatisfying marriages, people may be increasing the likelihood that their marriages will become unsatisfying in the long run.' It seems that the divorce culture feeds on itself."[3]

Sound familiar? People may have lots of high expectations for their marriage, but when they are not met, they see divorce as a simple solution. If your worldview includes feeling the freedom to divorce "because it just didn't work out," or "I just don't feel happy anymore," you just set yourself up for the very thing you don't want to happen—a marriage that doesn't work out! The foundation in your marriage is shaky from the very start.

Roughly half the marriages in the United States still end in divorce, and a rate nearly this high applies to those getting married again after they have been divorced.[4] While half the people getting married end up divorced, 81 percent of those same divorced people still believe marriage is a commitment for life![5] How can so many people with this view of marriage still end up getting divorced—again and again? It just isn't enough to try to be smart, choose a mate carefully, and then hope for the best. Instead, you need to understand what it really takes to succeed, then make sure the foundation for success is in place. Additionally, be clear on what your obligations are (and what they are not), be sure your partner understands and agrees with you, then live up to them. When, for example, is divorce acceptable to you? How did you determine your answer?

> *It just isn't enough to try to be smart, choose a mate carefully, and then hope for the best.*

Talk with your partner about what you believe your marital obligations are. Be specific. What is an okay reason for divorce? Does your answer provide the security to your partner that he/she wants?

## KEY ATTITUDE:
**Be honest about how real your belief in God is.**

Yes, our times are surely changing. How many times have you run into someone or overheard someone talking about living with a boyfriend or girlfriend for a while before getting married? It has become commonplace and, unfortunately, pretty widely accepted. While the Bible is clear that premarital sex is wrong,[6] many parents are fighting an uphill battle with their kids about such issues because our culture has become flooded with acceptance.

In one study, 73 percent of adolescents either had a positive view or no opinion about cohabitation. This flies in the face of most research, which shows that couples who cohabitate first have less marital success than those who do not.[7] Starting at a young age, we are all heavily influenced by what is going on in the culture around us.

We all know that divorce is not what God wants. If you are serious about your belief in God, you should know what the Bible says about marriage, sexuality, and divorce. Otherwise, your notion of God is only your notion, not necessarily the God of the Bible. If you are living a double standard, doing some things God's way and some things not, realize that much of the available research supports God's way of doing things. Setting your expectations accordingly can and will serve you well. Anything else lays an unreliable foundation for your marriage.

## WHAT DO YOU EXPECT FROM MARRIAGE?

Most people have never sat down and defined for themselves what constitutes the ideal marriage. Marriage changes, people change, life changes. What is marriage *supposed* to give you? And what if it doesn't? Do you just throw in the towel?

The fact is, popular American ideas are not the only way to pursue a satisfying marriage. The world is full of other cultures that have very different expectations about marriage. Consequently, day-to-day married life in these cultures looks different. Likewise, people around the world decide whether they are satisfied in their marriage in a variety of ways. Believe it or not, "happiness" is not the only or even the main marital goal everywhere! Think about it: imagine getting up every day and living for something other than personal happiness. So if you answered that marriage owes you happiness—especially your definition of happiness—you may want—no, you may *need*—to think again.

**KEY ATTITUDE:
Give up any sense of entitlement that is selfish.**

From culture to culture, other approaches to marriage can and do work. So what if your marriage doesn't meet all your expectations? Who said marriage owes you everything you have in your mind? Let's review just a few cultures to illustrate.

Before reading further, write down a short paragraph defining what an ideal marriage is to you. You might find your answer interesting as you continue with the chapter and see what you did and did not include with your answer.

Monica McGoldrick has written a widely used textbook about how different cultural histories *within* our culture trickle down into everyday life for families. While her ideas are not meant to be "absolute truth," she causes us to think about how our roots tend to affect everything we do. Here are just a few of the cultures she examined that may tend to look for marital "happiness" in different ways:

NATIVE AMERICANS—"Happy" when respectful listening is going on; partners think in terms of "we" versus "I" when it comes to family issues.[8]

AFRICAN AMERICANS—Historically, African women have had an easier time obtaining gainful employment,[9] so some of these couples have defined marital roles differently. This is rooted in generations of experience for some African Americans. Even as this trend evolves, some of these couples may be "happy" when the wife helps the husband maintain his rightful place of strength in the relationship.

AFRICAN AMERICAN MUSLIMS—This culture believes that the best husband is one who is very good to his wife. Divorce is among the worst of possible sins,[10] so both partners can be happy so long as he is good to her. When combined with the African American experience, this dynamic tends to be created. African Americans may be attracted to Islam because it provides order and structure to their lives that social injustices have taken away. In our mainstream culture, we often expect many things *in addition* to our partner being good to us.

There aren't too many Hollywood movies out there that depict this as the awesome marriage, are there? The American culture defines marital happiness very differently. Partners who are *unhappy* tend to base this condition on how it feels emotionally.

JAPANESE—Indirect communication characterizes the Japanese marriage out of respect for the male-dominated hierarchy. Therefore, asking direct questions or speaking out is very uncomfortable.[11] Happiness comes from living these roles well.

A Japanese woman in her seventies came to me for help with her adult married son. She was very upset because the son was not fulfilling his duties as the eldest son (and male) within the family (which includes aunts, uncles, etc.). She was convinced he was not happy in his marriage because of this. She had become convinced that her son's marriage—namely his wife—was holding him back from his duties. This created huge conflict throughout the whole family and put a lot of strain on his marriage. Having grown up in the United States, he finally told Mom that his marriage was not her concern (this is *not* the Japanese way). However, he *did* continue to try to meet family expectations to lead the family. Mom was confused about how he could say he was happy. Frankly, he was a bit confused himself from trying to blend the expectations of both cultures.

Just because Japanese tradition does not define marital happiness as romantic love, does that make it wrong? Hollywood would have us think so. What expectations did you bring into marriage, and are you sure that they are all realistic and clear to both of you? How much do your expectations depend on an emotional feeling?

ARAB—So you think the Japanese approach to marriage might be hard? Similar to the Japanese culture, the Arab family chooses your mate. Romantic love, or knowing each other for that matter, is not even a factor. Personal feelings are really not the priority.[12] Male domination is a clear expectation.

Here's another real-life example of how real this is behind closed doors:

A couple came to see me that was having intense conflict. He was an Arab who came to the United States for work. She was a white woman raised in the United States. His attitude focused so much on the dominance of the male that she felt overwhelmingly oppressed. At one point, she feared he would take their children to his home country and never return. When asked, he confirmed he might very well do just that!

Unfortunately, this couple did not make it. The wife had no idea what she was getting into when she got married. Their marital expectations were nowhere close to each other. While this approach to marriage seems strange to Americans, and we may not even agree with it as an acceptable approach, it has been working for centuries when both spouses are on the same page.

GREEK—This culture tends to think of love in terms of being a good provider (for the husband) and being faithful. Dating and engagements do not occur as they do in the United States. In fact, there is no word in the Greek language for dating! The couple has focused discussions about what they want out of marriage at various points in this courtship.

Once married, the wife should make few demands and give love with no expectations. The wife often settles conflicts by giving in to the husband's wishes. Marital "communication" is not an end-all when it comes to feeling secure in the relationship.[13]

This sounds crazy to most of us, doesn't it? I asked a Greek couple (born in the United States) in marriage counseling about this. The husband indicated that his grandmother sat him down when he started "seeing" his future wife and told him, "There is no dating. You either marry her or be done with it." This couple then had very pointed discussions about what they wanted out of marriage. Even though they came to me for help, the husband described the marriage as being like a 12-cylinder car and sometimes it was running on 11 cylinders. Many marriages in the United States, unfortunately, seem to be like 4-cylinder cars running on one. This Greek couple had *thoroughly* covered their expectations *before* they got married.

What are the dating expectations of the American dating scene? Sexual compatibility, having lots of fun together, getting personal needs met (that have not been identified and discussed), passion, romance, and personal "happiness," to name a few. What are the criteria you use to decide whether you are happy in your marriage?

ANGLO—The United States census of 1790 revealed that a quarter of all Americans were of Anglo descent, with direct ties to Great Britain. The Anglo people have a long history of being happy when individual freedom and self-determination exist. Marital happiness comes from fulfilling individual, personal needs.[14] Sounds like a recipe for failure, doesn't it?

Is all this just a bunch of academic hoopla? Hardly. It gets played out every day behind closed doors. It's probably playing out at your house, very likely in ways you don't realize.

I could go on and on discussing all the cultures out there, but I hope you get the point. *Your* cultural background is important to *your* marriage, regardless of what culture you come from. What your great-great-grandfather did to come to America still influences who you are today, whether you know it or not. We all have a fascinating story to tell, even though most of us know a small fraction of our ancestry. This may seem like a tedious way to question your view of happiness, but I guarantee it plays a huge role. I discuss past family influences in the chapter on stress, so you will have a chance to come back to this and look at it some more.

So if you believe you are entitled to certain things in your marriage, I would challenge you to take a second look at them to see if you aren't shooting yourself in the foot with them. Exactly what are your expectations? Write them down. Were they formed by your upbringing or culture, or based more consciously on some well-established ideals?

> Talk with your partner about what you believe your marital expectations are. Be specific and write them down. Are these expectations easily influenced by your circumstances? If so, what expectations would be more consistent and be reliable when life changes?

## UNSPOKEN RULES AND YOUR EXPECTATIONS

We're all familiar with "unspoken" rules. We go to kindergarten and learn from some teachers that free expression is the rule, but then find out later this only applies if you are always agreeable. Later, we join an athletic team or musical ensemble, only to discover that others may not say what they expect of you. You just have to "figure it out" from some unspoken rule.

Why this happens is well beyond the scope of this book, but suffice it to say it happens at home too. We all develop "habits" about how we go about living our lives because, well, they just work. These things turn into unspoken rules, even if that is not our intention.

Unspoken rules may work for a long time, but time and circumstances can change all that. Al and Debbie learned this the hard way. When I met them, she was twenty-five and he was forty-six. He married her when she was still a teen. She grew up right before his eyes and began to question most things about their relationship. Historically, he was very much in charge of everything and he expected her to fall in line with the role of a dependent. When I met her, she was already planning her divorce. Among other things, she rejected all the unspoken rules that had worked for years. These unspoken rules could not withstand the test of life's changes.

## *Key Attitude:*
**Be willing to admit what your behavior is really saying.**

Your behaviors reveal many of your expectations. Over time, our lives take on some central themes based on what we expect about life. We looked at this in the previous chapter from a different angle—the personality of your marriage. There are also certain recurring themes in your marriage that reflect your unspoken rules. The kinds of unspoken rules you have about a given theme could be very different from the couple next door. It all depends on your approach to marriage. Expectations play a major role.

As a little experiment, ask yourself the following questions about your life right now:[15]

1. What topics of concern keep coming up in my life?

2. What are some interactions at home that are pretty unique to us and seem to happen with regularity? What are they about?

3. What conflicts keep coming up that have a lot of emotion tied to them?

4. What is the main emotional tone in your marriage (and what is that all about)?

Your behavior around these questions says a lot about you. Be honest and take the time to look at them closely. You may have already thought of these questions, but most people get too busy to stop and take an objective look at themselves very often. What you will find is that the answers to these questions will help you identify what the themes are in your relationship. These themes provide the energy that drives much of your married (or family) life. Your expectations turn into unspoken rules.

An example that is very common in America is the theme of personal achievement. Many children grow up with the expectation they have to get above-average grades in school. (By the way, when did average become such a bad thing?) When they don't, they get some form of parental disapproval. Depending on how parents show this disapproval, and what rationale they give the child for needing As and Bs, a daughter may think she is an inferior person unless she performs at this level. So she grows up with an underlying obsession for high achievement, getting a lot of her self-esteem from this. When she does not reach high achievement for any reason, her self-esteem is threatened.

The high achiever grows up, gets married, and decides to be a stay-at-home mom. Then she has a huge dilemma: *How do I measure success now?* She becomes emotionally off balance and lots of insecurities begin driving family interactions.

Other themes that have unspoken rules could be a mistrust of outsiders, don't show your emotions (or even have any), always control the situation, keep people at a distance, be responsible for the happiness of others, be in charge of taking care of others, the pursuit of career or money, be morally upright, or do what you want when you want. Obviously, life and marital themes can be good or bad. It just depends on whether you manage them well and whether your partner is playing by the same rules.

*Name two unspoken rules in your marriage. If they are not helpful or desirable, discuss how to change them with your partner.*

So what exactly are you expecting out of marriage? How did you determine what you expect, and is it realistic? Using marriage as a venue to live out subconscious, unresolved issues from your past creates problems that just don't seem to go away. Be sure you understand the theme(s) of your life. If the rules (expectations) around those themes are not clear to you or your spouse, exposing them will clear up a lot of possible conflict or confusion.

## EXPECTATIONS IN THE CHRISTIAN HOME

### The Christian culture reflects God's expectations.

The roots of Christianity began with Israel of the Old Testament. There were centuries of Jewish tradition before the time of Christ. In Jewish families, everyone assumes that sons will be successful in the world, and a good marriage is part of that. For the Jews of Eastern Europe, a good marriage is one that has a good balance of learning (i.e., education) and money. The women have seen marriage as the first step toward childbearing. Maintaining the marriage is of utmost importance. Young Jewish couples spend a lot of time early on defining boundaries and expectations, which include extended family. Family obligations are central to daily life, the marriage being the main focal point for this. Historically, divorce was a violation of family obligations as well as a huge religious crisis.[16]

When Jesus walked the earth, He redefined a lot of things. He didn't eliminate teachings of the Old Testament, but took things to a whole new level. The Old Testament, for example, was designed to give us training wheels so we could learn how to ride the bike—which was an actual relationship with God. The New Testament did not negate anything, it just expanded on it. Among the many things Jesus challenged, He clarified marriage and the role of women.

*KEY ATTITUDE:*
**Be open to changing your values.**

Most Americans have heard the Bible story of Jesus with the Samaritan woman at the well.[17] He asked her to give Him a drink, and then went on to teach her about how to find God. Back in that day, Jews had nothing to do with Samaritans, most especially a Jewish man and a Samaritan woman. Jesus rose above the culture of the day to teach us a more universal lesson about how we interact with others. One lesson from this is that we should be willing to change our values, even if it runs counter to the culture around us.

In another story, Jesus talks to the crowd about how Moses permitted divorce because their hearts had become stubborn. This was never God's real intention, so He goes on to clarify that whoever divorces and remarries is committing adultery unless there was an affair.[18] Note that He does not say divorce is automatic if there was an affair, only permissible. So Jesus brought them back to the original meaning and intent of what God had wanted all along.

The scope of this book is not to cover all of what the Bible has to say about marriage, only to present a simple foundation. God never intended for His teachings to be complicated even though His ways are profound. God promises to "preserve the simple."[19] King David said that fearing God and keeping His commandments is all we have to remember.[20]

So what is the Christian understanding of marriage? Essentially, marriage should reflect the relationship each partner has with God. If there is an unbelieving partner, that partner can be set apart for God's purposes through the believing spouse.[21] This gives even people in these marriages a sense of purpose to keep trying no matter what. Christian couples are to be careful not to get distracted from their relationship with God by being preoccupied with each other.[22]

*Husbands are to love their wives the same way Jesus loved the church.*

The Bible discusses how the husband is expected to take a leadership role as he submits to God, while the wife is to respect and "submit" to this leadership.[23] As you can imagine, this concept has been highly misunderstood and abused by many husbands and wives. Husbands have used this teaching to be overly controlling, while some wives have used the women's equality movement to demand no distinction in roles. It is necessary to understand the context of the teaching. Husbands are to love their wives the same way Jesus loved the church. What did He do for the church? He died for her!

*Your marriage should act out the drama of God's redemption of man.*

So the woman's love and respect are a direct outgrowth of this kind of love. Imagine how good it would feel for either partner if *both* were living up to this. Husbands would never get arrogant or controlling, and wives would have no issue with feeling disrespected.

Without going into a detailed religious discussion here, the Bible clearly compares marriage with the relationship Jesus had with the church. The point is ultimate sacrifice for one another, not who gets the short end of the stick. It's a win-win situation on both sides. The best way to summarize what a Christian marriage should be is this: your marriage should act out the drama of God's redemption of man. That means sacrifice and absolute selflessness. Partners are to take on the character of God[24] and allow this to determine what they expect in their marriage.

Review your answer to defining the ideal marriage. Is there anything you would change about your answer if you base all your expectations on God's view of marriage? How will this change make a positive impact on your marriage?

## BUT "I JUST WANT TO BE HAPPY"

Every married person and every person thinking of getting married should be asking himself or herself what his or her real agenda is. In the United States, especially, many people view being married as *the* primary adult relationship. This simply places too much stress on a marriage.

*KEY ATTITUDE:*
**Base happiness on the things that are lasting.**

Don't fall into the trap of requiring some vague notion of "romance." Being romantically in love is also a notion the American culture generates, and this expectation in marriage leads to all sorts of problems. In fact, marriages that start out with less romance seem to last longer. Did you catch that? Romance can easily go up or down, leading to lots of intense emotional disappointment.[25] If we get disappointed enough, commitment goes out the window.

One study has even shown (over a four-year period) that couples who split up had lost a sense of commitment in the relationship even though the love hadn't changed much. The ones who stayed together experienced the biggest change in increased commitment, not love.[26] Sometimes working things out takes good old-fashioned commitment, regardless of emotions! Learning to value commitment more than romance may be just what your marriage needs.

One marriage researcher put it this way, "When the reality of marriage doesn't meet our expectations, we tend to blame reality." We take issue with reality when it doesn't fit our romanticized view of marriage. Many people think marriage will meet all their personal needs and they will live happily ever after. Mary Laner, professor of sociology at Arizona State University, believes Americans often tend to blame their spouse instead of modifying or lowering expectations. When comparing expectations held by couples married ten years with unmarried college students, she found the students had much higher expectations.[27] Obviously, this sets them up for big disappointments once married. Then, they may or may not "stick it out." The "veteran" couples had changed their expectations over time to match *reality*.

Many couples who come in for marriage counseling think better communication will solve all their problems. Sometimes it does, but when it does not, the reason is often one partner not following through on what he says he will do. Once again, the central issue is what kind of heart does the person really have and what is the conflict really about? A quick-fix book on communication often does nothing to address the real need.

*Sometimes the problem is that couples are unclear about what their expectations are. And sometimes one partner just isn't living up to the standards.*

Like it or not, there are many ways to approach marriage that have been shown to work. Sometimes the problem is that couples are unclear about what their expectations are. And sometimes one partner just isn't living up to the standards the couple started out with.

One study compared couples in Shanghai, China, to couples in suburban United States. Even though cultural expectations about marriage differed greatly, these two groups were virtually the same in a couple of key areas. Marital adjustment was good when (1) they agreed on what the standards were for the relationship and (2) both partners lived up to the standards.[28] In other words, both partners agree on the marital expectations and both live up to them.

So what's really the point of all this? You could be saying, "I just want to be happy." So when you say that, what does that really mean? What do you base your happiness on? Feeling "in love" or having certain emotions most of the time just may not be realistic. Know how you describe the ideal marriage. Then ask yourself if it is clear to you and your partner whether you agree with each other, and whether it is realistic. Most importantly, does your view of marriage stand up to the constant pressures and changes of life?

Some of the things you come up with will be unique to you as an individual, and that's great. Those things unique only to you are rarely *legitimate* relationship breakers; things like wanting to share certain interests or having different communication styles, for example.

♥ Share with your partner what the term "happiness" in life and in marriage really means to you. Are the things you base happiness on easily changeable with your circumstances? Discuss how this ties in with your marriage vows and unconditional love.

If you place a premium value on more universal principles like commitment, they will serve you well. And if you define your expectations based on the teachings of God, you will weather the storms of life in ways that will absolutely amaze you.

## THE BOTTOM LINE ABOUT MARITAL EXPECTATIONS

Many couples facing marital distress are in need of a big mental shift about their view of happiness and what marriage owes them. We are all familiar with the quote made famous by John F. Kennedy: "Ask not what your country can do for you, but ask what you can do for your country." Couples in distress, more often than not, are preoccupied with what their marriage is not giving them. In the grand scheme of things, chances are they have become takers in the relationship far more than givers.

There is probably no better description of what your main expectation should be than what Jesus said in his Sermon on the Mount.[29] In essence, He says that true happiness is a paradoxical byproduct of being concerned (which is your theme) with giving yourself to God and other people—things outside of yourself. You will be happiest when you stop thinking so much about being happy!

According to these "beatitudes," you will be blessed—or happy—if you have attitudes quite different from what most of the world has. Contrary to human nature, you should recognize your own inadequacy to meet your needs without God, understand your own imperfections, approach others with gentleness and humility, have true mercy in your heart, want what is right in God's eyes, and have a life filled with making peace with others. Apply this outlook to your marriage relationship and see what happens. Is it costly? You bet it is. But the finest things in life have a high price tag. It's *more* than worth it.

Certainly today's culture strongly influences what people expect when they get married. Problems are often a reflection of these expectations, which tend to be easily influenced by the pressures of the day. Each new generation has new challenges to face in order to fit in with "attitudes of the day." Most of these influences are subtle, chipping away at how we see things.

In 1960, the movie rating system was backward and old-fashioned compared to standards of the twenty-first century. Now, corporations use psychologists to learn how to market toys to children by appealing to their tendency to nag their parents.[30] Video games depicting brutal violence are widely accepted. The media and marketing appeal to our romantic side, with TV commercials setting the mood for us. The media tends to shove the importance of youth, good looks, and bigger-than-life romance down our throats. Just for fun, check out the commercials during an average evening in front of the TV, and pay attention to the techniques used to sell products. These are the very things pressuring how you think.

Chances are, if you are having relationship problems right now you are thinking you have some needs that your partner does not meet. The frustration always starts with that. The first question to ask yourself is whether it is truly a need. Do you base this "need" on depending too much on your partner? Ask yourself if you have stepped up to the plate and responded to defining moments with true character. Determine if you have made your expectations clear, and if they are based on things that last.

Most people are not even sure themselves what their true bottom-line needs are (these are also expectations). Jot them down on paper. Condense your list only to those things that are essential. Then see if your partner understands and agrees with those expectations. Instead of continuing to bicker over things, ask and listen closely for the answer. If you agree, that is a platform from which to begin finding solutions. If you don't agree, *that* is what you should be working on.

Remember: what you expect influences what is happening. If the things you want are actually contributing to conflicts, it makes sense to identify those things and make sure they represent a healthy outlook of give and take. You might have to change some of your expectations. That is part of Element #1, having the right personal character to create a shatterproof marriage.

So what do you expect? Before going further, it's worth taking some time to answer this question.

## Main Chapter Attitudes

✓ Be open to changing your expectations.
✓ Develop a clear sense of your obligations to your marriage and live up to them.
✓ Be honest about how real your belief in God is.
✓ Give up any sense of entitlement that is selfish.
✓ Be willing to admit what your behavior is really saying.
✓ Be open to changing your values.
✓ Base happiness on the things that are lasting.

## ATTITUDES IN ACTION

**1. Attitude: Be open to changing your expectations.**

Identify three or four of the biggest expectations you have in your marriage. Discuss their impact on the "mood" of your marriage and how much they include unconditional love.

**2. Attitude: Develop a clear sense of your obligations to your marriage and live up to them.**

What do you base your attitudes on for keeping promises, honoring your commitments, and love in relationships—religious beliefs, upbringing, or something else? Discuss with your partner what kinds of things keep you from being a giver in the relationship and why. Does this reflect strength or weakness of character? Tell your partner what you owe your marriage and what the limits are to this.

**3. Attitude: Be honest about how real your belief in God is.**

If you have a belief in God, how serious are you about this belief? How do your beliefs reflect (or not reflect) God's way of thinking about marriage and divorce? Talk about ways you would like to see this reflected more in your marriage interactions.

**4. Attitude: Give up any sense of entitlement that is selfish.**

Tell your partner what you think marriage does and does not owe you. Take some time to reflect on this before giving your answer.

**5. Attitude: Be willing to admit what your behavior is really saying.**

What are the biggest unspoken rules in your marriage? What unspoken relationship "rules" work well, and which ones do not work well? Discuss specific changes that either of you should meet.

**6. Attitude: Be open to changing your values.**

Consider your marriage vows in light of the popular ideas of marriage around you. How would your values need to change for your idea about marriage commitment to be more absolute? Talk about this with your partner.

**7. Attitude: Base happiness on the things that are lasting.**

What makes you happy, how have you determined what makes you happy, and how realistic is it? On a 1 to 10 scale, how much do feelings determine whether you consider yourself happy versus an overall state of mind? Discuss how your views about happiness differ, and whether one or both of you need to modify what you base it on.

# 5

# Define Love Carefully

*I promise to love you in sickness and health,*
*for better or worse.*

Repeated at most American weddings

*L*ove is either a fickle myth or a reality you can count on.

But one thing is for sure: it doesn't work both ways. You can't rely on it to be an anchor in your life yet let your feelings rule the day at the same time. Your idea of love is one way to take an even deeper look at your expectations. If you don't, you may be in for some very unpleasant surprises. Having the right kind of personal character means you define love in a way you can truly count on when times get tough.

Jeff found this out the hard way. He married later in life (in his early forties) for the first time to Paula, who was in her midthirties and had already been married three times. The first major issue in their marriage came up about a year into it. While they were still dating, Jeff had told Paula about some debt he acquired that he had not disclosed when they first started seeing each other. Unbeknownst to him, she apparently never resolved her feelings of anxiety about the way she found out about it. As soon as a few mild conflicts arose in the marriage, Paula wanted out, citing this premarital issue as the reason! Her original response was clearly an overreaction, yet her love commitment was tainted with it.

By the time he made it to my office, Jeff was utterly bewildered about what had just happened to him. Less than a year earlier, the couple had exchanged promises to stick with each other no matter what. What in the world happened? Believe it or not, this couple had dated for two years before getting married. Well, here's the catch. Jeff never really talked with her about the meaning of commitment and knew very little about Paula's views on marriage. And this after knowing she had been married three times before!

## YOUR COMMITMENT MUST HAVE DEEP ROOTS

Some people have very little depth of commitment. And then there are those who know enough to be saying the right things, but as soon as tough times hit, they find ways to rationalize or compromise their principles. What motivates you in life is ultimately what determines whether you stick to your principles in tough times. When life turns up the heat, some people have deep roots that anchor them—and some don't.

*What motivates you in life is ultimately what determines whether you stick to your principles in tough times.*

Jesus compared this to seeds being planted in different kinds of soils.[1] Referring to the way people respond to the truth about God, he said some seed (the truth) falls on rocky ground. Some roots grow, but pressures of tough times overcome them because the roots are weak. Other seed falls among thorns, which represent all the other concerns people have about life. Those concerns end up taking priority and choke out the plant. The seed that falls on the good ground develops a good root system, so the plants are strong and hearty. If you want the truth to be rooted in your life, that is half the battle.

In another story, Jesus was in a boat with his closest friends when a storm rolled in.[2] Jesus was asleep, so His friends began to panic. The waves were coming into the boat and it was clear they could all perish in these conditions. They woke Him up and He calmed the waves with a command! He pointed out their lack of faith and asked why they were so timid. The lesson here is that if you turn to God for guidance and strength when marital turbulence hits, He will empower you to meet any challenge. Living this way becomes your motivation. When tempted to compromise your principles, this will keep you on course every time.

Most people have never really sat down and asked themselves what they base relationship commitments on. If they depend on conditions that can easily change from one day to the next, like moods or how much money they have, the commitment will change right along with it. On some level, what motivates all human relationships is getting something out of interactions. Otherwise, why bother with relationships if we don't get anything out of them? What you get out of a given relationship is critical to understanding what your commitment is all about.

One of the foundational theories about how families operate says that all human interactions happen because there are certain costs and rewards connected to them. When you put them together, you get more than you lose. Otherwise, you stop being with someone. People also tend to think they deserve certain things as opposed to what they are actually getting. On top of this, they think about what kind of relationship or partner they are willing to accept considering all the options.[3]

For instance, let's say you have a job on the Alaska pipeline. I've never been there, but I'm imagining a life in which many choices are not available as they might be in the "lower 48" states. You live isolated from shopping malls, fast food, and certain forms of entertainment. The work is hard and often very cold. Hours are long, daylight is all but nonexistent certain times of the year, and the work can be risky at times. You are also physically isolated from loved ones. Those are some of the costs. But the pay is exceptionally good and the company pays for some of your expenses. You are able to save lots of money so that someday you can pay cash for a new house. The work, while risky at times, also has some real excitement to it. Plus, you love the outdoors and are able to hunt and fish almost every day.

So you feel torn about your situation. On the one hand, there are several things that make you unhappy, but on the other hand the advantages are awfully compelling. You ask yourself, *What do I think I deserve in life right now?* Your answer could surprise you, and you realize that in the grander scheme of things you deserve to have a life with some financial leverage. Saving the money—for now—is the net profit. And—you are not willing to give that up and settle for less.

If you've ever been on what I call a "relationship roller coaster," even for a while, you know what I'm talking about. You think about all the things in your relationship you don't like. Poor communication, feeling berated, lack of intimacy. You consider how much you don't like those things. Then you weigh those things against what you do get out of being with the person. Some level of emotional security, good memories, some fun times, more financial stability. Then what's the next thing you evaluate? Be honest! You ask yourself, *Could I do better? Should I have better?*

There are some rewards that are universal. Everybody wants them. Generally speaking, all people are seeking a sense of social approval (love and respect), the ability to choose and be themselves, security, enough money to be reasonably comfortable, equality with someone of similar status in life, agreement about their values and opinions, and they want to minimize uncertainty about the unknown.[4]

Some of these are more important than others to you. You may have an especially strong need for love and respect. Your neighbor may value agreement about values and opinions the most. Your coworker may really want to have lots of predictability and wants to be with someone who helps provide that.

There is one simple way to figure out what really influences your commitment when faced with problems. Ask yourself what makes you feel discouraged the most in your marriage. Whatever it is, the opposite of that is what you want. It's what floats your boat and it is likely that you connect much of your commitment to it. Do you feel most discouraged when your husband seems to dictate your freedom of choice? Does this make your full, 100 percent commitment much harder to come by every day? Perhaps you think your wife could be showing a lot more love and respect in some way. Does this have a weakening effect on how committed you feel? Whatever it is that has the power to weaken your commitment, you must identify it, be aware of it when it happens, and deal with it each and every time.

> *Remember that selflessness is ultimately the key to enduring happiness.*

## KEY ATTITUDE:
**Base your marriage commitment on things that last.**

In the last chapter, we talked about basing your expectations on things that last. The same holds true for your commitment. If the dissatisfaction continues to be a major problem, run it through the acid test. Ask yourself, *How good is the soil that my commitment is rooted in?* Do you base your commitment on things that tend to be changeable with your circumstances? Or do you base it more on things you can truly count on, things that just don't change with your circumstances? If you are still feeling a bit confused about how to tell the difference, remember that selflessness is ultimately the key to enduring happiness. Just like a grain of wheat cannot grow unless it falls to the ground and dies, neither can we experience lasting fulfillment focusing primarily on ourselves.[5] Survivors are not preoccupied with themselves. Instead, as we discussed earlier, they are in relationships that meet the other person's needs. They don't take themselves too seriously but make it their business to serve others.

You may be thinking, *This sounds good and I'm sure it works, but I'm not going to be stupid. If my partner acts in such and such a way, all bets are off.* This is where most people run into all kinds of problems. Our culture may tell us the above attitude is common sense, but survivor personalities don't think this way. That's why they are the *minority*. Those who follow in the footsteps of Jesus will always be a small group. Don't let that convince you to go down a different road. That road is a shortcut and *will* disappoint you. It isn't easy and it isn't our natural tendency to go against the grain of what most people do. But those who respond to each defining moment with strength of character succeed every time. There is no guarantee of the physical outcome, but the deeper sense of satisfaction and living with a higher purpose in life—the overall profit—is guaranteed.

Rick Warren, author of the bestselling book *The Purpose Driven Life*, puts it this way, "You were made for God, not vice-versa, and life is about letting God use you for *His* purposes, not your using *Him* for your purpose."[6] In the majority of marriages, it is past time to begin thinking this way. The divorce rate is proof enough. Just think of the power you would unleash the next time there is a problem at home if you stepped out of yourself. If you saw the issue the way your partner does, accepted him or her completely, and looked for solutions based on what would be good for your partner! Now we're getting closer to understanding a marital love most people never get to experience.

On one hand, name the things you get most out of interactions with your partner. If they are not about seeing your partner be happier, adjust your attitude starting now, and begin interacting more with your partner's interest at heart. Be specific. Name at least two behaviors that would be different.

## WHAT IS LOVE ANYWAY?

Depending on your value system and view of life, what you think love is determines a lot about how you conduct yourself in marriage. Most men, especially, are highly driven sexually. Hormones and pheromones are largely responsible for this. It's even true in the insect world, where some insecticides interfere with the pheromone production, thus blocking interest in mating.

Some people are so driven by this biological drive they confuse it with love. Even the term "making love"—the sexual act of intercourse—can contribute to this misconception.

The sexual issue alone messes up a lot of marriages. One couple in their early forties came in to talk about problems they were having in this area. She admitted to having a low libido, which had nothing to do with anything going on in their relationship. She had been to her primary care doctor and had tried several things to improve her sexual desire. The husband, however, had become so frustrated sexually that she could not do anything right when it came to their sex life. He developed elaborate sexual fantasies in which the woman was a sex maniac. He was spending more and more time every day with Internet pornography. His demands became more and more extreme, as did his criticism of her.

To be fair, I asked the wife on numerous occasions about her willingness to engage in a reasonable number of sexual encounters per week. Her husband reluctantly asked her a minimum number, and the couple agreed to start with a clean slate. After a few weeks, he was convinced she was not meeting this expectation even though she insisted she was. Finally she kept a daily calendar to prove she was meeting her end of the bargain (and she was).

Well, when she proved her willingness to engage in sex for the agreed-upon frequency, his irrational demands got worse. Feeding his fantasies with pornography took on a life of its own. He stopped coming to therapy while she continued. Finally, I advised her to put her foot down and tell him it was all his problem at this point and to "get over himself." She did, it brought him back to reality, and the couple's sex life stopped being a huge battleground. Surprisingly, this was the only major problem they had with each other, so all was fine after that. Sometimes, as this couple illustrates, you can get stuck in a self-indulgent attitude that clouds your thinking completely. Rational discussion gets you nowhere. This couple had finally hit bottom with the problem after discussing it and trying different solutions for at least a year. The only way for the husband to "snap out" of his self-indulgence was a bold, direct approach. It was clear to me that this husband had distorted sex so much because of hormones and unhealthy attitudes that love got lost in it all. His wife had gone overboard in her efforts to please him, and was becoming more and more distressed. For her sake, she needed to stop taking on all the responsibility for his selfish desires.

There are hundreds of theories about what love is. So it's no wonder the average marriage partner gets overwhelmed with the concept at times. One theory suggests the most complete definition of love consists of intimacy, passion, and commitment.[7] Partners feel close to each other, there is sexual and emotional passion, and commitment exists even if the feelings are not always there. Other theories believe love begins with lust and physical attraction. Most of us have had at least one relationship that began that way. You probably know some people who believe lust should always be there with his or her spouse, otherwise there is something very wrong. The "spark" is gone. When I ask people to define "spark," the closest they can come is romantic butterflies and sexual excitement.

Then there's the notion of being "in love." People every day are considering divorce because they have fallen "out of love." That's as tough to define as the spark. And is it necessary to be "in love" for people to be satisfied and have a strong marriage? As we've seen, that is not a universal requirement in every culture. In the American culture, feelings would say "yes" every time (and so would our hormones), but the state of being "in love" is awfully fragile. Do you honestly want a partner who only stays with you when she feels "in love" with you? If so, you will be biting your nails every day waiting for the other shoe to drop! That's no way to live!

There is a term called "limerance" that attempts to capture this concept of being in love. Dorothy Tennov invented the word while a professor of psychology at the University of Bridgeport, Connecticut, in the seventies. While love involves concern for the other person, limerance demands equal response from the other person. It's conditional. Sex is usually part of it, but not always. Limerance typically lasts from a few months to about a year and a half. If the other person returns the infatuation it can last longer. Obsessive longing for the other person characterizes limerance. The biological result of this state of mind is a decrease in serotonin. This leads to increased emotional sensitivity and instability. In short, people can become quite irrational when in this state. Being irrational leads to beliefs that are not based in reality, leading to more conflicts. This proves that things "aren't right" because the other partner is not living up to some unreachable ideal.

Another part of this is the image held of the other partner. The infatuated person falls in love with this ideal person and can carry this image around for years. We will touch on this a little more later, but it's incredible how the mind can accomplish this in the midst of all the other demands and relationships of life.

Tammie found herself in a real pickle, not unlike so many people. She and Dennis had been married more than twenty years, had two great kids, and were reasonably successful financially. Dennis had become infatuated with a girl he knew for just a short time while in college. For the first fifteen years of their marriage, Tammie found poetry and songs written for this girl. He was smitten with some magical image of this girl. He based it all on this infatuated state of mind. He even found the girl, who was happily married and had no inkling of wanting to be with him. Because of this preoccupation, Dennis felt so disenchanted with his marriage he thought he wanted out. In contrast, the marriage he was in could never live up to his fantasy relationship.

How sad to think that a promise to stick with someone through better or worse ends up looking like such a train wreck. And it all starts with buying into the idea that romance, sexual attraction, and feeling "in love" is what love is all about. The mind is capable of feeding off this idea until it becomes a two-headed monster in the closet.

♥ Discuss with your partner how much being "in love" has to do with your marriage commitment.

## DIFFERENT KINDS OF LOVE

As we have already seen, the way people define love differs from one culture to another. The Chinese have different love words to depict being in love, having moral love for all people, having bound destinies, and having a crush on someone. The Japanese have words for passionate love that is a fundamental desire and another one referring to self-indulgent dependence. Buddhists have words for sensual love (sexual) and one for benevolent love. The Jewish culture sees marital love as an essential ingredient to life, as reflected in the instruction to "Enjoy your life with the woman whom you love all the days of your fleeting life . . . "[8]

In the Christian culture, the Greek language (the language of the original New Testament) defines and translates words for love. They are:

### *Storge* Love

This word embraces the idea of affection and fondness that comes from being familiar with someone. It is comfortable and predictable. This term is not actually in the New Testament, but refers to a general type of love that binds families, races, and social groups together. An example of this would be the affection you might have for coworkers that you have known only at work for years. This kind of love can also serve to exclude certain types of people, like someone who is different from the group. If you are not a "good old boy," storge love might shut you out.

### *Philia* Love

This is the love of strong friendship and brotherly love. It involves people who share some similarities and grows with time. This kind of love does not happen among people who are very different from you, it only occurs between people of like mind. Closeness and intimacy arise out of philia love. It does appear in the New Testament in reference to a relationship like between God and Jesus.[9] Obviously, if the similarities end or a sense of betrayal occurs, this kind of love will be broken.

## Eros Love

This Greek word is the closest to the one referring to being "in love." It includes sensuality, romance, and sexual desire. There is an intense, passionate desire for the other person. This word is also not in the New Testament. In the Greek language, it does not relate to the higher levels of loving another person.

## Agape Love

This kind of love does not depend on the lovable qualities of the other person. This love is more of a decision and commitment, originating in the mind and not the emotions of a person. In the Greek language and the New Testament, it is certainly the highest form of love. This is the word used to describe the love God had for the world to give His son for it. Someone who loves in this manner does so unconditionally and out of decision, not feeling. It's the kind of love a mother has for her baby. She would die for her baby and will sacrifice for it, even when it cries all night. This kind of love involves a commitment decision that rises above circumstances or personal shortcomings of the other person.

For many people, agape love is something they have experienced very little or not at all. The closest they come to it is maybe having a sacrificial mother. But if it was not rooted from Christian motives, even that experience was somewhat limited compared to the real meaning of the term. Even "good Christian folk" may not have experienced a lot of this growing up. Agape love grips a person's mind and is not fully attainable without God's changing influence. But even then, we do it imperfectly since we are still human.

Many couples have developed a strong friendship love, philia, in their marriage. While not mandatory in order to have an enduring marriage, it is common and has its merits. But even the feeling of friendship love

*"This is love, not that we loved God, but that he loved us and sent his son as an atoning sacrifice for our sins."*

can deteriorate as problems fester, making it more and more conditional. Clearly, agape love provides an unshakable marriage foundation.

At this point, you may be thinking, "I don't disagree with what you're saying, but I don't think I can live with the disappointments I have in my partner." My friend, this is *the* ultimate defining moment for you in marriage. It's major gut check time. *Now* is the time you need the high form of love most. As the Bible puts it, "This is love, not that we loved God, but that he loved us and sent his son as an atoning sacrifice for our sins."[10] The simple fact of the matter is that you and I, deep down, have messed up so much in our lives that we are guilty—guilty of negative thoughts, saying hurtful things, being dishonest, acting selfishly, wanting things our way at the expense of someone else. Yet all too often, we offer our love in marriage only as long as we are getting what we want out of it. At some point every married person on the planet has to decide whether to live by faith or by feelings. If you're looking for a more complicated or sophisticated explanation, there isn't one.

Everyone is familiar with the warning: "What goes around comes around." It's a cliché, but all clichés come from people experiencing something predictable and universal. Jesus said it better—"For in the same way you judge others, you will be judged, and with the measure you use, it will be measured to you."[11] When we love with anything short of selfless love, we put standards onto our partner and they either measure up or they don't. That's the core of our discontent.

**KEY ATTITUDE: Love unconditionally.** When you base your love and subsequent actions on how well it's going, how good it feels, or what you get out of it, your partner may very well apply those same criteria to you. And unless you are not being honest, you know you don't want that! Most people live their lives being motivated by what they get out of something. On the most basic level, that's normal. But when applied to the marriage commitment, it quickly turns to a self-serving attitude that their desires are requirements.

Don't mistake this for those times when you and your partner agree to something and your partner does not hold up his end of the bargain. That is a legitimate bone to pick. The problem comes in when you can't be happy because of something you demand or some standard you have set. Or you can't accept your partner *anyway*. Your partner may have even agreed to it, but only under pressure. Weighing the costs and rewards of your relationship, which is how most people operate, most of your marital behavior comes from knowing you will get something back you like. It works beautifully when both of you buy into it and are doing it. But what about when your husband is sick and unable to give you attention? Or your wife has clinical depression and is unable to give much to the relationship at all?

I don't know about you, but I want a relationship based on far more than that. I want to know in my heart that my life takes the higher road and, more importantly, that I am choosing to respond to what God has done for me by loving others out of what I call a commitment decision. It's the stuff that makes for quiet heroes. I want to be one, and I want my wife to be one, for sure!

Does this sound impossible? Certainly. And actually, it is if you're relying on your own intellect. You may have already done terrible things in your life, in your marriage. Your actions did some damage and you're trying to assess the damage. Well, here is the good news. Trusting in God and following His pattern for relating to others gives you total reprieve from your guilt, even if your partner does not forgive you. Nothing is impossible when you accept that, pick yourself up, and aim for the target one more day. When you mess up, it is the heart that God looks at, not how "together" you appear on the outside.[12] The Bible says nothing can separate us from the love of God—*nothing!*[13] It doesn't matter that you feel hopeless. It doesn't matter that the situation has gotten out of control. Stop trying to fix your problems your way. As we've seen, your way probably included a number of false assumptions about reality. Love your partner unconditionally no matter what. There isn't anything more powerful on the planet.

The personal character in Element #1 defines love as being unconditional and it transcends your feelings. You might be exceptionally smart, good-looking, have lots of money, hold a position of prestige in the community, be a gifted arguer, be able to talk yourself out of anything, and still have a marriage relationship that is struggling. Maybe you just feel empty.

If you are ready, things don't have to stay this way. It's a big "if." But if you are ready, hang on. Instead of what you've been doing, I will show you a better way. This brings us to the second vital element of a shatterproof marriage.

## MAIN CHAPTER ATTITUDES

✓ Base your marriage commitment on things that last.
✓ Love unconditionally.

### ATTITUDES IN ACTION

**1. Attitude: Base your marriage commitment on things that last.**

a) Discuss, in detail, what your marriage commitment is based on. Do you both feel good about your answers?

b) When is it okay to back out of a marriage commitment? Is your answer complete, including all possible scenarios? Discuss what you are basing your answer on and how this fits in with your marriage vows.

**2. Attitude: Love unconditionally.**

What definition of love have you been living your life by? Talk about how much of this is conditional and how much is unconditional. Discuss how your definitions of love differ. Then imagine together how the marriage would be different if *both* of you lived with each of the definitions at the same time.

# The Right Kind of Love

*Truly love for better or for worse.*

The one unique thing about chemical elements is that they can't be reduced down any more than they are without changing their properties. In their basic form, they *always* possess the same qualities and are foundational to all the rest of chemistry. One element, hafnium, is used to make control rods in nuclear reactors. The reason is that this element has a high melting point and is resistant to corrosion. In other words, its properties provide the structural integrity needed for something that potentially would have a high level of risk associated with it. Additionally, these properties never change, since hafnium is one of the basic elements. So for something as dangerous as a nuclear reactor, it is a substance we can always count on.

Like hafnium, unconditional love gives your marriage the structural integrity it has to have if it is going to be shatterproof. It's easy to say that you should love unconditionally, but it is an entirely different matter to understand just how this is done. Marriage is full of hazardous conditions—both present and future—that make this marital "element" essential. Without it, your marriage might perform just fine under ideal conditions, but when an unexpected severe test comes your way, the strength of your bond is torn to shreds. You have to understand what the properties of unconditional love are in detailed terms. Then your love will be the real McCoy instead of some substitute that does not hold up when times get tough.

If this hasn't grabbed your attention, I wish I could let you talk to Jackie. She married Paul thinking she had found the man of her dreams. For a couple of years, this was true. They had three wonderful kids together. Well, Jackie had some medical problems that included postpartum depression. She tended to be insecure and a bit needy to begin with, so when the depression hit she really needed all of Paul's attention. Frankly, she became hard to live with. The kids were beginning to pick up some of her dependency behaviors. But postpartum depression is a known medical condition, and loving for better or for worse means hanging in there, doesn't it?

Paul became disillusioned despite his promise to love Jackie no matter what happened. During the three-year period of Jackie's depression, many of his personal needs and wants received little attention. They tried the "swinging" lifestyle for a while, exchanging sex partners with another couple in hopes it would "draw them closer" somehow (which makes no sense to me). This was a dead-end street, leaving them both emptier than before. So Paul took it to a new level and had an affair. He had just ended the affair when I met this couple.

While all of this was going on, Jackie had received treatment for her depression and was working her way back to her old self. But this was no longer enough for Paul. He had grown disenchanted with even the old Jackie. His emotional bank account was empty. He did not have certain feelings of being "in love," and he was trying to avoid divorce "for the sake of the kids," the oldest of whom was a teenager.

You see, Paul never did love Jackie unconditionally. He made lots of promises when they got married, but they were empty. Like most couples, both were overwhelmed with being in love and did not give enough thought to the implications of their promises. Once real life set in, his love proved to be fickle. Element #2 is knowing what unconditional love is really all about. If you or your partner don't have this knowledge, your marriage is missing a critical element required to be shatterproof. Let's explore this in some detail so you can consider making any changes to how you love your mate.

# 6

# Importance of a Well-Conditioned Heart

*Let the words of my mouth and the meditation of my heart be acceptable in Thy sight, O Lord, my rock and my redeemer.*

Psalm 19:14

A heart that is working at full potential is truly a miracle.

The heart muscle, about the size of your fist, beats on average about 108,000 times a day. That's roughly 39,420,000 times a year! The heart is responsible for pumping nourishment and oxygen through the bloodstream to every cell in your body. Accident victims whose hearts stop beating have just a couple of minutes before there is irreparable damage to their brains. The nourishment accomplished by your heart is at the center of survival every minute of your life.

Your circulatory system starts with the blood leaving your heart into arteries, then into tiny tubes called capillaries, and finally into veins leading back to the heart. The whole process takes about 60 seconds, during which time your tissues, organs, muscles, and bones receive what they need to stay strong and healthy. There are even arteries that wind around your heart so it can receive the same lifeblood as the rest of your body. As your lungs breathe, your bloodstream releases carbon dioxide and replaces it with fresh oxygen.

The heart all by itself is a wonderful, amazing gift when it is healthy. Your heart beats whether you are asleep or awake, thinking about it or not, laughing or crying. There are four chambers in your heart, two on the left and two on the right side. They are the right and left ventricles and the right and left atriums. A valve connects each ventricle to its respective atrium. As the heart beats, the valves release blood to the next chamber and eventually out to the body. Simple and miraculous. All parts working in perfect harmony all the time.

The heart muscle contracts from a built-in electrical system. Electrical impulses provide the energy needed to make it work. The impulses work their way through the heart, enabling all parts to work. Sometimes these impulses don't work exactly right, which affects blood flow to one or more parts of the body. In some of these instances, people need pacemakers to regulate this process artificially.

Exercising your heart is key to its health and long-term durability. If it's abused or even neglected, eventually it weakens and can develop a life-threatening condition. Developing an exceptionally strong heart takes hard work and requires the momentary pain of exercise. Unfortunately, many people (if not most) are unwilling to experience even twenty minutes of discomfort a day (or even two times a week) to improve the length and quality of their lives.

## KEY ATTITUDE:
**Desire to examine the condition of your heart regularly.**

What we know about the workings of the human heart is strikingly similar to what we need to develop a heart that makes your marriage virtually shatterproof. When two marriage partners come together and become one, they create a single heart that governs the relationship. If one spouse's heart grows faint, problems occur and the other spouse's heart is affected. If they allow this to continue unchecked, the couple begins to spiral. The very heart of the marriage gets sick. Recognizing the true condition of things is the first step toward recovery. Loving unconditionally is not for the faint of heart. And it requires some serious thought if it is to be achieved. Element #2, knowing how to love unconditionally, possesses some properties most people rarely experience or give. This section of the book attempts to show you what it really takes.

Like the physical heart, the heart of your character needs to be working fully every second of your life. It's that second, or precious few minutes, when it is not working properly that can so easily destroy you. Think about all the everyday situations in which this is true. The temptation to look at a pornographic picture that is right in front of you, a spontaneous response of irritability, being short with someone only to find out later that was the person who will be interviewing you for a job later that day.

Another similarity is that your character needs to permeate every fiber of your being, just like the physical heart must pump blood to every cell of the body. If it doesn't, that part of your body begins to deteriorate. If it spreads, eventually the whole body is threatened. The common term for this condition is gangrene. It tends to be common with war injuries in which injury disrupts blood flow to part of the body. Bacterial infection sets in, causing tissue to become necrotic (dead). Without treatment, it will spread and kill the victim. Character functions the same way. Having strong character *most* of the time is just not enough to carry you through situations that are the most challenging. Likewise, allowing yourself little "pockets" here and there of weakness will usually come back to haunt you.

**KEY ATTITUDE:**
**Have a "work ethic" to strengthen your heart of character.**

As the human heart purges carbon dioxide waste through the lungs and brings in fresh oxygen, character continually requires renewal with those things worthy of your attention. The Bible says that ". . . whatever is true, whatever is honorable, whatever is right, whatever is pure, whatever is lovely, whatever is attractive, if there is any excellence and if anything worthy of praise, let your mind dwell on these things."[1] Furthermore, we get rid of unhelpful attitudes and thinking by having our minds renewed with these things.[2] As the human heart achieves renewal with every beat, so must we make this our goal with character. Focusing on the right things and making this a habit throughout the course of every day is the only way to do it. If we get sloppy or lazy, the poor attitudes creep in. We focus on our own comfort and opt for the easy way rather than living life deliberately.

> *Character that has had consistent practice and repetition becomes second nature.*

This points to another similarity between the physical heart and the kind of partner you are: both need to be automatic. Your heart beats without thinking. You need to develop your love habits enough for them to become your first reaction under tough circumstances. This comes through practice, repetition, and consistency. It's no different from any refined skill you've developed. Responses that have had consistent practice and repetition become second nature. If they are not second nature, responding to challenging situations takes more effort and there is a higher possibility you won't be up to the challenge.

**KEY ATTITUDE:**
**Always look for ways to live your life—and marriage—with true character.**

The electrical energy impulses making the heart beat are very much like the actions required for an unbreakable heart of character. It starts with desire. There has to be a vision for being more than you are. This is the electrical energy before it transmits throughout the heart. The civil rights leader Whitney Young (1921–1971) put it this way, "The truth is that there is nothing noble in being superior to somebody else. The only real nobility is in being superior to your former self." The Bible says it this way, ". . . in reference to your former manner of life, you lay aside the old self . . . and put on the new self."[3]

In addition to having the right desire, you must be willing to put your good intentions into action. Just having electrical energy isn't good enough. It has to be directed someplace where it will do what it needs to do. In the physical heart, impulses travel through all four chambers so each chamber is working in conjunction with the others. With character, *knowing* what you should do is only half the equation. The other half is *acting* on it. God certainly understands this tendency for us to stop short of action. The Bible says, "But prove yourselves doers of the word, and not merely hearers who delude themselves. For if anyone is a hearer of the word and not a doer, he is like a man who looks intently at his nature in a mirror; for once he has looked at himself and gone away, he has immediately forgotten what kind of person he was."[4]

In other words, you can say you have the right attitude all you want. But if you don't live out your attitude in each and every situation, it's like forgetting what the attitude was to begin with. Just thinking right does no one any good. Making the decision to live with true character, followed by daily actions consistent with it, leads to all kinds of blessings. The heart of a shatterproof marriage is one that is focusing daily on the right things, then putting these things into practice.

> Decide what some things are that you know will make your marriage stronger. Over a three-day period, focus on these things like never before. Think about them and then act on them. Then determine if the advantages outweigh the disadvantages.

Remember: the advantages might only be that you live consistently being the kind of person you want to be. What is that worth to you? When tough times come, this kind of character is much more "fit" to overcome the challenges.

## YOUR HEART MUST ALWAYS BE PUMPING

The heart of your character must fill up with the right desires, attitudes, and habits so they can pump into your life continually.

Just as the heart operates to pump blood to the entire body, the heart of your character must fill up with the attitudes and heart of Jesus so it can pump "lifeblood" into every part of your life. Marriage is a classic test for this, for without this lifeblood your marriage will be anemic at best. Lack of oxygen in the blood makes us lazy and tired. At best, weak character makes us the same way in how we live. At worst, your marriage may be facing a life-threatening condition. Once a life-threatening condition progresses beyond a certain point, too much damage exists and recovery is much more difficult. Not that recovery is impossible—but it will be fighting an uphill battle. The key is not to let it get to that point.

**KEY ATTITUDE: Choose to love selflessly.**

As we have seen, unconditional love is what we all want in life. Although life in this world can be utterly confusing, following God's pattern suddenly brings everything into focus. God has nothing to do with confusion, but has everything to do with clarity and peace.[5] To pattern your life—and your character—after God's own heart is the simple answer to any marital issue you are facing. Well, what is God's heart? Jesus described it about as plainly as anyone could, saying we should love God with all our heart, soul, mind, and strength. Following at a close second to this is to love one another as we love ourselves.[6]

You might have extra intelligence, or the gift of winning an argument, good looks, abilities few people have, or more understanding and insight than most people. Maybe you've been wronged one too many times in your life and think the world owes you something. Or perhaps you just think you are entitled to certain things and become frustrated when they don't come your way. Other people pride themselves on being "good people," thinking that passive compliance in life is their noble contribution. Whatever light you see yourself in, if your burning desire is anything but loving God and others with everything you have, you may have some great things going but are still missing something. If it hasn't happened yet, your marriage is still quite vulnerable to situations that will challenge the very essence of the marriage commitment. Furthermore, if you are one of the lucky ones who doesn't experience this kind of challenge, having any other focus will make the stresses you do have greater than they need to be.

Fortunately for all of us, the Bible says there is a better way than relying on our insights, abilities, and good efforts. This applies even to "good church folk." How many people have you encountered who claim to be followers of Jesus who ended up divorced? This better way is simple: love because God first loved us.[7] That's the what and the why. It's what we do, and why we do it is because God first gave it to us. To hold out on our partner because "he just doesn't deserve it" is unacceptable. To say, "She's making it too hard to love her (she's not lovable enough)" doesn't cut it.

The heart of a shatterproof marriage has eternal, unconditional love at its center. There is one short section of the Bible—I Corinthians 13—that best describes eternal, unconditional love, the only love that is unshakable. It goes like this, "And if I have the gift of prophesy, and know all mysteries and all knowledge, and if I have all faith, so as to remove mountains, but do not have love, I am nothing. And if I give all my possessions to feed the poor, and if I deliver my body to be burned, but do not have love, it profits me nothing. Love is patient, love is kind, and is not jealous; love does not brag and is not arrogant, does not act unbecomingly; it does not seek

> *There is one short section of the Bible— I Corinthians 13— that best describes eternal, unconditional love, the only love that is unshakable.*

its own, is not provoked, does not take into account a wrong suffered, does not rejoice in unrighteousness, but rejoices with the truth; bears all things, believes all things, hopes all things, endures all things. Love never fails."[8]

This definition of love NEVER FAILS! Not most of the time. *Never!* Think about that. Think of all the situations you have felt were impossible. This kind of love overcomes everything! Will it always feel like it? No. Thankfully, we don't rely on just feelings. Agape love is a commitment to love no matter what. It's hard, but it sure is comforting to be on the receiving end of this. It's worth basing your whole life around this kind of love.

If you are not a Christian believer, you may be thinking this is a nice platitude to think about or even strive for, but that's all it is. It is not attainable. If you are a believer, you probably know this teaching but may have found it doesn't work all the time in your life. There are just some situations, some problems that are too big for this. Jesus understood this is an awfully tall order. He understood that even well-intentioned people are likely to get frustrated and discouraged trying to live up to this kind of love. That's why He said that He is the vine and we are the branches. Like the branches must connect to the vine, we have to connect to Him. If we do not, we will be unable to love this way. Our human tendencies—past attitudes and upbringing—will take over. If we *are* connected, we *will* be able to love this way.[9]

If you are trying to rely on your upbringing, your natural abilities, a view of the world based on anything but God's love, you are marching toward a destiny whether you know it or not. That destiny leads to frustrations and disappointments and a life that breaks down after a certain point. It leads to a life that is less than what it could be. Dealing with marital problems is like facing a ferocious army with no shields and plastic baseball bats. Your approach to love (as well as your partner's) has strings attached. When the strings come loose, the foundation of your marriage begins to unravel. It happens a little bit at a time until one day you wake up and realize it's fallen apart. A big marital crisis almost always happens after lots of little disappointments and unresolved issues. It usually doesn't just suddenly happen. Some people have entered the relationship from the beginning with the wrong understanding of love and commitment. Those relationships often have been eroding slowly from the very beginning. They met the first sign of life's challenges with a weak heart.

Talk to your partner about whether you have ever experienced a love that has "never failed." If not, how has this affected what you expect from love? Share what you think about God's love and whether you have given God a chance in your heart.

## CHAMBERS OF THE CONDITIONED HEART

Just as the heart has four chambers working together, I view the heart of the shatterproof marriage as having four primary working chambers. When they are all functioning at full capacity, they make up a complete heart that is like God's heart for us. Element #2, knowing how to love unconditionally, consists of a heart that is open and ready to be strengthened. The next few chapters describe each of the chambers of a heart that loves unconditionally. These are the "atoms" inside of Element #2.

Based on the love description just discussed, the four heart sections reflecting God's love are based on the famous love chapter in the Bible—I Corinthians 13.

### The Selfless Heart

This part of the loving heart is unselfish and makes you a servant and a giver.

### The Humble Heart

The humble part of the heart is patient, gentle, able to exercise self-control, not provoked to anger, not arrogant or jealous, and does not act unbecomingly. Humility is at the core of these things.

## The Devoted Heart

The devoted heart has joy, peace, kindness, goodness, and faithfulness, and has a thirst for what is right.

## The Enduring Heart

This part of the heart believes, hopes, and endures all things. It never gives up; it overcomes any obstacle.

In the next several chapters we will be looking more closely at each of these heart chambers. Developing all four of these areas of the heart leads to a fully healthy heart of love. This paves the way to a survivor personality and, more importantly, to a life—and marriage—that is unshakable. Allow your heart to change by experiencing, then following, a life of love as God has provided. Explore it. Try it. Risk it. Trust it. This kind of love lasts forever. I don't know about you, but this is what I want filling my life and marriage.

You may be looking at what makes up a strong, healthy heart of love and realize you have been neglectful. Your heart has become weak and lazy. Maybe your heart never has functioned fully and you have all kinds of habits and unresolved issues keeping you from developing a strong one. Or maybe you have certain chambers working very well but not all of them. If this is the case, your heart as a whole is struggling to keep up. I can imagine that heart patients have a hard time visualizing ever being strong again. But with proper medical attention and lots of hard work in rehab, it happens. Why would we ever think the same thing could not happen with our character?

All you have to do is remember the "what" and the "why" and the "how." *What* we do is decide to love God and others with all our being. *Why* we do it is because God loved us first. *How* we are able to achieve it is by drawing the power from God. Will you do it imperfectly? Most certainly. Is that a deal breaker? Most certainly not. If this kind of love is your foremost value in life, even your imperfect efforts will sustain you. The reason this is true is that God forgives you if you ask for it and "rights" the course again and again.

Doing it His way enables you to get up and brush yourself off.

Some of you reading this will stop here and never finish reading this book. The challenge will seem too big. It's big, but not too big. If this is you, you're already forgetting a crucial point: God is the only one powerful enough to love this way. Deepen your relationship with Him and learn His ways. Then you will be deeply fulfilled and amazed. Your marriage will weather virtually anything.

Don't be like so many who walk away discouraged and defeated. Dare to let go of what is familiar, looking instead outside of yourself for the answers you know you want. As impressive as the human heart is, an even bigger miracle is developing the heart of a shatterproof marriage. It has to start with a decision. Decide to give your heart over to the rigors of an overhaul. That's what Element #2 would have you do: give more than you receive. And know how to do this in everyday, practical terms. The payoff comes later, just as it does with physical conditioning.

If you dare, let's take a closer look at what this involves. But be ready—this could literally revolutionize your marriage.

## MAIN CHAPTER ATTITUDES

✓ Desire to examine the condition of your heart regularly.
✓ Have a "work ethic" to strengthen your character.
✓ Always look for ways to live your life—and marriage—with true character.
✓ Choose to love selflessly.

## ATTITUDES IN ACTION

**1. Attitude: Desire to examine the condition of your heart regularly.**

Identify which heart chamber(s) needs the most exercise to work at full capacity. Tell your partner a couple of small things you will start doing immediately to get started.

**2. Attitude: Have a "work ethic" to strengthen your heart of character.**

Are you willing to exercise your "heart of character"? Discuss with your partner what is most likely to get in the way, and how you can overcome that. Schedule a time to review your progress in a few days.

**3. Attitude: Always look for ways to live your life—and marriage— with true character.**

Do you consciously—knowingly—apply (exercise) a heart of character when you encounter challenges in life and in your marriage? Discuss when you have the hardest time with this and what you have to do differently to live with more character. How will you have to change, and what will it take?

**4. Attitude: Choose to love selflessly.**

Ask your partner if selfless love describes you in your marriage. Invite your partner to tell you some ways you can show this kind of attitude more. Make this your goal for a few weeks, checking in weekly with your partner to see how you are doing. Then talk about what that was like.

# 7

# True Love Must Be Selfless

*[Love] does not seek its own or is jealous,*

*but is patient and kind.*

I Corinthians 13:4–5

Ralph Waldo Emerson once said, "Self-sacrifice is the real miracle out of which all the reported miracles grow." Finding your life by losing it is arguably the greatest paradox in the universe.

Even people who do not believe in God have discovered this principle. Survivor personalities understand that giving freely to others eventually benefits them. Sayings like, "What goes around comes around" reflect this universal idea. Cancer patients forgetting about their own problems by helping others have blessed themselves with more joy and, not uncommonly, improved health. Jesus summed it up in a one-liner, only He took it a step further when He said, "He who has found his life shall lose it, and he who has lost his life for my sake shall find it."[1] Losing

*Losing your life with purpose— in order to follow God's way—gives you promise of a great life now and even beyond this Earth.*

your life with purpose—in order to follow God's way—gives you promise of a great life now *and* even beyond this Earth. We accept so many miracles because they are not new to us, whether it is the human heart, or the birth of a new baby, or the unexplainable recovery of an accident victim. Is the miracle in this statement by Jesus really so inconsistent with what we already know from these everyday miracles?

## WE CAN ALL MAKE THE WORLD A BETTER PLACE BY GIVING UP OUR "RIGHTS" VOLUNTARILY

In a world that has become so concerned with personal rights, this way of thinking has become more old-fashioned than ever. Just look at some of the lawsuits that fill up many American courts. In 2001, a couple in New Jersey sued the Kellogg Company and Black & Decker for $100,000. The cherry Pop-Tart they put into the toaster caught fire and burned the house down.[2] Gee whiz, what kind of flammable food are they making nowadays? A closer look at this case reveals the couple left the house with the toaster on, despite the warning on the box not to leave it unattended!

Also that year, a Levittown, Pennsylvania, teenager sued her former soft-ball coach for a whopping $700,000. *Probably sexual abuse*, you say? No, she claimed that bad coaching cost her a college athletic scholarship.[3] In 2002, a convicted rapist sued the hospital where he raped a patient in her bed. His complaint was the hospital failed to protect visitors and patients, which in turn made it possible for him to commit the crime. He wanted $2,000,000 for this "injustice."[4] Then later that year in another court, lawyers filed a class action suit in New York on behalf of the state's children against McDonald's. Why? The state's kids were too fat! One thirteen-year-old boy, weighing in at 5'4" and 278 pounds, contended he didn't realize eating three to four fast-food meals a week would compound his problems.[5]

The list goes on and on every year of people who go out of their way to protect their "rights." What drives much of this is a desire to profit off some kind of loophole in the system, but many of these people actually begin believing their complaint. People often bring this mentality into marriage, where one or both partners are determined not to be "violated." Couples get into all kinds of situations in which their biggest concern is others taking advantage of them. Instead of taking personal responsibility, we are in a world of blaming others for anything and everything.

Some partners have a low tolerance for any kind of perceived injustice, so they overreact with anger or pouting. All this amounts to is personal insecurity and mistrust. Surely you've had a friend who became absolutely indignant because his wife wronged him in some way. This is also the root of jealousies. Whether it is a fear of rejection, a pronounced aversion to being humiliated, or an exaggerated desire for your partner to do everything "correctly," much of the world tells us to "take care of number one." The world considers us fools if we don't.

Jesus challenged this way of thinking with some radical teaching. His way of thinking requires us to eliminate "self" from our vocabulary. There are lots of well-intentioned Christian believers who have a hard time getting their arms around His approach. In a world where most people pay someone back for a wrong, Jesus said if someone slaps you, turn to him the other cheek. If someone forces you to go a mile for him, go an extra mile.[6] Most people are familiar with these words of Jesus and would agree the lesson is a noble one. And as long as the situation isn't too ridiculous, it's the way to be. But there is a line most people draw in the sand and, if you cross the line, all bets are off.

**KEY ATTITUDE:**
**Know the difference between wants and true needs.**

One way we rationalize stopping short of this radical view of our rights is to use Maslow's Hierarchy of Needs. We have all heard of it. This theory says our most basic needs are hunger and thirst. We *have* to get those needs met. Then we need security and protection. After that, we are concerned with a sense of belonging and being loved, followed by needs for recognition, status, and self-esteem. Once we get all these needs met, we reach "self-actualization." In other words, we have reached our personal potential.[7]

💜 Discuss some of the routine things that happen in your marriage where you feel a sense of injustice, unfairness, or that your "rights" have been violated. Tell your partner what you would honestly like from him or her, then express a commitment to surrender these rights voluntarily in the interest of harmony and love. Can you do it?

We often say we *need* love and to have our self-esteem built up. Our marriage partner lets us down in these areas, so we say he or she isn't meeting our basic personal needs. Suddenly you call the marriage into question and blame it for the problem. That was a fast conclusion, wasn't it?

There are a couple of major problems with this logic, though. Remember the old song, "Looking for Love in All the Wrong Places"? Love begins with *us*. If you don't love yourself, you can't expect to get any fulfillment from another person's love. If you are constantly upset or disappointed in your partner, chances are you are looking at it all wrong. Don't get me wrong, there are some terrible marriage partners out there and the reasons are obvious. But before you come to that conclusion, be sure you are not projecting your own inability to be satisfied onto your partner. *Most people need a major attitude adjustment about their partner at least once in their marriage.*

> *If you don't love yourself, you can't expect to get any fulfillment from another person's love.*

**KEY ATTITUDE:**
**Choose today to be selfless the way Jesus was.**

Love starts as an infant with your parents, primarily your mother, and then as you get older you make some kind of judgment about God and your relationship to Him. The Bible tells us, "In this is love, not that we loved God, but that he loved us . . ."[8] It starts with your being loved before you ever did anything. If you are constantly feeling unloved or bad about yourself, you have become preoccupied with yourself and lost sight of the truth about love. It's easy sometimes to blame the marriage. Even if your partner is behaving poorly, this does not threaten your source of love if it comes from God.

The result of relying on this kind of love is the ability to let go of yourself and have a selfless heart. If you choose to follow the teachings of Jesus and respond to the love God has already given you, then you will put aside the "old you" in exchange for the "new you" every day.[9] You will have the strength to bear the burdens of your partner whether he or she asks for it or not[10] and look out for the interests of others instead of yourself.[11] By remembering God's love every time you are hurt, wronged, or disappointed, you will be empowered to follow the example set by Jesus. He did not come to be served, but to serve.[12] He encouraged us by reminding us, ". . . freely you received, freely give."[13] This is what it means to find your life by losing it.

Find one small way this week to be a servant to your partner, then put it into practice consistently, even if your partner does not pat you on the back.

Don't worry that life isn't fair. By voluntarily surrendering your "rights," you can't really be "violated" like you thought you were before. This is not to say you become a doormat. Being treated that way clearly hurts intimacy. But it does not have to mean you spend all your energy looking out for yourself.

You will be amazed when you stop being so concerned about whether life is always completely fair; life gets easier and you get along with others better.

*KEY ATTITUDE:*
**Commit to a lifelong process of becoming a selfless person.**

You know when you want to be selfish and self-centered. It is important you stop and take some time to think about these times. Otherwise, you go about your day out of habit and your selfish tendencies just keep on happening. This may sound silly, but make a list of these times. This forces you to get specific and makes it real. Take two minutes a day to review the list. After a couple of days you won't need the list anymore because your awareness level will be higher.

Most people have predictable times they tend to be more selfish than other times. If you are tired, under stress, wake up in a bad mood, or feel ill, you are not at your best and probably tend to think of yourself first. With the busyness of life, it's easy to get sloppy and let your guard down during these times. Train yourself to be aware of these times as they happen and notice how selfishness takes over.

## WE ALL STRUGGLE WITH SELFISHNESS, BUT WE HAVE TO FIGHT THAT BATTLE EVERY DAY

Sometimes just getting through the day is about all we can do. You may not be doing anything that is obviously selfish, but you aren't exactly putting energy into the marriage relationship either. This builds up and takes a toll on the relationship, so be careful not to let this happen too long.

We all have some selfish habits, some big and some little. Once you have been in a relationship for a while, you both develop certain roles around these habits. One couple I knew perfected this idea. Rochelle had very definite ideas about where she wanted to live. She liked the change of seasons, the northwest part of the country, and lots of snow. Clarence had a good job in a warm climate, both of which he valued highly. Rochelle claimed she didn't care—she wanted what she wanted. "I'm a cold-weather person," she proclaimed. All of this couple's planning revolved around Rochelle's insistence on getting what she wanted regardless of Clarence's desires. After many years of this, she was in the habit of getting her way. Although Clarence has cooperated for years, he was also not a very satisfied marriage partner. If you want to know what your selfish habits are, ask your partner once. As long as it's safe to be honest, he or she will tell you what you need to know!

Then there are all those times you feel like just about anything is an inconvenience to you. Perhaps you grew up having others serve you much of the time. Getting your partner a glass of water or running an errand for her becomes a huge thing for some reason. If you really want to develop a selfless heart, start with these little things. Habits change one small behavior at a time. They eventually change your attitudes—they become more second nature. Don't underestimate this principle. Besides modifying the behavior, doing this also serves to remind you to think of your partner before yourself.

One selfish moment worth mentioning is when you feel discouraged in your marriage. You might be thinking your mate is never going to change, she doesn't meet your "needs," or you have tried everything you know to make things better. At some point discouragement can set in and you feel the need to lick your wounds. You might do this by withdrawing, getting angry, acting spitefully, or simply putting little energy into being a good partner yourself. These responses almost always backfire. The reason they do is because your behavior influences what your partner does next, so you become a coproducer of a bad movie; only the movie is your life. It is never okay to indulge the temptation to feel sorry for yourself. It's human to feel discouraged, but letting the feeling determine your behavior is destructive. It might just be time for a new strategy, but this does not include indulging in self-pity.

*It is never okay to indulge the temptation to feel sorry for yourself.*

*Consider which day-to-day issues discourage you the most in your marriage. Rehearse in your mind what you will do instead of letting your discouragement get the best of you. The next time it comes up, do what you practiced in your mind.*

## WHEN TO STEP UP TO THE PLATE AND BE GIVING

Marriage is like baseball. There is a time to receive, which could be the trophy at the end of a great season. Before that can ever happen, there are lots of times to step up to the plate and bat, which means you have to produce. Life is like that, as summed up in the great philosophical saying, "No pain, no gain." If you are serious about wanting to step up and contribute your share to making a great marriage, there are some key opportunities to look for.

First, notice those situations that are important to *your partner*. Keeping your socks picked up off the floor may seem like a stupid thing to be concerned about, but your wife may consider it being considerate. The fact is that living with another adult cooperatively is not a snap. Going out of your way to do something that you don't value but your partner does has great value. But it probably won't happen unless you go out of your way to pay attention to what those things are. It's great to be selfless in everything you do, but focusing especially on the things your partner values is especially great.

 *Ask your partner what little things you could do this week that would make his or her week a little easier, then do them.*

Next, learn what kinds of things really contribute to your partner's happiness from day to day. What motivates your partner? What kinds of things can you do—big or small—that will brighten up your partner's life? Maybe it involves you stopping a behavior. This is a time to dig deep and do (or don't do) whatever it is. Sometimes when things have not been going so well just using common courtesy would make a big difference. Quit thinking for a moment about *your* happiness and ask yourself what you can do that will contribute to your partner's happiness. Don't be stupid about it—this is an investment in *you!*

Another opportunity to be selfless is to think about what you can do to make your partner better in some way. It could be learning to be a better father. Some people are trying to learn how to take time for themselves more, while others want to quit smoking or exercise more regularly. Whatever it is, consider how to encourage (not pressure) and help (not make) your partner to grow and reach personal goals. In your efforts, be sensitive to how your partner perceives your good intentions. If just bringing up a certain subject causes hard feelings, ask how you can be supportive and listen closely to the answer. Be careful here not to have your own agenda and force-feed him or her with it.

Tell your partner you want to be more supportive and ask how you could be.

Then there are those situations that are inconvenient to you. Now you're relating to this, aren't you? Changing your plans at the last minute, getting up off the couch, getting up in the middle of the night, eating later than you wanted, fixing your own food, stopping by the store on the way home, missing a TV show. The list is as long as there are seconds in the day. At some point, on some level, we're all lazy creatures. To develop a selfless heart, one of the disciplines you must work on is learning to experience inconvenience as a way of life. Accept it. A friend of mine used to say, "John, tomorrow you won't even remember the pain." He was referring to doing a job that was physically demanding. How much truer is this statement about little inconveniences?

A habit closely related to allowing inconvenience in your life is going out of your way to make life easier for your partner. Clean up the dishes whether it's your chore or not. Offer to watch the kids so your wife can do whatever she wants. Pick up something at the store your husband wants. Look at your partner's normal routine and consider what would make that routine a little easier today. The answer sometimes will require something of you that you really don't want to do.

So what are you going to do with this moment? You can shy away from it and nobody will notice. Or you can step up to the plate and inch just a little closer toward having a selfless heart.

Look around you and think of ways you could make life a little easier for your partner. Start doing things without being asked.

There's one more opportunity to step up to the plate worthy of an honorable mention. There are times when you can act in a completely selfless manner as an appeal to your partner to be reasonable. One or both of you may have been pretty unreasonable and this has now gotten a little out of hand. You recognize this, but your partner won't let up. You've tried everything—staying calm, talking about it, arguing about it, keeping your distance. His unreasonable behavior only leaves you with one logical choice: be unreasonable back or let him run over you.

At times like this, sometimes it makes sense to do the most unexpected thing. Instead of engaging like this, you not only give in but you do something totally selfless for your partner. It's a great way to ask for peace. And if even this does not work, you know you did the right thing and can say with confidence the ball is in your partner's court.

Think of one way you could give in to your partner on something that would be somewhat out of character for you. Look for the next opportunity to give in.

## PRACTICAL SUGGESTIONS FOR A SELFLESS HEART

In addition to looking for certain kinds of situations that give you the opportunity to be selfless, here are a few other ideas you can work on.

*Do one behavior a day.* Considering all the opportunities that exist every day to be selfless, make a commitment to yourself to intentionally do at least one selfless thing a day for your partner. This will typically lead you to do something you would not normally do. Wake up each morning with this in mind, training yourself to remember it periodically through the day.

*Ask your partner.* Express to your partner you want to be more giving. Ask him for a few ideas, then be ready for the answer! I can guarantee you that he will have an answer, and the things he mentions may very well hit on some of your shortcomings. Being the gracious person you are, you thank him for such helpful feedback and commit to working on those things every day. Ask him in a week if he has noticed any improvement. Again, thank him for his answer!

*Learn from others.* There are three important ways to learn about being selfless from others. First, observe any selfless attitudes in other people, especially your mate. Add these attitudes to your own. Second, think about if and how you learned about personal sacrifice from your parents. Third, talk to friends about how they learned from their parents about personal sacrifice. These are easy questions to ask, and are easy to present casually over coffee. You will get some great ideas as well as some inspiration from hearing these stories.

*Take personal inventory.* Make a list of all your selfish habits. Include attitudes as well as behaviors. The reason to write them down is to make them real. Otherwise, it is really easy to lose track of them or minimize them. Then hold yourself accountable to catching yourself "in the act," and then behave differently. If you're really brave, share the list with your partner and ask for help in noticing them if they occur.

**Give in.** Go out of your way to give in to your partner when you normally would not. It doesn't matter if it's fair. Just do it because you have a bigger purpose in mind. Parent the kids today the way your wife wants to do it. If it backfires, you've still accomplished a great deal. You have shown good faith, flexibility, and still made your point because it backfired. If it doesn't backfire, you gain in every way possible. Don't keep insisting on your own way of doing things, but instead just give in. It isn't weakness; it takes a strong and courageous heart to do that.

**Practice empathy.** Empathy is recognizing and understanding the beliefs, desires, and emotions of others. Most of us know this definition so well we can brush it off pretty easily. It goes deeper than just taking a minute every now and then to consider your partner's viewpoint. True empathy means understanding the viewpoint, then imagining *what it's like* to live life with that viewpoint. When you are angry or hurt because of your spouse, how often do you honestly exercise empathy then? Empathy requires you to let go of yourself—what preoccupies you—and become 100 percent focused on listening. When you are upset or unhappy, use this opportunity to listen more than ever and imagine *being* your partner. Even if you still disagree, your partner will feel validated and your approach will be much gentler.

**Admit your shortcomings.** Having a selfless heart empowers you to lose your concern about having faults of your own. When we are not getting along with our partner, the last thing we want to do is give him or her any more ammunition. But the more you deny your shortcomings, the more this forces you to go on the defensive. This locks you in with an offensive/defensive kind of interaction you can't escape. During a conflict, playing the blame game gets nowhere. Be quick to admit your contribution to an unhappy situation and place the focus on solutions. This is an art and can be learned. I will say much more about this in a later chapter.

**Get control of your dependencies.** Any habit that you like to indulge is self-centered. That is not to say it is necessarily bad. But since its purpose is to indulge a desire you have, it always has potential to interfere with placing your partner first. It could range from TV to sleep to alcohol, but you should review whatever it is continually to be sure it is not destructive to your higher goal of being selfless. Deep down, you know when this is happening, but listen to what your partner has to say about it. If he keeps bringing the same thing up, chances are you are letting something self-centered get in the way.

**Get into the world of others.** This suggestion is a little different from empathy. It is one thing to imagine being the other person, and that is important. You can take this a step further by sharing part of your spouse's world. Guys, tag along sometimes when your wife goes shopping. Gals, help your husband rake the leaves. Sometimes couples have a hard time seeing where they have common interests. If that is the case, put some work into creating interests together. Maybe they aren't your first choice, but the goal is sharing life together, not the activity! Commit to working at this by slowly changing your lifestyle to include some shared activities.

I've said it already, but the key with any of these ideas is to start small. The operative word here is "start." Even the smallest change has the potential to start a chain reaction leading to great things. One couple was having problems because the husband kept daydreaming about things he could not have. This self-centered indulgence became a bad habit and prevented him from focusing on his wife. It made him moody and preoccupied. He started to break out of this by making a weekly date with his wife and living that date "in the moment," enjoying it for what it was. This began a chain reaction of positive responses from her that made staying in the moment better than it ever was in the past or future. Pick some of the suggestions made here and start with *something*. Even if you stay small for a while, keep going. Just like a little yeast expands a big lump of dough, even our smallest efforts, whether positive or negative, have a huge influence.[14]

Common sense tells us being completely selfless is unattainable, doesn't it? Making a selfless heart your *goal* is the point. Christian people who speak in platitudes and act like you are just missing the point if you experience weak moments do us all a disservice. The Bible clearly says those who follow God's way have not already become perfect. Instead, we keep pressing forward so we can "lay hold of that" for which we were laid hold of by Jesus.[15] In other words, Jesus made the first move and paved the way. He did this so we could walk with God in this life and the life to come. Understanding His continual forgiveness enables us to keep getting up and pursuing a selfless attitude every day, relying on God's power to pull it off one more day even after we blow it.

Finally, you will never develop a selfless heart without facing all your fears and insecurities. Being selfless requires trust. You have to believe that if you let go of concerns about yourself, everything will be okay. Some people have learned to be selfless, at least partially, by simply observing how life works. They understand that giving of yourself turns into a blessing for everyone involved and they trust that process.

It's hard to let go of ourselves. In one of the first and most famous stories of the Bible, God tested Abraham by asking him to sacrifice his son Isaac. Put yourself in Abraham's spot: Take your son . . . kill him . . . show your trust in God. What did he do? What would you do? Abraham actually raised the knife to kill Isaac, and God stopped him.[16] God did not require the sacrifice, so don't get hung up there. This is the point: Abraham trusted God's love enough to be willing to give up his son! He believed God would make everything okay, even if he didn't understand how. Trusting this much takes away any need you could ever have to hold on to your own insecurities. God has shown his faithfulness throughout history. You have every reason to believe that emptying yourself for your partner because of His love will result in great things.

One of the main properties of the "atoms" in Element #2 is understanding how to let go of yourself, then putting that into action. The prospect of forgetting yourself and focusing on others is going to challenge you to the core. It will not be easy, but greatness never is. *You* can be the start of a modern-day miracle. Turn your trust to God and empty yourself for the sake of your spouse.

The miracle will start in your heart.

## Main Chapter Attitudes

✓ Know the difference between wants and true needs.
✓ Choose today to be selfless the way Jesus was.
✓ Commit to a lifelong process of becoming a selfless person.

### Attitudes in Action

**1. Attitude: Know the difference between wants and true needs.**

What do you think your real needs are versus your wants? Share these with your partner and discuss ways you can help each other meet both needs and wants. Does getting closer to God affect your answer?

**2. Attitude: Choose today to be selfless the way Jesus was.**

**a)** Talk to your partner about whether you ever really step outside yourself and focus completely on the needs of someone else. Do you do that in your marriage, and does it show patience and kindness? Agree on realistic ways you can start being more selfless at home.

**b)** Discuss situations that come up in your marriage that require each of you to be selfless the most. This includes any jealousies you may have (we are not talking about current behaviors your partner really does need to change). Talk about how you can both be more selfless in these situations.

**3. Attitude: Commit to a lifelong process of becoming a selfless person.**

Have you committed to any of the practical suggestions to strengthen a selfless heart? If not, explain to your partner why you think things will get better in your marriage anyway. Commit to several of the suggestions in this chapter and schedule times to review your efforts together.

# 8

# True Love Must
# Be Humble

*[Love] does not brag, is not arrogant or act
unbecomingly, but instead is patient.*

I Corinthians 13:4–5

Helen Nielsen said, "Humility is like underwear; essential, but indecent if it shows." Where would humility be without mercy? Without it, life would be too painful to bear. Like so many people, I grew up in a broken home, my parents divorcing when I was in sixth grade. There was so much I did not understand about my parents and their roots. Once I had grown and received training as a marriage and family therapist, I went back and had a long talk with my mother about her life and what she knew about our ancestors. She grew up the youngest of six children, being rather shy. Her father owned a business until the Great Depression, at which time he lost everything he had. When he died, he was a janitor. His father, my great-grandfather, died when my grandfather was only nine. He had grown up in the New York Bowery after fleeing the military draft in Ireland. My grandmother died when my mother was six. My mother admitted to having low self-esteem, and grew up with a negative, pessimistic outlook on life. I wonder how that could have happened! Early deaths and major hardship were all too familiar in her family.

**KEY ATTITUDE:**
**Be humble enough to accept your partner for who he or she is.**

I remember arriving at the out-of-state hospital just two hours before she took her last breath. By this time, she was comatose. I took her hand and talked to her, telling her, "I am here." Her head moved as if she heard me. The only word that came into my mind for the next several hours was "mercy." So much of life on this Earth is hard, and then we die. It happens to all of us, and we are in such dire need of mercy. We need acceptance despite our many shortcomings—and we all have many. Despite any unattractive aspects of my mother's pessimism, she needed mercy more than anything. She didn't need judgment from me, and I certainly didn't need to remember any wrong she ever committed toward me. Rather than being concerned with myself, the caring and concern needed to be 100 percent on her. This is the beginning of humility.

The simple truth is, if you strip away all of our titles, circumstances, and accomplishments, we are all the same. Every last one of us has hurt someone else and acted pridefully at times. None of us is free of guilt and our fate is the same. This is one reason we all find inspiration from our heroes. Peter Gibbon, a research associate at the Harvard Graduate School of Education, says that heroes teach us because they transcend suffering and triumph over human weakness.[1] Intuitively, we know that everyone possesses the same basic human condition, so when someone does something truly heroic, we all celebrate.

Most people would rather not think much about mortality. Instead, we would prefer to focus on those times when we feel invincible. When we're young, it feels as if we could live forever. You are hardwired to feel this way; in fact, God created you with a connection to eternity. The great King David from the Bible wrote more than two thousand years ago, "He has also set eternity in their heart, yet so that man will not find out the work which God has done from the beginning even to the end."[2] God made you to yearn for eternity, yet not quite be able to grasp it. This leaves us with an itch that we have to scratch; all too often we scratch too hard the wrong way.

## $\mathcal{K}$EY $\mathcal{A}$TTITUDE:
### Always keep your ego in check.

All too often in life, our own ego gets in the way and we get carried away with ourselves. We have a sense of immortality that often gets off track. Whatever builds us up—whatever feeds our ego—is what many of us learn to crave. Advertising companies know this all too well. They appeal to our wish to see ourselves a certain way through our desires and even our pride. No one is completely immune to it. Complete ad campaigns center around this desire to live up to a certain image we want to have.

If you are young and have a certain body shape, the world says you are special. How many new "ab-builder" machines (to build your abdominal muscles) have hit the marketplace since the turn of the twenty-first century? New fad diets to give you that perfect body have made millions for their proponents. Physical prowess, like that of professional athletes, has taken center stage in the media. Many people identify with athletes, living vicariously through their favorite team or player. Some of us care too much about what the world defines as "success," including the pursuit of lots of money, a good position with the company, living in the right neighborhood. Or maybe your attention is on anything that elevates power, your intellect, or skill in a certain area. The world seems to think well of us if we fill a role exceptionally well or if we are able to "one-up" the guy next to us.

Then there's the big one—sex appeal. According to Richard F. Taflinger, Ph.D., sex is second only to self-preservation as the strongest psychological force.[3] Just using women's bodies in advertising is enough to influence the average man. For the average woman, romance is the big appeal. Sexual self-image—good or bad—keeps many of us preoccupied with ourselves. Not all advertising uses self-image. Some ads just appeal to our cravings for things. But all of the strategies just mentioned make an appeal to how you want to see yourself.

♥ Write down a short paragraph describing how you see your-self overall. This is a hard thing to do but well worth the effort. Then discuss how this does or doesn't influence the way you approach things in your marriage. Don't argue here and don't criticize, but instead be open to an honest self-examination.

Either we're prideful about certain parts of ourselves or, on the other extreme, we're struggling just to feel a healthy sense of self-respect about ourselves in some areas. They are flip sides of the same coin—pride. When someone triggers either one of them, they lead to problems in marriage and neither extreme is healthy. Humility does not mean you think poorly of yourself or put yourself down. Charles Hadden Spurgeon said, "Humility is to make a right estimate of one's self. It is not humility for a man to think less of himself than he ought, though it might rather puzzle him to do that."[4] Real humility occurs when you have an accurate truth about your-self. You are no worse, but also no better, than anyone else.

> Real humility occurs when you have an accurate truth about yourself.

If you have a bruised ego, any suggestion that you are not good enough makes you desperate to feel good about yourself. Feeling pride in yourself becomes your goal. This kind of pride goes beyond a healthy sense of dignity and self-worth. The root is usually some kind of shame you experienced in your life. It won't be possible for you to be able to let go of this pursuit until you resolve the issues that put you in this condition.

Now if your ego is too big, seeing yourself truthfully will seem too threatening. Anything suggesting that you have flaws does not fit in with your exaggerated sense of yourself. Denial becomes your best friend. I especially like what William Temple had to say about the definition of humility. By his way of thinking, "Humility does not mean thinking less of yourself than other people, nor does it mean having a low opinion of your own gifts. It means freedom from thinking about yourself at all."[5] Preoccupation with yourself, whether it is thinking too highly or too little of yourself, is the essence of pride.

## THE DIFFERENT FACES OF PRIDE

There are several ways that either side of the "pride" coin can turn up in marriage, whether it is the prideful side or the insecure side. To confuse things even more, they often look the same. Pride steps in when we get too full of ourselves. The Bible tells us it is so easy to become consumed with the desires of our flesh, desires of the things we see, and feeling too good about ourselves.[6] It's called the "boastful pride of life." As my mother used to tell me, "You are getting too big for your britches." We think we can do what we want, when we want, and that we completely control our own destinies. We may have some things figured out and things are going our way, but the fact is that none of us is ultimately in control.[7] Every good thing you have in life—even the things you worked hard for—are ultimately from God.[8] If you are not actively thankful and humbled by this every day, chances are you tend to get too full of yourself.

One way pride comes out in marriage is to become preoccupied with wanting recognition and credit for your efforts. Going the extra mile for your partner is more difficult if you don't think she will notice or acknowledge your effort. Don't get me wrong, it's great to see the smile on your wife's face when the flowers arrive. But cleaning the toilet whenever it needs it, even if she won't notice what you did, that's another matter! Maybe you think cleaning toilets is below you. Or perhaps you just need lots of positive strokes, so you make sure she knows what you did to contribute.

Another classic way to be prideful is to see yourself as being a great arguer. You "always win" and have a need to be right all the time. Admit it, either your ego is too big or you are too insecure to accept the feeling of defeat. We'll talk more about this later, but disagreements should never have a winner and a loser anyway. If this characterizes you, it means you are too concerned with yourself being better than someone else—or not good enough.

Some people have made a habit of putting other people down or finding fault much of the time. Hopefully you are a step ahead of me on this one— yes, this form of pride is habit-forming and feeds on itself. It could be making fun of how other people look, ridiculing them, or just finding something wrong with them. The effect of this is to elevate yourself over others for your own ego. Even if this habit started because you were trying to be funny, it really is habit-forming and quickly takes on an ugly and unhealthy nature.

Depending on your past experiences, one form of pride you may slip into is thinking the world owes you something. You have developed a sense of entitlement, often expressed in being presumptuous with others. You just assume it's okay to borrow something and return it when you feel like it. You may just expect your partner to cater to you, even if she is getting the short end of the stick. If this describes you, the world centers around you a lot. It's about what you think, what you want, what's going on with you. Like your partner doesn't have concerns of her own! If you wrestle with the insecure side of pride, you may just have a chip on your shoulder. Something hasn't gone your way so you walk around as though others should cater to you. Nothing they do is good enough. Until you admit this to yourself, you will drive your partner away rather than creating intimacy.

*The less we think we deserve, the closer we are to understanding true humility.*

Essentially, your prideful nature takes over anytime your ego is threatened. If you pursue a right relationship with God, the Bible tells us you will "put on a new self" that is being continually renewed. This makes us all the same to God, so we should put on a heart of humility because of it.[9] Just understanding that God created us all equal is enough to give us a healthy dose of humility. The less we think we deserve, the closer we are to understanding true humility. The New Testament says you should not be wise in your own estimation. Instead, you should accommodate yourself to lowly things,[10] whether it be people, how you're seen, or what is asked of you. There are some marriage relationships characterized by partners who are never willing to appear weak. Maybe you feel threatened too much to let your guard down. If this describes your marriage, there is something very wrong. Either you have become too prideful, or your partner is way too hurtful, or both. It's crucial to discern which because it will determine what you need to do about it.

I see lots of folks in marriage counseling who describe themselves as stubborn, hardheaded, and quick to anger. Some people recognize this is a problem but keep giving themselves permission to be this way. They want to keep being this kind of person but also want me to fix their problems. It doesn't work that way! If this is you, you need to soften your heart and be willing to swallow some pride. Just about everyone in the Western civilized world has heard this saying of Jesus, "Blessed are the gentle, for they shall inherit the earth."[11] In another part of the Bible we are told, "God is opposed to the proud, but gives grace to the humble."[12]

## KEY ATTITUDE:
### Always be ready to admit wrongdoing and apologize.

We will address this in more detail later in the book, but being angry for any reason that involves self-interest is wrong in God's eyes. The only times Jesus became angry were occasions where He saw God being offended. Even then, His anger did not make Him want to lash out and be hurtful to others.

Stubbornness and anger are rooted in rigid thinking. Either self-interest or your need to control the situation produces this kind of thinking. Either one of these is destructive and is a form of pride. Jesus did not get angry from self-interest, nor did He control people. It's human nature to struggle with anger, but we must recognize when it is out of self-interest (it usually is) and resolve it quickly. We do this by taking ownership for it, not blaming the other person for our reaction, and getting back to an attitude of being reasonable. The better you are at this, the less likely you are to feel anger to begin with.

I know we are all imperfect and blow it sometimes. That really isn't the point, though, is it? It's what you do afterward that counts. We would all do well to apologize more and justify ourselves less. And if you have an "anger problem," admit it, apologize for it, then do what it takes to address it.

## Sometimes Life Requires Us to Quit Thinking so Highly of Ourselves

Some people are so full of themselves they become overconfident and disregard the feelings of others. Confidence is a great virtue, but when it gets cocky it quickly becomes ugly. These people feel little obligation to others, taking from the relationship and reciprocating little. Or they may just think that your giving in the relationship is automatic. Your "giving is a given." They spend little time thinking or investing themselves into being givers themselves. This reflects a selfish heart but is also symptomatic of a prideful one.

*Again, here's the rule: Being humble means we do not act or react out of self-interest.*

When one is no longer concerned with self-promotion, there are a lot of very human—and prideful—attitudes that disappear. One of the many faces of pride is when you deny your mistakes and refuse to really look at yourself honestly. This may be due to a low self-esteem (the insecure side of pride). A close cousin to this is when you "make" yourself humble in order to feel okay about yourself. This is fairly common and includes even some well-intentioned people. These are people who recognize some prideful tendencies and try to "work harder" at acting in a more humble manner. They are quick to put themselves down or cannot accept a compliment. While a step in the right direction, this still falls short of the proper understanding of humility. Again, here's the rule: Being humble means we do not act or react out of self-interest.

Discuss the things you pride yourself in the most. Then explore how this can interfere with marital interactions. Confessing this openly and honestly is a big first step toward the right attitude.

## *Key Attitude:*
**Have the humility of Jesus in all situations.**

When we finally "get" the truth about ourselves, we have the right frame of mind as we relate to our spouse. The Bible says to be subject to one another in the fear (reverence) of Christ.[13] This instruction comes right before a section talking about marriage. We are further told to give preference to one another[14] and to consider one another as more important than ourselves, having an attitude of humility.[15]

In virtually *everything* that happens between you and your partner, the humble heart thinks of your partner's best interest *first*. Challenging? Yes, but equally as powerful. Even if your partner is being unreasonable, humility like this can't help but have a positive effect. You may not change your partner—that's his choice—but you will have shown him something special with this kind of heart.

## When Humility Is Especially Important in Marriage

There are several situations requiring an extra dose of humility in marriage. Undoubtedly, you will encounter times when your abilities just aren't strong enough (or they don't fit the situation) to resolve an issue.

I'm generally a pretty good handyman, able to tackle many jobs and figure out how to fix things. But don't ask me to diagnose an electrical problem. I have learned some things about electricity but just don't have a very good aptitude for how it works. The same can be true for some people in relationships. You may be very talented at seeing what the real issue is with your wife, but every time you offer to help she gets upset. Sometimes she just wants you to listen! You say, "But I'm such a good fixer!" She says, "Who cares? I don't want you to fix it. Just listen." Be humble enough to do what your partner really wants and needs from you, not necessarily what you are good at. If your wife is better at managing the budget, swallow your pride and enjoy the fact she can do something better than you can.

When you have done something wrong, just swallow your pride about it. Sometimes you give a situation your very best and it still hasn't been good enough. Back when I first got married, we had some hedges that needed to be trimmed. Wanting to be a good husband and take care of our property, I volunteered to go out and trim them. The only problem was that I had no idea what I was doing. I'll never forget what happened next. I trimmed the bushes so far back there were no buds remaining on the branches. For those of you who don't know what you're doing in the yard either, that means there was no way for the bush to sprout again in the spring. In other words, I killed the hedges! Nothing but grotesque sticks in the ground! Just because you have good intentions doesn't mean you are making the right contribution to a situation. Be humble enough to admit it when this happens. To this day, I still have to swallow my pride when the topic of the hedges comes up.

> Ask your partner what he or she thinks you need to admit more about yourself. Thank your partner for the honesty.

Another common situation is when your approach is clearly a logical one but the issue continues to be a problem. Speaking reasonably to your wife about her mood swings makes perfect sense, after all. But have you ever tried having a logical conversation with PMS? Sitting down and telling your partner he has had too much to drink, then going on to discuss the details of how it is affecting your marriage, is probably not going to work. What you have to say is right, but your efforts do not work. An old college professor used to say, "You can't talk to alcohol." Whatever the situation is, even strategies that make sense may not be working. You may have to think outside the box, considering approaches outside your normal way of thinking. This can be humbling, and your own pride can block you from giving other approaches a chance. Give up being stubborn.

Identify a strategy you have tried with a problem that has not worked. Then consider a completely different kind of strategy and try it for a while.

One of the toughest times in marriage is when you are under the fire of criticism. Your husband is telling you that you are going about something all wrong. This is hard enough when he is being diplomatic, but there may be times he is just coming right at you. It triggers your pride and your defense mode kicks in. I am not suggesting you should not defend yourself, only that you stay rational and keep your pride in check. Keep focusing on the issue at hand, not on proving your worthiness. He may be insisting on his own way, inviting you to become stubborn in your effort to counteract his extreme approach. This is what gives birth to a world-class power struggle. The quickest way to interrupt a power struggle is by staying humble.

Finally, a common situation that arises is when you allow your circumstances to affect your willingness to try. This can be good or it can be bad. Let me illustrate. You have been trying to get your husband to treat you with the kind of affection you want. He does what you like for a while, then gets lazy. So you make a big issue of it and he does what you like for a while, then gets lazy again. After several rounds of this, you just don't bring it up anymore.

Sound familiar? If you realize your husband can't or won't change this behavior, you could accept the situation by modifying your expectations. This is probably a good resolution to the problem. It isn't your first choice, but it works. But if you are quietly resentful, you could become passive-aggressive. You will find indirect ways to show your displeasure. You might not cooperate with small requests your husband makes. Or you might find ways to annoy your husband in small things. Of course, you might just be out of ideas and don't bring it up for that reason. That is another matter, and we will look at it more in a later chapter. The key here is your willingness to try. Don't allow these situations to influence how much effort you make to achieve a good relationship. And don't let it become a reason to pump negative energy into the marriage.

## PRACTICAL SUGGESTIONS
## FOR A HUMBLE HEART

*Listen, listen, listen.* The less concerned you are with yourself, the better listener you are. If you just train yourself to do this one thing you will be amazed at how much difference it makes. The Bible says for "everyone to be quick to hear, slow to speak and slow to anger."[16] When you are passionate about something and someone disagrees with you, be careful to listen instead of thinking what you want to say next. But how do you do that when the other person is talking a mile a minute? You listen by relaxing and *slowing down*. If you start to feel anger, catch those feelings early and have strategies to keep it in check. A humble heart not only listens, it *wants* to hear what your spouse has to say. Remember: you are listening only if your partner says you are.

*Accept your partner.* This is another extremely basic and critical attitude. In probably nine out of ten marriage counseling cases that come to my office, one or both partners are not practicing real acceptance. It means you accept your partner as he is without insisting or demanding he is perfect. This does not mean you never have requests of your partner. But if he has a habit you don't like, a personality trait or certain viewpoints, you discuss it, then drop it. It comes down to allowing your partner to have weaknesses.

This can get tricky because some people want to use this as an excuse to be selfish or lazy. If that is the case, beating your partner into submission is never a good option anyway. You can make your appeal to him, then if he continues to be selfish, your closeness may be affected. It is not the best solution but it takes two people to achieve the ideal relationship. The Bible tells us to accept one another[17] and to "bear the weaknesses of those without strength and not just please ourselves."[18] State your case, then be sure to affirm your partner.

**Do the Hokey Pokey.** No one wants to be with someone who never has an opinion. It's Friday night and you ask your wife where she wants to eat. "I don't care, wherever you want," is her answer every time. After a while, this becomes monotonous. Plus, this kind of interaction does not offer much companionship. Put your two cents in and have an opinion. So you put your right foot in. Then be flexible enough to accommodate your partner. It should not always be your way. So you take your left foot out. Work on having a balance of asserting your views and preferences, while remaining flexible enough to have give and take in the relationship.

**Get out of yourself.** Simply put, take a couple of minutes every morning to review the focus of your concerns for the day. Are they all about you? Take the time necessary to reflect on the big picture. Be sure you are aware of what concerns the people around you have. Carry this awareness through your day and be ready to interact accordingly. One valuable habit is that of asking your partner questions about his or her world. This gets him talking about himself (we all like to do that) and shows him you are tuned in to him and not just yourself.

**Become an anonymous donor.** Make it a habit to consider ways to contribute to daily household routines in ways your mate never knows about. Pick up some extra clutter, clean something not on the schedule, call the repair person for something you have both been procrastinating about. This will not only make life go more smoothly, but humility will bud in your heart and begin to grow. It will start to show in ways you don't even see in yourself.

**Love the wrongdoer.** Probably the hardest time to love someone is when he wrongs you. Remember that when he has wronged you, this represents an important defining moment. Your emotions may be strong, and if you have not disciplined yourself to manage them, they will take over. In the midst of your emotions teach yourself to remember to step back and see the big picture. Jesus told us to love our enemies.[19] Even if it *feels* like your partner is "the enemy," that is no reason to treat him like one. You may be convinced his intentions are self-centered or meant to hurt you, but the Bible says we should "overcome evil with good."[20] There is a good chance your assessment of his intentions is inaccurate, but even if it is accurate your response should be the same either way. Train yourself to think this way.

*The real truth is, nice guys finish first.*

**Become more childlike.** In a world where everyone is scratching and clawing to compete for his fair share, this advice may seem foreign to you. Everyone has heard the saying, "Nice guys finish last." If you're competitive and have ever found yourself thinking this, chances are you carry this attitude into your marriage in some form or fashion. You might be thinking, *If I don't stand up for myself he's going to run all over me.* The real truth is, nice guys finish first. Jesus said, "Whoever then humbles himself as this child, he is the greatest in the kingdom of heaven."[21] Why would He use a child to make his point? A child is the perfect example of humility! While we know that little children like to throw temper tantrums, they are pliable and more capable of learning new things than us grown-ups.

I have played the guitar since my early twenties and just wish I had started when I was ten. I missed the magical years of childhood where learning happens exponentially faster than it does as an adult. My advice is to approach your marriage in a childlike manner (not child*ish*), with the wonder, curiosity, willingness to learn, and intuition that says you can't do a lot of things on your own. When you do, you will be open to change when it becomes necessary.

**Go to confession.** This is not the Catholic practice of going to the priest and telling him your sins. Instead, make a practice of admitting—with painful honesty—your mistakes and faults to God and to your marriage partner. In the old movie *Love Story* with Ryan O'Neal and Ali MacGraw, the character of Oliver told Jennifer that love means never having to say you're sorry. It was a moving moment in the movie, but I completely disagree. Say you're sorry and mean it! However, one apology should be enough. Then commit to working on yourself to prevent the same mistakes from happening over and over. Tell your partner you are open to his or her constructive criticism and be willing to acknowledge any truth to it.

*Be transparent.* Genuine humility means there is no reason to cover up any of your feelings, weaknesses, intentions, or desires. By being transparent you open yourself up to your mate in all ways. Shutting down, pouting, or having little to say is unfair to your spouse. After thinking about it, if you still have nothing to say on a regular basis, you may need to spend more time getting in touch with your thoughts and feelings. Some people spend such little time on this they really don't know themselves.

A young lady came to me for help controlling her stress reactions in relationships. In talking with her, it became obvious she had almost no insight into what kinds of things upset her and why. The first order of business for her was to begin paying attention every day to what was going on inside of her. Then letting others see her truthfully was the next step.

*Practice gratitude.* Realizing that everything good in your life ultimately comes from God, stop patting yourself on the back or spending so much energy "controlling" your destiny. I put that word in quotes because our being in control is mostly an illusion. Yes, we can be well organized, work harder, or apply ourselves intelligently. Get rid of the notion that you deserve what you have and recognize that you control very little on this planet. Be thankful for the strengths your wife has. Be glad for what your husband does offer the relationship. In the midst of struggle, don't lose sight of your gratitude. Find ways to show your partner this attitude in actions and words every day. Does your wife always cook the dinner? Thank her today for it. Does your husband always write checks to pay bills? Thank him today for it. If you can do this even when things are not going well you will bless yourself and your partner.

**Submit to your partner.** Whatever your view is on the husband/wife roles and who is in charge of what, an attitude of submission should be overflowing in your marriage like the swelling of a river after a hard rain. Submit to the desires and needs of your partner. This has nothing to do with power and control. It also has nothing to do with the husband being a leader. Instead, the Bible says we are all to serve one another through love.[22] In your marriage, who is the greater servant? In most marriages it seems the wife is better in this area. If this is the case, husbands will do well to follow the example of their wives and learn how to serve, not have the attitude she should serve him. I have met many women who have said they would fall out of their chairs if their husband did something for them! Whether you are a husband or a wife, give thought to how you could be a better servant to your partner starting right now. Be specific and put it into action immediately.

**Just let go.** If you are serious about wanting a humble heart, the only way to do it—the only way—is to let go of all the things that make you want to focus on *you*. It doesn't get any more challenging than that. Things that tempt you, things that worry you, catering to your weaknesses, things that make you feel important, things that upset you, things that make you jealous—you need to surrender all these things. What do you put your confidence in? Is it your career, your looks, your ability to figure most things out, your youth, your personality, your intelligence, your money, your ability to control your situation, or the things you enjoy?

A skiing buddy told me one day as we stopped on the side of the mountain and looked out at a spectacular panoramic view, "This is my church. I feel the most spiritual when I'm up here looking at this." The Bible warns us not to put our confidence in ourselves[23] and to worship the creator, not the creature.[24] It's even possible to place so much of your confidence in your marriage partner that when things go wrong at home, your world falls apart. Take the time to identify the things that give you the most confidence. If they serve to put the focus on you—your desires and wants—they probably won't help too much when you need humility the most. Placing your confidence outside yourself and onto God is the simple answer. Then approaching your mate with this accurate view of yourself will lead to nothing but growth and blessing.

Once you empty yourself of you, only then can you begin to understand the kind of humility that Jesus has shown the world. Once you do, the spirit of God has room in your heart to fill it with such things as love, joy, peace, patience, kindness, goodness, faithfulness, gentleness, and self-control.[25] Your primary concern will be what will build up your partner, not worrying about your own "needs."

Another property of Element #2 is authentic humility. Without it, it may look like Element #2, but it is not. You can't love unconditionally without pure humility. Conflicts and differences will always arise. A humble heart will meet them with an attitude of helping to find solutions. This kind of heart directs the emotions and behaviors toward a gentle demeanor not found among the proud. Every response of the humble heart will be to exalt your mate, not yourself. If your partner is receptive at all, he or she will have a very hard time resisting this. Empty yourself of self-promotion and look outside yourself for your confidence. Make this your daily quest, working at it consciously.

Remember who you are before God and start conditioning your heart to be humble.

## MAIN CHAPTER ATTITUDES

✓ Be humble enough to accept your partner for who he or she is.

✓ Always keep your ego in check.

✓ Always be ready to admit wrongdoing and apologize.

✓ Have the humility of Jesus in all situations.

## ATTITUDES IN ACTION

1. **Attitude: Be humble enough to accept your partner for who he or she is.**

   **a)** Discuss some of the criticisms you have made of each other in your marriage. Explore how these would vanish if you simply showed unconditional acceptance of each other. Commit to showing this for three days, then sit down and review what it was like.

   **b)** Have you committed to any of the practical suggestions to strengthen a humble heart? If not, explain to your partner why you think things will get better in your marriage anyway.

2. **Attitude: Always keep your ego in check.**

   How does your ego sometimes get "bruised" in your marriage relationship? Talk this over with your partner and determine how much of it is an oversensitive ego and how much of it is really triggered by your partner.

3. **Attitude: Always be ready to admit wrongdoing and apologize.**

   Is apologizing a regular part of your personality? Ask your partner if there is anything he thinks you have not apologized for that you should have, including too much bragging or thinking too highly of yourself.

4. **Attitude: Have the humility of Jesus in all situations.**

   When do you find yourself being the most prideful in life? Determine how this can affect your marriage and begin changing the thoughts that reinforce this pride. Identify what those specific thoughts or ideas are. Discuss how you could humble yourself more completely with your marriage partner.

# 9

# True Love Must
# Be Devoted

*[Love] does not rejoice in unrighteousness,*
*but rejoices with the truth.*

I Corinthians 13:6

Everyone is devoted to something. As Vince Lombardi, famous football coach said, "Once a man has made a commitment to a way of life, he puts the greatest strength in the world behind him. It's something we call heart power. Once a man has made this commitment, nothing will stop him short of success."

The sad thing is many people are devoted in ways they don't realize. The definition for devotion is ardent, often selfless affection and dedication to a person or principle. Another word that is close to this is "commitment," defined as the act of binding yourself to a course of action. Most people are devoted to things that are mostly self-serving—the things in life that are not lasting—and give them most of their time and energy. For the vast majority of people this means taking the path of least resistance, giving in to laziness and the pleasures of immediate gratification. They are passively devoted. Their devotion is by default—it's not a conscious decision so much as a pattern of life they fall into. Marriage is a common place to see this; just look at all the people that do the same things over and over without thinking much. But the net result is they are pouring their time and energy into thoughtless mediocrity.

Many years ago there was a young man who eventually made writing his career. He spent twenty years in the Coast Guard and decided to become a freelance writer. He moved into a cleaned-out storage room in a Greenwich Village apartment building. It was not heated and had no bathroom. He bought a used manual typewriter to get started. He spent a year at this with no success of any kind! He had a dream to be a successful writer, but began to have serious doubts about his plan.

One day he got a call from an old friend from the Coast Guard offering him a job as a public information assistant that paid $6,000 a year. In 1960, this was great money! Yet this young aspiring writer wanted to write full-time, so he turned down the job. As frightening as this was, he knew what he really wanted. The struggle continued, as he had the daily challenge of figuring out how he was even going to eat. Gradually, he began to sell an article here, an article there.

Slowly but surely, this young man managed to make a career for himself. Long after he moved out of Greenwich Village and had become successful, one day he was unpacking some personal things. He came across a brown paper bag. What happened next is pretty impressive. Opening it, he found two corroded sardine cans, a nickel, a dime, and three pennies. It was an overwhelming reminder of his struggles in previous years, and he realized these things were part of his roots. He told himself he could never allow himself to forget that.

Today, Alex Haley, the author of *Roots*, keeps these items framed on the wall next to his Pulitzer Prize. Haley still tells people that doubt is part of having a dream.[1] We must continue to focus and maintain our dedication, for this is the only road to big achievements. Developing a devoted heart in your marriage is not easy and there will be many times of doubt. But it's worthy of your time and energy. It is a big achievement.

Single-minded devotion is a rare thing these days. The average person lacks follow-through when it's needed the most. You can say you are committed to something all you want, but in the end your behavior betrays you if you don't maintain your focus. Telling your wife all your good intentions and not following through produces more frustration than if you had not said anything at all. Weak devotion is simply a halfhearted effort.

*Anything worth having requires a price of admission.*

Anything worth having requires a price of admission. If you don't know what the price is to have a devoted heart in your marriage, take the time to consider what would have to change in you to be this way. Jesus knew how important this is. He said that if you want to build a tower, you should sit down and estimate the cost to be sure you can complete it. Otherwise, you won't finish and end up looking foolish.[2] Don't be too quick to say, "Yeah, I'm really going to work on having a devoted heart." First, consider what it will really take and prepare yourself to follow through on your commitment.

♥ *Discuss what "price of admission" you will have to pay to be a more devoted marriage partner. Tell your partner how he or she can help make that easier, and ask how he would like you to be more devoted. Find a time this week to begin paying that price.*

Many people fall short in their devotion to something by being too quick to compromise. They begin to doubt the course they are on, thinking it will not work for some reason. This leads to changing what has been proven to work and replacing it with some other course of action that "makes more sense" at the time. A perfect example of this is when people find themselves stranded in their cars during a winter blizzard. Instead of waiting out a storm, they make the decision to leave their cars and look for help. There have been many tragic stories like this where people were found within 200 yards of their car frozen to death.

## KEY ATTITUDE:
**Be devoted to being a good marriage partner.**

Learning what works in marriage, then abandoning it due to "exceptions" in your relationship, is a quick way to defeat yourself. These exceptions are usually rooted in being concerned with how someone has wronged us. In reality, this just amounts to making excuses for being less than fully devoted to your partner. Most often, this happens when you are not getting along and can't seem to resolve an issue. You think to yourself that you will get back to investing the way you need to in the relationship once you get past the issue. This reaction is common, yet it represents a change of course that puts you right into a downward spiral. It's critical that once you decide how you will devote yourself, you stick with it and don't deviate. Otherwise, you will be all over the map in your efforts—and not getting anywhere.

Blind devotion is a second cousin to this, where people make erroneous judgments about how they should devote themselves. Devoting yourself to your job so you can be a great provider for your wife is awesome, but only if that is what she really wants. She may prefer less money and more of your time and companionship. Be careful about the assumptions you make in your devotion. Make sure you don't outsmart yourself, but instead take a little extra time every now and then to make sure your commitment focuses on the right things. A final thought on this: don't fall into the common trap of thinking there is really an end point with your marital devotion. It's a daily decision to live this way for as long as you live.

Much of the world tends to be impressed with passionate devotion regardless of its object. Some people make money and worldly success the object of their passion. Others focus on family or even some definition of "marital happiness" that can be easily affected by changing circumstances. Some marriage partners focus heavily on their own personal enjoyment in life, making that their biggest priority. Still others just want their fair share in life.

Roger, a young, good-looking, and well-educated black man, came to see me for couples counseling. His wife, an attractive black woman, was also successful in the business world. She, however, had a pretty laid-back attitude and was not very concerned with what other people thought of her. Roger was focusing heavily—devoting himself—on success in a business world that tended to discriminate against him and require more talent of him than of his white counterparts. This stress began to creep into their marital interactions. He started thinking her efforts were not strong enough and began to pick at her in lots of small ways. When Roger finally realized what the focus of his energy really was, and how it was preventing him from accepting his wife, he came to tears. He began to shift the object of his energies.

## KEY ATTITUDE:
### Be devoted to complete openness and truthfulness.

To have the kind of love Jesus had, we must learn to rejoice with the truth.[3] One of the famous beatitudes of Jesus is that we are to thirst for righteousness.[4] What in the world does that mean? Well, righteousness—and truth—is whatever conforms to the true nature and heart of God. Righteousness is whatever is consistent with who God is. It means you are upright, just, straight, innocent, true, and sincere. Jesus Himself, when He was talking about people who become anxious about the material things of life, said to ". . . seek first [God's] kingdom and his righteousness, and all these things shall be added to you."[5]

The Bible tells us that God exercises his will through "the word of truth."[6] Profoundly, that word has always been with God, and in fact is Jesus Himself.[7] It isn't a complicated bunch of theology. Simply put, Jesus is our example of all truth and righteousness. He is our standard. Follow His example and we can rest assured we are doing the right thing. Jesus is God personified. Make the cliché, "What would Jesus do?" your guiding princi-

*If there is any doubt about what the heart of Jesus is, or what the truth of His word is, the Bible is the ultimate reference book.*

ple and you can't go wrong. Do what He would do and, to go one step further, develop His heart. If there is any doubt about what the heart of Jesus is, or what the truth of His word is, the Bible is the ultimate reference book. Don't look at people in churches, or what the popular opinion is, or what most people are doing. Don't rely on this book to tell you. Make it a point to *know* what the truth is about Jesus and His teachings.

## KEY ATTITUDE:
**Learn how God thinks and desire to think that way.**

So we are to devote ourselves to knowing, and following, the nature, character, and heart of God. Knowing God personally and intimately in this way is the message of the whole Bible. That is to be the focus of our devotion. In Old Testament times, the warning was to live our lives with righteousness and justice. If we cheat others and focus on material things, we miss the point of life. Instead, we should be champions of those in need and care about others. In fact, that is when we start to know God personally.[8]

*Adopt one new habit that will enable you to know God more personally, starting today. Be realistic, starting small enough that you will follow through with this new habit daily. Then look for ways to show the changes this creates in you within your marriage.*

## KEY ATTITUDE:
**Be devoted to doing things God's way.**

Allowing this to change us, then, is what enables you to be a great marriage partner. Trusting in God and His ways gives you a single-minded focus that will carry you through any marital difficulty.

Otherwise, the Bible says we will just become double-minded and unstable because we are not focusing on the right thing.[9] But if we turn to God and follow His way of doing things, He will "never allow the righteous to be shaken."[10] The Bible says to commit our way to God, to trust Him and He will bless us.[11]

So what does rejoicing with the truth of God and thirsting for righteousness have to do with your marriage? First, it sets a standard for what your relationship should be like. It gives you clear direction. It not only creates a thirst in you for what is true and right, but it gives you the gentleness of heart needed when things are not that way. When your marriage veers off course you are not satisfied until things are right again. When it is on the right course you couldn't be happier. Your whole definition of happiness becomes one in which circumstance makes little difference. It makes you focus on principles that have worked for centuries and opens the door to tap into the very power of God if you are open to this.

> *Your life's agenda is now the pursuit of attitudes, emotions, and behaviors patterned after the heart of Jesus.*

Second, it creates an "agenda" for your life every day that comes from something greater than you. It comes from a higher source. Your life's agenda is now the pursuit of attitudes, emotions, and behaviors patterned after the heart of Jesus. When you finally comprehend how powerful and effective this way of living is, you can't help but get excited. It is then that you are motivated to commit yourself in this way to your marriage and devote yourself to it every day. Even in the face of doubt and discouragement, your dream is now big enough to keep you focused and inspired to do what's *right* where your partner is concerned. When tempted to lash out in anger, your devotion to truth reminds you that is not the response you want. When you make peace with your partner—even if it didn't seem fair on your end of it— you rejoice. Peace is your passion—not avoiding conflict, but the peace that comes from confronting issues calmly and respectfully.

♥ Consider situations in your marriage in which you know you are not thinking or behaving the way Jesus would. Name a couple out loud with your partner. Spend a few minutes (at least) every day thinking about this, developing a hunger for what is right in these situations. Then show that you are rejoicing in the truth by acting on this hunger with attitudes and behavior.

The results of this kind of devotion only come from daily effort and focus. You can't be hot one day and cold the next. It would be like exercising hard one day, then taking two weeks off. That isn't devotion at all! To devote yourself—to anything—means you pour yourself into it consistently. If you do, results will come. Just remember that it's a cumulative effect. It usually takes time to build up before you start to see the result of your devotion. Dieting is the perfect example. You can starve yourself, lose weight, and then gain it all back again (isn't that what most people do?). Or you can commit to a new lifestyle of eating more modestly every day for the rest of your life. Results come more slowly, but they are much more lasting.

## WHEN DEVOTION IS ESPECIALLY IMPORTANT

You need a devoted heart most when either problems or pleasures of the moment tempt and sidetrack you.

*KEY ATTITUDE:*
**Want to do what's right in God's eyes.**

We all want to indulge ourselves at times. This isn't a bad thing in your marriage unless it interferes with your commitment to give yourself wholly. Spending the day golfing when you haven't had time with your wife may be acceptable if it is an exception, but if it is a common occurrence it is not loving at all. Wanting to be self-indulgent only shows that you are devoted mostly to yourself, which doesn't exactly promote a good marital relationship. Another key situation that calls on your devotion to truth is when that truth reveals something negative about you. How badly do you love the truth? What's right is right. If the tone of your voice is coming across to your wife as harsh or defensive, even if that is not your intention, don't you want to know about it? It makes no sense to get defensive about this and argue about it. If she approaches you with an accusing attitude, talk to her about *that*. Don't just dismiss her point, though. To be devoted to what is right and true, you will always be open to constructive criticism.

> Find out what your partner's biggest criticism is of you. Invite his or her input. Look for any and all truth in it, then begin changing whatever attitude or behavior is required to take this information to heart.

Sometimes the same old problems keep coming up. You have talked to your husband over and over about the way he jokes with you. He is too sarcastic and makes fun of you. You've talked until you are blue in the face about how it makes you feel. He agrees to stop doing it, then the next day it happens all over again—in front of friends. "I shouldn't *have* to keep bringing this up," you say. Maybe you're right. So what! If you are devoted to what is right and true as Jesus showed us, you will quickly remember He said to forgive someone seven times seventy times.[12] Your devotion will keep your response within an acceptable range.

Okay, so far so good. As if that's not hard enough! How about those times when you repeatedly do the right thing, leading the way for your partner to do the same, and he doesn't want to have anything to do with it? As long as we feel as if we can control the outcome at some point, all this stuff works. The biggest test of your devotion to what is right and true is when your partner just isn't responding.

An overly controlling—but very tender—father came to therapy wanting to restore a damaged relationship with his fifteen-year-old daughter. She wanted to trust him not to be demeaning to her when they had a disagreement but was unsure if she could. He was quick to say he would just be patient with her and give her time, indicating he would communicate with her very respectfully. What stopped him dead in his tracks was when I asked him what he would do if she still wanted to have nothing to do with him. That would mean he couldn't control the outcome on his terms. He had never entertained that idea before. This challenged him to be devoted to the right thing more than he ever had before—even if the outcome was undesirable. He realized he was doing this in his marriage, too, and had a lot of things to think about at home.

Some situations escalate to the point where your partner just gets downright ugly. Maybe his pattern is yelling, name-calling, withdrawal, sabotaging your good efforts, or irritating you on purpose. Well, there *are* exceptions, right? Wrong! This is where most people bail out, even the tough people who are really trying to have a devoted heart. You start rationalizing how this is going too far and that it's time to put your foot down. Now don't get me wrong. We all should have personal limits and a healthy capacity to be assertive with them. But that never gives you a license to act poorly yourself. You may have to pull back a bit just to keep your own behavior in check. Assertiveness means you can enforce limits respectfully and with love.

♥ Choose one behavior you could do differently when your partner does not behave well and begin implementing it the next time it happens.

It's easy to think we have it so rough, then let our devotion become weak. A young husband came to me alone asking me to help him improve his marriage. He and his young wife had a child together who had a medical condition requiring twenty-four-hour nursing support. She had gone to school to become a licensed practical nurse so they would qualify for insurance reimbursement. While the couple could get some relief sometimes by having another nurse come in, they were utterly convinced this could not be trusted. On more than one occasion, their son almost died when they brought in outside help. They believed only they knew how to care for him in a way that would keep him alive. Whether this was really true, I was unqualified to say. This couple was virtually under house arrest from the circumstances. It had been three years since they had both left the house at the same time! Their devotion to their son was remarkable. For almost every one of you reading this, you have not devoted yourself with this kind of ferocity yet to your marriage.

A final thought here on when you most need a devoted heart. We looked at this earlier but it is worth mentioning again because it is such a common challenge. Life puts your heart to the test constantly when it doesn't measure up to your expectations. Most expectations are really about *you* and *your* desires, and it is really hard sometimes to give them up. A devoted heart takes the greatest pleasure in the "agape" kind of love, which is selfless and unconcerned with what we are getting out of it. If you are with a partner that just doesn't respond to that, you both probably need marriage therapy to get help sorting it all out. Otherwise, it is when you are disappointed that a heart devoted to what is true and right is especially needed. Train yourself during these times to see if it is because of a self-serving desire or because something actually does need to change. If it is the latter, your devoted heart will point you in a direction that will make things better, not lead to more problems.

> *Life puts your heart to the test constantly when it doesn't measure up to your expectations.*

## PRACTICAL SUGGESTIONS FOR A DEVOTED HEART

**Determine the object of your devotion.** Most people do not have a clearly defined set of standards for their marriage. You can say you are devoted to having a good marriage, but what exactly are you devoted *to*? Is it based on what you get out of it, or is your partner's well-being 100 percent of what you are devoted to? If what you are devoted to is not something bigger than you are it will prove to be unreliable and disappointing. Commit yourself to what is true and right by God's standards and you will not be disappointed. When Jesus was teaching on this Earth, skeptics tried to trick Him into saying something that they could attack. Even when they approached Him with this motive, they acknowledged that He was truthful and was teaching the way of God in truth.[13] Following Jesus and making His simple teachings the object of our daily devotion will produce great success.

**Establish daily habits.** The only way to be devoted to something is to put some time in. It is not possible to be devoted to something by deciding what is important to you then never thinking about it. If your desire is for your marriage to exemplify what is right and true, there are a couple of habits that will help a lot.

Make it a habit to spend at least a few minutes every day to ask your partner (you find the words that work for you) if he or she is doing well. *Really* doing well. If you are doing anything unhelpful or if there is anything you can do to make things better, be ready to hear that. Second, spend at least a few minutes every day reflecting on the object of your devotion. Think about God and how the life of Jesus gives your life direction. Some call this a daily devotional time. It includes thinking about God and yourself, some prayer, and ideally reading even a short excerpt from the Bible. Then try to remember what you thought about throughout the day. Even five minutes a day can make a huge difference.

*Think about God and how the life of Jesus gives your life direction.*

Try it once if you have not been doing something like this. If you manage to remember your thoughts throughout the day you will see a difference in yourself that day. This little habit will also help you develop a taste (or thirst) for what is true and right. If you already have one it will just make it stronger.

*Identify chinks in your armor.* Think about the situations, people, stresses, and times when you tend to get distracted from what you value. You may tend to become distracted when tired, sick, overscheduled, have unexpected bills, or your partner acts distant. Whatever it is that weakens your devotion, the first thing to do is identify it. Once you identify your weak spots, decide on a new behavior at the very moment it happens. Remind yourself somehow that this is a time you need to be devoted the most and choose a behavior consistent with that.

*Keep your motives in check.* The Bible says, "The heart is more deceitful than all else."[14] Be careful not to get too comfortable and think everything is just fine. Without consistent honesty with yourself, your own selfish agendas will creep in ever so subtly. Beyond identifying those situations that are distracting, it is critical to make a habit of taking a close look at your motives and intentions. Don't give in just to get your wife off your back. Give in because you know it's the right thing to do at the time. When conflicts arise, your first response should be to make sure that your attitude—your heart—is really one of devotion.

*Become self-disciplined.* Staying focused on anything takes discipline. Being obsessive is not discipline because it is out of your control. The average person cannot focus only on one thing for very long at all. For example, if you love ice cream, it's impossible to think about only that for hours. Most people couldn't focus just on ice cream even for fifteen minutes. Train yourself to concentrate with consistency.

> *Train yourself to concentrate with consistency.*

Reading is a great way to do this. Find a book that inspires you, fiction or nonfiction. Meditation, yoga, prayer, martial arts—these all require concentration. The Bible urges us to be devoted to prayer.[15] Start with just three minutes of concentrated prayer a day. See if you can really do that. Set a goal for yourself of prayer and meditation every day for at least a few minutes. Many Christians know they should do this but still don't. Then they wonder why their marriage seems to be all over the place.

**Consider the price of admission daily.** Make this a conscious, deliberate, and specific process. It's human nature when you hear something over and over again to say, "Yeah, yeah, yeah. We've been over this already." But to develop a fully devoted heart requires lots of repetition even when it seems unnecessary. Remind yourself often what it is going to take to be this committed. Honestly consider the challenge and recommit yourself to it all over again each day. Remember why this is what you want your life to be about. Then watch for situations throughout the day that enable you to live it out.

**Always tell the truth.** Couples tend not to be 100 percent honest with each other for a lot of reasons. Sometimes it's to avoid conflict, hurting the other person's feelings, "pushing" your opinion onto someone else, thinking the other person will not listen, or admitting something you have done wrong. Whatever the reason, being less than honest goes against the grain of being devoted to what is true. Holding on to truth sometimes has consequences. Make it a habit to be truthful at all times and be willing to deal with any fallout from doing so. If being truthful causes problems, there is something wrong anyway!

**Welcome ambiguity.** Uncertainty and lack of control are a part of life. Living with them securely is a *way* of life. Sometimes life is like driving in a blizzard with cliffs on both sides. It can be terrifying because you can't see where you're going. Like it or not, life is like that. Trying to resist that reality does nothing but stress you out, and often makes things worse. Trying to control the way your partner feels or naturally thinks is, well, not very intelligent. Trying to make someone respect you usually has the opposite effect. Life gets a whole lot easier when we accept the fact that ambiguity is the natural way of many things. Do what you know to be constructive, then sit back and let things happen. An old friend of mine told me once, "Things always happen slower than they do." That includes not being sure how they will happen or when. You know that if you put a healthy seed in fertile soil, provide adequate light, and water it, it will grow. Learn to live your life that way. Don't force or try to control the growth, just nurture it.

There is so much about life—about being married—that is bigger than we are. We never really become experts at marriage. What we know is so much less than what we don't know. So hanging on to the things we can rely on merits our wholehearted devotion. Thirsting for what is right and learning to be passionate about what is true *are* things we can count on. Injecting this kind of wholehearted devotion into your marriage provides a compass for the relationship that never steers you wrong.

Another property of Element #2 is wholehearted devotion to the highest form of love, which comes from God. It takes a willingness to change what you have been doing and to begin doing things a new way. All change is painful and we humans love to avoid it. Being passionate about what is right and true is not an easy course. But as tough as it can be sometimes, the reward is worth it. Jesus has told us that if we live by what He says we shall know the truth, and that truth frees us.[16] Instead of being enslaved to our old way of doing things we are free to do things His way. No one would argue that if you treated your partner the way Jesus would, your marriage would see dramatic improvements.

You have a compass available to you. Do you trust it and remember to use it enough for it to lead the way? You could continue relying on your own wisdom to figure everything out, allowing your human weaknesses to influence your decision making. The question is whether you will choose to use the compass and, more importantly, follow it every day. Putting the compass down will most certainly lead you off course.

## MAIN CHAPTER ATTITUDES

✓ Be devoted to being a good marriage partner.

✓ Be devoted to complete openness and truthfulness.

✓ Learn how God thinks and desire to think that way.

✓ Be devoted to doing things God's way.

✓ Want to do what's right in God's eyes.

## ATTITUDES IN ACTION

1. **Attitude: Be devoted to being a good marriage partner.**

   What parts of being a good marriage partner for your spouse deserve more of your undivided attention and effort? Share your desire to do this with your spouse and identify specific ways you will do this more.

2. **Attitude: Be devoted to complete openness and truthfulness.**

   Discuss ways you or your partner are not always completely open, forthright, and truthful with each other. Explore reasons for this and plan together how to make needed changes.

3. **Attitude: Learn how God thinks and desire to think that way.**

   How much does God's way of doing things influence your thinking? Does that need to change? If so, how can you begin pursuing this more? Habits are hard to change—commit just a few minutes a day to this. If you don't follow through, count the cost all over again and keep fighting to make this a new habit.

4. **Attitude: Be devoted to doing things God's way.**

   What in life are you most devoted to (based on what consumes your time, attention, and energy)? If you haven't already, set some goals for devoting yourself to what is right and true in your marriage. Identify specifically what that means.

**5. Attitude: Want to do what's right in God's eyes.**

Is doing the right thing as God would have it at the center of your marital devotion? Talk to your partner about any ways either of you see this not happening in your relationship and commit to doing things differently.

# 10

# True Love Must
# Be Enduring

*[Love] bears all things, believes all things,*
*hopes all things, endures all things.*
*Love never fails . . .*

I Corinthians 13:7–8

When you and I are long gone, there won't be many things about our lives that last. Remember the ancient Greek poet, Homer? Centuries ago, he said, "Men are haunted by the vastness of eternity. And so we ask ourselves: Will our actions echo across the centuries? Will strangers hear our names long after we are gone, and wonder who we were, how bravely we fought, how fiercely we loved?" Will the love you show your partner endure the test of time?

Life has a way of finding our greatest weakness and playing with it. If you had to boil it all down, you'd discover that there are one or two themes that come up in your life with regularity. When you are under the greatest stress, you have one primary weakness that challenges you the most. It could be discouragement, pessimism, anger, fear, a desire to flee the scene, or something else.

Likewise, whatever in life impresses you the most, there is one primary reason it does. I asked a friend once what impressed him the most about God. He was a Christian believer who tried to center his life on following God every day. His answer was, "I'm impressed with God's power." Interestingly, much of his life focused on things of power—certain pro football teams, fast cars, positions of financial power in the workplace. He liked things that showed power.

## KEY ATTITUDE:
**Desire to learn what makes you want to give up in order to make changes.**

At the end of the day, your life is largely a reflection of what impresses you and what your biggest weakness is under stress. It usually shows up in subtle ways, like being impatient, negative, or identifying with the things that impress you. Much of the time these are not big issues for you, but they can become problems if not kept in check.

The story of Achilles illustrates this element of life quite well. Achilles is depicted in a lengthy poetic story written by Homer of Greece, who is believed to have lived sometime around 750 BC to 850 BC. Brad Pitt made the story even more popular in 2004 in the movie *Troy*. Achilles is a bigger-than-life, unbeatable warrior. We've all heard of having an "Achilles' heel," which refers to our biggest weakness. In the movie, Achilles gets shot by an arrow through the heel, which completely disables him and eventually leads to his demise. Some critics of the original story by Homer believe the real weakness of Achilles was his pride, and this is what really led to his defeat.

*Your greatest strength can quickly turn into your greatest weakness, and your biggest shortcoming can predict what will keep you from weathering tough times.*

It doesn't matter who you are, how strong you are, how talented or even how troubled you are. Your greatest strength can quickly turn into your greatest weakness, and your biggest shortcoming can predict what will keep you from weathering tough times. Enduring the challenges of life, especially married life, takes a determination too few people possess. Many people put conditions on endurance, telling themselves what their limits are before they even get started. They set their sights low to begin with. Either they don't know what is possible, they won't pay the price, or they just don't have the life skills to negotiate life's problems. Many years ago the world thought it was impossible to run a mile under four minutes. Now that time isn't even competitive in world competition!

When I go running, I know before I start how fast and how long I am willing to go. Do you do that with life?

You may filter what you think is possible through your view of "common sense." It isn't reasonable to endure this or that. You're a fool if you put up with this or that. We humans are awfully good at rationalizing why we can stop short of enduring too much pain or discomfort. You tell yourself you will exercise tomorrow. Sometimes we even recruit other people to agree with our decision to quit trying. Turning to extended family in times of trouble is an excellent way to get needed support, but we have to be careful about biasing them. After all, they are already on your side. Be careful your family support doesn't turn into a family excuse to give up on your partner. Feeding negative attitudes just gives those attitudes a bigger appetite.

When marital problems arise and won't go away, it's usually because you are not thinking outside the box. This trap is a closed "loop" of thought in which solutions don't exist. The thought of enduring a situation that offers no hope of a solution becomes too much to bear. Of course, it is also possible to bear with situations that are too destructive to you.

Linda, a single middle-aged woman, was overly concerned with giving people a chance in love relationships. She was dating a man who had been in jail numerous times, was self-employed but could not support himself, and his pattern was to live off other people for little or nothing. He was insecure and exhibited a lot of controlling behaviors. Linda was a successful businesswoman who had a long history of stability. She was so open to new solutions she boxed herself in with her openness! Nothing was ever definite. This trapped her in a way of thinking that had very little hope of a successful relationship with this man. When you have used an approach for a long time with no success, it is often time to let go of the approach and try something—anything—new.

♥ *Think of a situation in your marriage that hasn't changed, despite your wishes that it would. Whatever your effort has been to change it, identify your reasons for doing what you do. Then change your approach significantly. What change of thought is required for this to be considered a permanent change—is the change required really so bad?*

Much of the world thinks of enduring problems in a relationship as biting your tongue and waiting it out. There is definitely a place for that. The Bible says that as small as the tongue is, it gets us in way too much trouble.[1] We make mountains out of molehills and make issues out of unimportant things. But just waiting out a bad situation with gritted teeth is often not helpful or even noble. You have probably known people whose marriage is so bad they are waiting for the kids to graduate from high school so they can get divorced. Most kids would be happier if the parents split up under these conditions! It's sad to realize there are a lot of people "enduring" a life like this when it could be so much more. Having a heart of endurance is more than taking the pain! It is much more positive than that. An enduring heart bears all things and believes all things.[2] It has hope that's based on knowing how powerful it is to pattern your life after the teachings of Jesus.

*An enduring heart bears all things and believes all things.*

Enduring with hope does not guarantee what your partner will do, but it's the best chance the relationship has, and does guarantee you will be the best partner possible. Having hope is not to say you walk around being unrealistic about your situation. If your husband has a drinking problem and is in heavy denial, hope doesn't make you roll over and smile as he takes his next drink. And it doesn't mean you cater to his selfish demands. You may have to assert your personal limits quietly by excusing yourself politely or making alternative plans for the evening. But you endure by continuing to be the person you should be, gently speaking up as appropriate, hoping your good behavior sends a strong message to your husband. If he won't get help and won't talk about it, what else can you do short of divorce? Endurance with inner peace is the other option.

♥ Discuss with your partner what the concept of endurance means to you in marriage. Identify where you ultimately get your strength from, and if your source is not always sufficient, explore why not.

Believe me, after doing marriage therapy work for over twenty years, I am not naive enough to think every relationship out there can work out. Some marriages are DOA by the time I see them. Feelings have turned ice-cold, behaviors are outrageous, and damage done from years of unresolved problems have made it impossible to find a place to start. Bitterness has set in and grown into a big monster in the closet. But I also know that even the tiniest spark can ignite the fires of caring and commitment.

## KEY ATTITUDE:
**Be enduring in your love for others, giving the benefit of the doubt.**

Until you believe that big things are possible, big things probably won't happen. Heimo Korth is a living example. In 1975, at the age of twenty, this Wisconsin native lit out for

Alaska to build himself a cabin. Romantic, right? The cabin was fourteen feet by fourteen feet and you had to bend over to get in the door. He ended up building two more cabins, and now migrates between them as he follows the best hunting patterns. He and his wife are now the only year-round residents of the Arctic National Wildlife Refuge, an area the size of South Carolina. Korth lives off the land, hunting for his meat and trapping for furs to pay for basic supplies. His story is bigger than life, but believing he could do it made it his life.[3] He was married with children living in this environment. Their very survival was based on unfailing endurance together against the forces of nature.

If you don't believe something is possible, you will never endure hardships. God's people throughout history believed that heaven awaited them, and there is story after story of remarkable endurance because of this belief. When Moses grew up, he refused all the treasures of Egypt and chose a life of mistreatment along with God's people because of this belief. He was able to pass through the middle of the Red Sea with the Egyptians chasing him because of this belief. David, when he was still a boy, was able to kill Goliath because of this belief. God's people were sawn in two, stabbed with swords, and wandered the earth homeless because of this belief.[4] If you believe that living your marriage based on the teachings of Jesus is worth any hardship, you have opened the door for great things.

*Problems have become raw nerves and the remedy is to believe things can be different.*

On the other hand, when you waver in your hope of what's possible, you open the door to all kinds of trouble. One way you know this has happened is when you or your partner becomes reactive and harsh. This is a sure symptom that you are giving in to impatience and frustration. I often see couples whose emotional barometer is about as high as it can get. Emotions are so strained they fill the room with tension like the airwaves of a high-powered radio. These couples have surrendered to their feelings and attitudes. Problems have become raw nerves and the remedy is to believe things can be different.

These frustrations lead to believing the worst about your partner instead of giving the benefit of the doubt. Common courtesies go out the window and partners are routinely rude to each other. Lack of courtesy alone tends to ignite an already volatile situation, leading to what I call "rude rage." Rude rage is about as irrational as road rage, and we all know how destructive and dangerous that is. Some partners just lose hope completely, which leaves the door cracked open for finding comfort outside the marriage relationship. It could be another person or any number of things outside the relationship.

Many couples settle for a growth stoppage in their relationship. They become frozen in their problems and carve out a daily routine to accommodate this condition. One way you can do this is to go underground. You privately do things your way, even if it turns out to be destructive. Just cooperate a little less and stop thinking about how it affects your partner. Ignoring issues is another great way to settle for a growth stoppage. I can't tell you how many couples I have seen who have not openly addressed important issues for years—even decades! Then at some point they can't take it anymore and their relationship is bankrupt.

*When we stop listening we isolate ourselves from our partner.*

Maybe the biggest symptom of a growth stoppage is when couples just stop listening to each other. John and Faith came to see me because they were arguing all the time. This was the fourth marriage for both of them (a good sign that some fundamental relationship skills were lacking). John was convinced that Faith felt superior to him and talked down to him. She had no idea why he felt this way, but didn't exactly ask so she could find out either. After listening to them talk to each other for about five minutes, it was clear they had no interest in what the other person was saying. If listening ever was part of their relationship it wasn't now. When we stop listening we isolate ourselves from our partner. We have no idea what their world is like. Growth is no longer possible.

As mentioned earlier, an enduring heart is based on much more than gutting something out and being miserable. It has to come from hope that better things are possible and that following the teachings of Jesus is worth any hardship regardless of what your partner does. This is hard, but doing things God's way—the right way—rises above any circumstance you can imagine. The Bible says God's "righteousness endures forever."[5] You may not be able to guarantee what your partner will do, but you do know you are developing a heart for things that withstand the test of time. Jesus addressed the need for His followers to have endurance. Because of unrighteousness, He said men's love would grow cold, but those who endure will be saved.[6] Just changing some behaviors does not create a heart for those things. Believing in God's ways, and that He rewards those who follow them, is the foundation for an enduring heart.

*Recognizing who we are at all times arms us with the information we need to choose a response out of character instead of reacting selfishly.*

**KEY ATTITUDE:**
**Do what it takes to build your faith in God.**

The Bible goes on to say that believers wait with *perseverance* for a hope they do not see physically.[7] This is referring to the return of Jesus. Developing a heart in marriage based on selflessness, humility, devotion, and endurance—a heart like Jesus—enables you to see the bigger picture in life. Your eyes will open to see possibility because of the power in this kind of heart. The Bible tells us God is love.[8] We all instinctively know that love is a tremendous power in this world. There was even a popular rock song about it called "The Power of Love" by Huey Lewis and the News. Developing four healthy chambers in a heart of love gives you the foundation needed for a shatterproof marriage.

The Bible presents us with a strange idea about enduring tough times. We are told to "exult" in difficult times, turning to God for strength and guidance. We exult because this leads to perseverance, which then leads to proven character. This kind of character gives us hope since God's love fills our hearts.[9] And if that isn't direct enough, we are to ". . . let endurance have its perfect result, that you may be perfect and complete, lacking in nothing."[10] You see, paying the price of endurance is critical to the health of your heart. If you do everything else we have talked about but fall short in this area, it's all for nothing. That's called a character heart attack! Train yourself to welcome adversity. Receive it with open arms. At first this sounds crazy. But adversity is just the beginning to a great opportunity for strengthening your heart. Once that heart develops, bearing, believing, and enduring all things will be second nature to you. The way you communicate, respond to criticism, handle disappointment—everything about you—will inspire those around you, especially your spouse.

## WHEN ENDURANCE IN MARRIAGE IS ESPECIALLY IMPORTANT

Fortunately, life is just full of situations that require an enduring heart. You're probably thinking how that does not sound fortunate at all. Ups and downs in life are what make it interesting, and all the down times represent defining moments. When you start viewing life this way, it becomes an exciting ride. And if you draw near to God along the way it couldn't possibly get any better.

It would be impossible to discuss all the situations in life requiring an enduring heart, but a few in marriage are especially worth mentioning. One common situation is when you discover that you have some basic philosophical differences with your partner. As a result, you clash with each other on how to go about certain things. A perfect example is raising children. He wants to be strict and emphasize raising a responsible child, and she wants to comfort, nurture, and show their child flexibility. We

> An enduring heart never gives up talking about this issue and bears with it when talks are not getting the desired result.

all know people who have had this conflict. Getting either spouse to modify his or her view is difficult at best. Some kind of compromise is usually the best solution, but even compromising can feel wrong to one or both partners. The fact is, we all know that being too permissive *or* too strict leads to problems. Both have elements that are good. Even after pointing this out, some partners simply will not agree to meet each other in the middle, continuing with an extreme approach. An enduring heart never gives up talking about this issue and bears with it when talks are not getting the desired result. I am not talking about cases that are so extreme the kids are displaying some alarming behaviors. I recommend marriage therapy if that is going on.

♥ *Talk about ways you both have had to make compromises in your marriage. Also discuss ways you feel pressured to compromise but have not. What is the price you are paying for maintaining your present stance?*

Sometimes you discover that your partner has some big flaws in his character or personality. Maybe he continues being less than fully honest with you about his feelings. Perhaps your wife becomes a different person when you are out in public and you don't like her personality at those times. Whatever it is, talking about it has not resolved this for you. The bottom line is, this is not a legitimate relationship-breaker, so learn to bear with it and remember that you still believe in *her*.

There may be some immaturity in your partner that drives you crazy. Your husband can't resist playing video games after work, or your wife still wants to party with her girlfriends every week despite the fact that you and she have little time together. If it really is an immature behavior, in most cases it needs to be changed. But if your partner won't change, or it takes a lot longer than you want, you may have no other choice but to endure this in the name of love and commitment.

Sometimes circumstances create stress in our lives, which in turn puts strain on the marriage. Starting a family by having children, for example, makes marital intimacy a lot harder to achieve every day. As the kids get older they place a heavy demand on the energy of the parents. Circumstances might be very stressful, time (and privacy!) is always short, or maybe you just slip into a huge rut that is boring and stagnant. Just being aware of it does not always fix the problem. Change your circumstances if you can. Your circumstances may be impossible to change, making endurance your only option. If you have an enduring heart you will find ways to be creative and make the most of whatever you *do* have.

Most of us can fill in the blank with things we believe we have to endure with our partners. You might have a partner who does not take very good care of herself by gaining weight, or making little effort at fixing her hair. Or a husband who has lots of annoying habits. Some situations require all the endurance we can muster. He may have crossed the line with some extreme behavior, such as drinking, using drugs, being abusive, or even having an affair. One couple came to me after the husband had an affair and both asked, "Is it possible to continue marriage successfully after an affair?" Of course it is! It's extremely difficult and requires a big heart of endurance, but people are overcoming all these issues every day! People make mistakes, some of them terrible ones. But when both partners have big hearts, a bond exists that makes it possible to overcome virtually anything. Mercy and forgiveness characterized the whole life of Jesus.

## PRACTICAL SUGGESTIONS FOR
## AN ENDURING HEART

*Identify your excuses.* Take the time to think about the kinds of situations that tend to weaken you the most. Do you get discouraged when your partner does or does not act a certain way? Do you want to keep your partner at arm's length when she nags you? It is important to figure out what kinds of things you tell yourself at the times you give in to your feelings. These usually amount to little more than excuses for being less than persevering. Don't give yourself permission any longer to make these excuses. Instead, welcome this opportunity to bear with and believe in your partner.

*Eliminate substitutes.* If you do not have a strong heart of endurance, you are likely turning to something (or even someone) else for comfort, satisfaction, enjoyment, or distraction. Self-medicating with alcohol to numb unpleasant feelings only adds to your problems. Burying yourself in the garage workshop, if done too much, makes matters worse. Make it a point to get rid of anything you use to avoid addressing issues. Be careful not to let anything in your life (outside of your relationship with God) take precedence over your marriage relationship.

*Accept your partner.* You may not like some habits, quirks, behaviors, or weaknesses your partner possesses, but it's imperative to keep your frustrations in check by accepting him or her. I see people in therapy on a daily basis who have forgotten this simple but powerful principle. Their intolerance has reached a point that is completely unreasonable and inflexible. The Bible instructs us to accept one another just as Jesus has accepted us.[11] Even minor bickering and irritability are a reflection we are not being very accepting of our partners by giving in to our own selfish wishes. You have lots of imperfections, as does your partner. Jesus himself said not to judge others because you would be judged accordingly. Stop making a big deal about things when you have plenty of your own shortcomings to worry about.[12]

*Expect problems.* Many people live most of their lives in their heads. Their heads are full of thoughts and feelings that become their reality. Live in the moment and accept the fact that life doesn't go as smoothly as the scripts we create in our heads. Maybe life is really going your way and you are on top of the world, but sooner or later there are difficulties. Don't be surprised when this happens. Prepare yourself now for these times by learning to bear with your partner and believing all things are possible with the small, daily things. Then when the bigger problems come, you will already have a heart conditioned for endurance.

**Learn to discern reality.** When your partner *seems* to be distant and uncaring, my experience is this is not what's going on. I often filter her behavior through my lens, which says if she isn't focusing on me this morning she must not care to be close. Make a habit of checking out your assumptions whenever you don't feel good about something. Many people still struggle with how to do that even after I give them this advice. It really is quite simple—ask! Say, "You seem distant today and it *seems* like you don't want to be close. Is that right?" If it is true, then you can talk about it. If it is not true you can drop it. We do the same thing with God. If we don't *feel* close we begin to feel less confidence. The Bible says that believers have a kingdom that cannot be shaken.[13] It doesn't matter how bleak things look or feel. Certain realities just are. Learn to keep your life centered on what is real, not what is imagined.

**Give the benefit of the doubt.** This is a little secret that can unlock the door to all kinds of solutions. Most people make assumptions about the intentions, attitudes, or feelings of their partner without even knowing they are doing it. A certain facial expression must mean a look of disgust. A certain behavior must mean a selfish intent. When you are having conflict, ask yourself what assumptions you are making about your partner. If you are coming up empty, ask your partner after an argument is over if he thought you were making any assumptions about him. You might be surprised. Everyone wants to receive credit for having good motives. Likewise, everyone is tempted to feel defensive when that does not happen.

**Accept the things you cannot change.** One of the quickest ways to become fainthearted is to try to control things well beyond your ability. When things aren't changing, we try harder and harder, only to become more frustrated and tired. A good example is a mother of a five-year-old who came to see me because her daughter was running the house. This little girl would attack both parents physically. Dad was about six-foot-five inches tall! He was afraid to respond because of the size difference. I had one simple instruction for them. When she threw a fit I directed them to gently but firmly put her in a bear hug restraint for as long as it took for her to calm down. It took some convincing because both were skeptical this would make any difference. They tried it even though the little girl would struggle for up to thirty or forty minutes. Within one week the little monster became a little princess. She learned she could no longer control her parents, accepted it, and life was just fine. If we adults could just do that with our issues!

*Choose to be happy.* Your feelings are not "caused" by anything or anyone but *you.* I mentioned this in a previous chapter, but something is not a problem in my life until I say it is. It also stops being a problem when I say it does. It can be that simple sometimes. Do the things that upset you in your marriage really have to make or keep you unhappy? Develop the habit of putting problems into perspective with the bigger picture of life. Worrying and being upset just leads to hypervigilance. Then you become reactive to every little thing. Determine to find ways to be happy and enjoy each and every day. There was a time I did landscaping work on the side to make some extra money. A friend who worked with me could never enjoy the day. He complained about hating the work. It was sunny, we were working for ourselves outdoors, and getting some exercise! They call it "work" for a reason, so why not enjoy what you can?

*Count your blessings.* During troubled times it can become easy to view everything through a negative lens. We can't enjoy anything. One effective way to counter this is to spend a few minutes reflecting on the good things in your life. If you can't think of any you aren't thinking clearly. Emotions have gotten a stranglehold on you. Even pessimistic people can make this a habit, which, in turn, negates much of the pessimism. Take all of the negative thoughts you have about a problem and finish them with the phrase, "but it's still a good thing that—," and fill in the blank with something good. If you are unable to do this you have lost the perspective you need about the problem and this is blocking the way to solutions.

*Draw near to God.* One of the easiest things to do when problems arise is to become preoccupied with them. As soon as we do, we shut everything else out and have blinders on. We get careless with our attitudes, filling our minds up with mostly negative stuff. It doesn't affect us too badly at first, but if it goes on very long it brings us down. The Bible promises that if we draw near to God he will draw near to us.[14] Furthermore, as unstable as life is at times, Jesus is "the same yesterday and today, yes and forever."[15] The reality of God and His way of doing things never changes. When you feel those negativity blinders blocking your vision—and you will—learn to recognize that is a special time to remember God and get closer to Him.

*Remember why you endure.* People who endure the greatest hardships remember who they are and what they believe in. Doubt is a normal part of enduring. When you are feeling the most doubt, I recommend you write down specific thoughts that keep you doubting your commitment to endure a situation. This makes them more real and workable.

I was counseling a woman who had become suicidal. She refused to write down her negative thoughts as part of her therapy. The rationale for this kind of assignment will be covered later, but Becky's reason for refusing to write her thoughts down was it would then be "a declaration I am imperfect and have weakness." Until she wrote it down, she just had a million things flying through her head when she became suicidal and she couldn't manage any of them. When she began writing them down she had something concrete to work on. Once you write down the thoughts of doubt, compare them to everything you have learned about a loving heart of self-lessness, humility, devotion, and endurance. You will quickly see how you are stuck. Get back to the right focus.

> Go out of your way to look for defining moments in your life and practice what people with big hearts do.

*Be proactive about your heart.* No one is born with a heart that naturally stays strong enough to run a marathon. Some hearts are physically bigger than others and are naturally more adept to long-distance running. But no one can go out and compete in a marathon without training. Likewise, why would anyone think they will have the heart needed for major challenges in marriage if they don't do some kind of training? I'm not talking about classes and workshops, or even books like this one. Don't spend your life looking for the best self-help programs you can find. Go out of your way to look for defining moments in your life and *practice* what people with big hearts *do*. The Bible says that physical fathers disciplined us as well as they knew how, but God disciplines us so we might be like Him.[16] Most of us are like "marathon wannabes" who look for the couch the instant we get home instead of our running shoes.

## *K*EY *A*TTITUDE:
**Have a "work ethic" to strengthen your endurance.**

View marital problems as true opportunities. The human response to relationship problems often includes mild embarrassment and even shame. Some people have had the blessing of smooth-sailing marriages for decades. That is not the norm. If you are weak because you are self-centered there is no honor in that.

However, if you decide to think outside yourself and pattern your life after the example set by Jesus—even if you blow it sometimes—there is nothing more honorable than that. The Bible tells us that one of Jesus' disciples was "well content with weakness" for the sake of following Jesus because that is when he was really the strongest.[17] It is human to be imperfect. Just don't stop there. Use your imperfections to point you toward growth. If things are rough in your marriage, you don't have to act like a martyr, but you can see it as an opportunity to live out what you say you believe in.

## PUTTING ALL PARTS OF THE HEART TOGETHER

Just like the physical heart, the heart of your character has to be fully functioning or it breaks down quickly. At the end of Chapter 5 I promised to show you a better way to live your marriage than what so many people are doing. This better way is to love the way God—and Jesus—love us. It was actually the Bible that made this promise to show a better way than focusing on our abilities and achievements.

Most people completely misunderstand what real endurance is. They think they have to bite their lips and suffer in silence. As we have seen, the endurance of Element #2 gives a whole new meaning to things. It includes hope. It accepts the fact that what we like and what we want are not the only issues. In marriage, there is often a "higher calling" that enables us to forgo wants and desires—and ultimately *feel good about it!*

We have looked at the four chambers of the heart of love based on what the Bible says love is. If even one of these chambers is weak, big problems are likely. You are ripe for a character heart attack. You may be pretty giving and selfless in your marriage but have a prideful streak. Your partner might be selfless, humble, and pretty enduring, but never devotes himself to what is fully honest, true, and right. The key to developing the heart of an unbreakable marriage is to be diligent at all times to take care of all four chambers of your heart.

> *The key to developing the heart of an unbreakable marriage is to be diligent at all times to take care of all four chambers of your heart.*

There are lots of relationship skills people think are the magic solution to their problems. "If we just communicated better" everything would be okay. We are going to cover some very helpful marriage tools next, but without a strong heart of love they are useless. By all means learn and practice using the tools that follow. They represent the tools I have continued to use over and over with great success in marriage therapy. They are the best of the best.

Just remember this: I would take a couple with a big heart over one with lots of relationship savvy any day. Tools are pretty easy to learn when you have the heart to use them. You could have a giant toolbox in the garage with all the mechanic's tools available, but they will just sit there until you are able to use each tool *in the right way*.

My easiest marital cases have sometimes had the messiest problems. Once given a few good tools and an appeal to remember their commitment to each other, the couple goes home and uses them around the clock. Commit yourself to spending the rest of your life strengthening the heart of your character. Get closer to God and do what Jesus would do in your marriage.

Next, we will turn to some important aspects of marital functioning and look at a few invaluable tools to negotiate them effectively. Element #3 encompasses a vast number of things, but in the end, it is relatively simple and basic. It's the ability to track down problems and convert them into solutions.

## MAIN CHAPTER ATTITUDES

✓ Desire to learn what makes you want to give up in order to make changes.

✓ Be enduring in your love for others, giving the benefit of the doubt.

✓ Do what it takes to build your faith in God.

✓ Have a "work ethic" to strengthen your endurance.

# ATTITUDES IN ACTION

1. **Attitude: Desire to learn what makes you want to give up in order to make changes.**

   **a)** What is your Achilles' heel? Admit it to your spouse and discuss a strategy that will make you stronger in this area.

   **b)** If you are stuck and having trouble accepting a situation you cannot change in your marriage, try everything you know to do. Then ask others for ideas. Then let go of your stubbornness and accept the reality. Stop making matters worse by insisting on doing whatever you have been doing about it.

2. **Attitude: Be enduring in your love for others, giving the benefit of the doubt.**

   Ask your partner if there are times you do not seem to think the best of him or her. Commit to changing this, asking your partner to tell you when that seems to be happening.

3. **Attitude: Do what it takes to build your faith in God.**

   What keeps you from trusting God's ways and His power more in your life and marriage? Face whatever it is and wrestle with it until you rely on God more deeply.

4. **Attitude: Have a "work ethic" to strengthen your endurance.**

   Which practical suggestion(s) from this chapter have you committed to working on starting this week? Share them with your partner.

# The Right Spirit

*Always find a way to turn every problem into a solution.*

*I*n conflicts, having the right spirit means always converting problems into solutions—this attitude and spirit is always present.

Nitrogen is a common element that comprises 78.1 percent by volume of our atmosphere, which is the largest single component in our atmosphere. It's also a primary element in all living tissues. Nitrogen is mostly inert by itself, which means that it does not do much and is not considered chemically active. Chemicals that contain this element have even been observed by astronomers, and when combined with other elements, nitrogen has an unbelievable number of uses. Certain compounds containing nitrogen can cause instant frostbite (this property can be very useful), remove warts, produce integrated circuits, make stainless steel, and change the very nature of air for practical uses. However, nitrogen is not without its dangers. If it is released too quickly, it can displace air and asphyxiate us. It is also the key element involved when divers go to the surface too quickly, resulting in decompression sickness.

Element #3 of a shatterproof marriage is very much like nitrogen. Its properties include the ability to communicate well, address stress, sort through problems, identify areas of concern, and get rid of power struggles. But without the first two elements, the right personal character and the right kind of love, this element has no real effect. You can do a great job of getting your point across, or be extra insightful about why a problem exists, but by themselves they do nothing to keep your marriage safe from everything.

Having good relationship skills alone is no different from having an empty canteen in the desert. You have the canteen, but what good is it? Likewise, what good is water in the desert if you have nothing to put it in? But when your marriage possesses the first two elements, then you add Element #3, you can stand back and watch great things happen! There will not be any situation life can throw at you that you can't handle.

Like nitrogen, however, overuse of this element is also not without its dangers. In today's culture of quick fixes and TV therapists who have great style, it can be easy to rely too heavily on techniques. I have included some great techniques within Element #3, but don't trust in them too much. If you do, I guarantee you will be disappointed. Some people pride themselves on learning great relationship tools, but improper use does nothing but make matters worse instead of better.

Through the years, I have seen people with great relationship skills who have the wrong spirit about them. For a long time I couldn't put my finger on just what it was exactly. We could have great discussions in marriage-counseling sessions, but then when it came time to end with a solution, things would fall apart. I realized some people don't have a spirit of *wanting* solutions that has the greater good of the marriage at its core. Once you realize that is what is going on, it is easy to identify.

Roy can tell you exactly what I mean. He is no different from a lot of people I have seen through the years, so I know that Element #3 is the final element needed for a shatterproof marriage. He had been to several counselors previously for marriage counseling, with no success. Roy and his wife, Donna, had been married twenty-two years. They had three great kids, he had a well-paying job, and they were blessed in many ways. Roy worked very hard and both were high achievers. They had some major personality and temperament differences, though. Donna was kind of a people pleaser who had a history of giving in to the wishes of those around her. Well, she had a near-death experience with a medical problem and her whole perspective changed. Life was short and she was no longer willing to cater so much to others.

Donna became too focused on everything being fair at home. Roy, being the high achiever he was, took the challenge! He had a low tolerance for incompetence to begin with, but when Donna no longer did things his way he became critical and negative. This led to her being critical and negative and, well, I think you know what life at home was like for them. They *never* went out alone together anymore, in fact they *never* took fifteen minutes a day to sit down alone and have some quality time. Both partners were defensive, hurt, discouraged, and angry.

At first, therapy focused on their goals of learning to communicate better and work better "as a team." Just like the previous counseling, we would have great talks, then everything fell apart at the solution-finding stage. When things would deteriorate like this, Roy had learned to back off and offer little resistance. This was real progress for him. But Donna continued to express her anger and wanted extreme changes right now.

Then something wonderful happened. It felt almost miraculous to all of us. Donna's walls of defensiveness and anger cracked. She came in one day and was ready to let go of those feelings and allow solutions in. How do I know? She came right out and said so. She said, "All I want is for things to be right with my husband and me." She was eager for me to load them up with homework. She couldn't wait to get started!

This is a perfect example of Element #3. When relationship problems come up, you not only learn any new skills you might need to have, but you approach all conflicts with a *spirit* of making peace. This is different from keeping the peace and someone paying too high a price for it. It's a heartfelt desire to work toward making things good between you. You let go of your upset enough to let possibility in.

That's the main property of Element #3. Without it, the first two elements are ineffective. When you add this spirit to the mix, exciting things happen. Donna combined her strong personal character and unwavering love with a true spirit of peace. When she did, rapid change was set in motion. She learned and applied some helpful relationship techniques, but they were only useful when all three elements were present. Like nitrogen, adding this spirit to this couple's situation created a compound that made their relationship shatterproof. At that point, I could not have stopped progress if I had wanted to.

The first element, the right personal character, is similar to the properties of carbon dioxide. It is essential to all of life, but a slight deviation of it can have devastating results. Donna's character was being put to the test in her marriage. Their conflicts had been worsening for more than two years. When her character refused to succumb to the discouragement, she brought Element #1 to the situation. The second element, knowing how to love unconditionally, is a lot like hafnium. This element provides the stability and reliability needed in marriage. Donna never lost her commitment to love her husband no matter how upset she got. Without this element, her love would depend more on Roy's performance and her emotions. Once she brought all three elements to the marriage, creating solutions was just a matter of time and some work.

The following chapters are full of relationship skills. I teach them here because you need them. They can make life a whole lot easier and problems can be resolved more quickly with them. But remember: Element #3 is about having the right spirit about you. You must let go of your upset and your personal agendas for the greater good. I have found there are some fundamental skills necessary in marriage, and these skills are also like nitrogen in the sense that they accomplish nothing in and of themselves. If you have good skills but do not have the right spirit, they are worthless. You should only proceed with learning these skills if you are prepared to "use them well." With the right heart, they can all help convert conflicts into solutions. I teach these skills only with the presumption you will use them with a genuine desire to make things right at home.

Now let's take a closer look at what I call the "secondary properties" of this element—good relationship skills—so you too can experience the power of these three elements working together.

# 11

# Make Sure Stress Is Not the Problem

*I don't like this game.*

Spike Milligan

efore you can hope for things in your marriage to get better, you have to make sure stress has not become the main problem. Stress can be easy to figure out, but sometimes it can be really complex and confusing. Jesus Himself said to be anxious about nothing because it won't add anything to your life span.[1]

For the remainder of the book, exercises based on therapy tools and techniques—with accompanying attitudes—are included in each chapter. This is so you can put everything we have discussed into practice.

Stress comes from several possible sources. There are usually several symptoms of stress in your life, and the list of them is even longer when you include those of your partner. In this chapter, we will be looking at stress symptoms, personality factors, and how close you need to feel with your partner. These things affect your marriage every day. Understanding them leads to good stress management. And if stress is the main issue causing problems in your marriage, it's important to identify it as such. If you are going to convert marital problems into solutions, you first have to be sure stress is not the main thing causing conflict. This is in keeping with the spirit of Element #3. You have to examine your life honestly, being open to what you might find.

Starting in this chapter, we will be following the marriage therapy progress of a real couple I saw—I will call them Russ and Mary Flanagan. Russ and Mary met each other through work and married after dating about a year. Both were in their upper thirties, and Russ had a stepson, Jack, from a previous marriage. Jack was thirteen when the couple got married. Russ was a very accommodating and patient man and Jack felt loved by his father. Jack had learned to use childish whining to influence his father, and his father would often give in. Russ loved his son so much that it often resulted in giving in to Jack instead of saying "no" when he should sometimes.

Mary was clearly a no-nonsense, bottom-line woman who spoke very directly when she was concerned about something. Shortly after marrying, this couple found themselves arguing, feeling a lot of stress, and repeating the same vicious cycles over and over again. As we work through the remainder of the book, we will take a few moments to check in on our friends, the Flanagans, to see how they're doing.

## SOURCES OF STRESS

This section gives you a pretty exhaustive listing of different symptoms and sources of stress. Jesus said that we become anxious because we get preoccupied with what is going to happen tomorrow. Instead, we should concern ourselves only with today.[2] But there is more to stress than just anxiety. Sometimes there are some very real demands on us *today*. But in the final analysis, we can only do what we can do. Sometimes, most of us find ourselves trying to do more than what is reasonable. The Bible says not to brag about what we will do tomorrow because we don't know "what a day may bring forth."[3] You are better off getting good at managing what you have today. This starts by examining the sources of your stress.

You will see lots of lists in this chapter to make it easy and quick to pick out what is helpful to you. The point here is not to get bogged down with boring, dry information. The point is to identify *your* signs of stress, figure out what causes them, and develop some kind of plan to do what you can about them.

Any marriage partner can be feeling stress from several possible places. Look at these sources and identify where you feel stress the most in your life:

1. Personal relationships other than your marriage
2. Demands from your physical surroundings (like crime in the neighborhood or a bad economy)
3. Personal tragedy
4. Life-cycle changes (such as turning forty, or a child leaving home)
5. Internal pressures (such as feeling responsible for the happiness of your partner)
6. Changes in routine
7. Financial problems
8. Legal problems
9. Job problems
10. Good things that have happened
11. Bad things that have happened
12. Anticipated changes
13. Ongoing frustrations
14. Young children at home
15. Friends or extended family living with you
16. A house or apartment too small to fit everyone
17. Legitimate time shortages
18. Transportation problems
19. Drinking or drug usage

20. A partner with a destructive behavior habit

21. Chronic illness

What else did I leave out? Add your own things to this list. Any *one* of these can make life difficult. If you happen to have identified several, these areas of stress are placing a significant strain on your marriage—whether you notice it or not. Research has shown that whenever people experience any big event they feel stress. This includes positive things such as getting married, graduating, going on vacation, or getting an award. Any change in our routine adds stress. How much more will the stress of problems add to the demand on us?!

Not knowing how to manage stress effectively just makes it that much worse. If one partner is not managing her own stress well, the other partner is affected. This can easily turn into one partner turning on the other. Then couples get sidetracked from addressing the stress itself and take it all out on each other.

When your partner is preoccupied with her own stress, be careful not to take it personally. Even if it makes her impatient and irritable, extend a little grace. Letting things get to her is not right, but it's often not personal. Remembering this can save you a lot of grief. All married couples experience their fair share of stress on a regular basis. It is important to remember that stress to some degree is healthy and even desired. Without any stress—either from within ourselves or from outside—we would all be couch potatoes!

*If you and your partner have been under a lot of stress—or if there have just been a lot of things happening—it would be helpful for each of you to write down as many stressors as you remember of the following over the past year or so. Then share your list with your partner. Talk about the effect it has had on you. Think about your emotions, attitudes, and behaviors. Discuss if and how it has affected your marital interactions. When you do this, blame the stress, not each other.*

## Symptoms of Stress

The big reference book used by psychiatrists is the *Diagnostic and Statistical Manual of Mental Disorders* (DSM-IV). It says that many symptoms are common to certain conditions and are predictable. It's actually an easy reference (when condensed) to help the average person begin to get a better understanding of their stress symptoms. It helps you begin to see that your symptoms *might* be stress-related. If they are, then you can look more closely at them and learn a lot about yourself.

Here is a list of different symptoms. They may or may not be the result of stress, but they merit your quick review. Check off the ones that apply to you.

1. Sleep disturbance
2. Appetite change
3. A long history of health problems
4. Rash
5. Muscle tightness
6. Pounding heart
7. Excessive sweating
8. Feeling faint
9. Nervous energy
10. Fatigue
11. Numbness
12. Mood swings
13. Nightmares
14. Flashbacks
15. Irritability
16. Nervousness
17. Inability to feel happy
18. Worry and obsessiveness
19. Forgetfulness
20. Poor concentration
21. Confusion
22. Boredom
23. Spacing out
24. Racing thoughts
25. Negative self-talk
26. Hallucinations
27. Hitting
28. Yelling
29. Breaking things
30. Breaking the law
31. Rebelling against rules
32. Drinking
33. Hurting yourself on purpose
34. Social withdrawal
35. Power struggles
36. Nagging
37. Arguing
38. Impatience
39. Lashing out

40. Blaming
41. Making threats
42. A sense of emptiness
43. Loss of meaning
44. Loss of direction
45. Being negative about life and the world
46. Lack of inner peace
47. Inability to forgive
48. Inability to care for others

A widely used standardized test on stress examines a person's response in nine more areas.[4]

49. Physical/health complaints (i.e., recent problems with headaches, stomachaches, etc.)
50. Having obsessions or behavioral habits that are out of your control
51. Being overly sensitive in relationships
52. Depressive tendencies
53. Anxiety
54. Hostility
55. Irrational fears (phobias)
56. Paranoia
57. Separating yourself from the reality of a situation in extreme ways (i.e., minimizing or denying you are being physically abused)

*Ask yourself, when you are in a crisis, which of these comes out the most? What about your partner? What are these symptoms all about? How does your behavior trigger something in your partner?*

All of these symptoms can be explained in several possible ways. Don't automatically assume they are caused by outside stress. And by all means, don't use them to excuse bad behavior. This is where application of the three Key Elements of a shatterproof marriage comes in. Look at yourself honestly. Earnestly desire to know the truth about you and your situation. Take personal responsibility and "own" these as yours instead of pressuring your spouse somehow. Otherwise, none of this information is worth two cents.

**KEY ATTITUDE:**

**Be proactive under stress instead of reactive.**

As you can see, there are lots of ways stress can come out. The biggest trap you can fall into is to see the symptoms as bad things that you should avoid at all costs. This couldn't be further from the truth. Without symptoms we would all be dead! A symptom of fire danger is to feel pain when it burns us. Learn to avoid the things that cause symptoms for you. A good way to try this is to work backward. Once the symptom is already there, find out what it is trying to tell you.

One of the best interventions for someone with major anxiety problems is when I tell the client to "make best friends with your anxiety." At first, they think I'm nuts! But I explain that anxiety is merely trying to tell you something important. Although it is a terrible feeling, don't panic when you feel anxiety coming on. Instead, learn from it. When you feel anxious, look at every minute in slow motion. Learn every detail about what is going on, including your thoughts at every stage. Then you can attend to what the symptom is really telling you. For example, it might be telling you to learn how to live with uncertainty about your job. This really does work!

Once people stop worrying about the symptoms themselves, they are no longer a distraction from the real issue. If I become preoccupied with fear of speaking in front of a large group, that distracts me from the real issue—I'm worried about how I look to others. That is a self-image issue. Fear is just warning me that I haven't really come to terms with my self-consciousness.

There are three important questions for you to answer that might help you understand what the symptoms are and what they mean:[5]

1. Is the stress coming from within your home or from the outside in?
   A partner who works night shift when everyone else has a different schedule is an example of stress within your home.

2. Is the stress falling mostly on one partner or on both of you equally?

3. How much time do each of you have to adjust to stress? If there is
   little time, there is more chance of coping difficulties.

> Answer the above questions as a couple and discuss
> whether there are any adjustments you can make. If not,
> how can you manage your situation better?

When any of these symptoms appear, instead of avoiding them at all cost, *pay close attention* to what they might be saying to you. You might easily learn something that points you to the solution needed. Make it a habit to keep an eye on the symptoms of stress regularly to prevent buildup. Otherwise, these symptoms can distract you from the things that are important, especially in your marriage. The Bible urges us to examine and test ourselves to see if we are really holding true to our belief in God.[6]

## COPING BEHAVIORS

Your mind and body go through certain changes when you are feeling stress.[7] These changes tend to affect the way you act with your partner. Learning what these changes are for you will point to specific points where you can manage your response the way you want.

The first physical response is "alarm." This is where certain physical changes happen in your body. It could be muscle tightness in certain parts of your body, increased breathing, or sweaty palms. Believe it or not, you can use these changes to remind you that stress has arrived and to be ready.

Then the body goes through a "resistance" where we more or less brace ourselves for the situation. Have you ever sensed that in your partner when you told her how much you spent on a fishing trip? You not only go into defensive mode, your body language even corresponds to your anticipation of what comes next.

When the stress goes on long enough, there is the "stage of exhaustion." This is where you can't take one more minute of a situation. When we reach this point, we give off all kinds of nonverbal signals that are not helpful at all. If you have reached a point of "low tolerance" or "zero tolerance" for the same problem that keeps coming up over and over, take ownership for this. Folks, this quickly replaces whatever problem you were having and becomes *the* problem if it is not kept in check. If you need to back off the problem for a while until you can up your tolerance, by all means do so. Being a hero here and continuing to address the problem while having zero tolerance does no one any good.

Many people do not have much insight about their physical responses to stress. Marriage partners should be aware (or beware!) of their common coping responses—physical, emotional, psychological, and behavioral.

**KEY ATTITUDE: Always manage your daily routine to minimize stress.**

Like so many things in life, the best way to approach stress is one day at a time. Otherwise, it will creep into your marriage and begin causing all sorts of problems. One helpful way to do this is to examine the coping cycle you have.[8] Your coping cycle is the typical way you and your partner respond to stress on any given day. Everyone's cycle is unique. Once you identify your typical cycle, changing it as needed becomes much easier.

This simple coping cycle goes as follows:

1. **The stress event.** Pinpoint the stress events that keep plaguing you and/or your marriage.
2. **Define the stress.** This refers to how you interpret the stress, or what meaning you attach to it. For example, is losing your job *really* the "end of the world"? Eliminate any exaggerated ways you define the situation.
3. **Coping skills and behaviors.** What is the usual response by you and your partner? What are the personal and relationship skills you each

bring to the situation? Are your responses flexible enough to meet changing stresses? What do you need to learn how to do better?

4. **Crisis or stress.** The stress event continues to be stressful if it is not resolved effectively. Then additional patterns develop. An entirely new approach to your situation is called for.

♥ Try to identify the specific coping cycle that you go through typically, both individually and as a couple. Identify at least one behavior that you can change to make a positive difference. Which stage is it in?

Take some time to discuss this with your partner. If you have been together for any length of time at all, you undoubtedly have established at least one predictable coping cycle. The power to make changes in your life starts with seeing clearly what needs to change. Then, look at your typical daily routine to see if you act or feel stressed at any point. Work on your reaction, but also review needed changes in routine. There is no such thing as being trapped in your stress. You can make changes, even if it is just in how you think about your situation.

*The power to make changes in your life starts with seeing clearly what needs to change.*

To help you further examine your typical coping responses, I have put a little inventory together. It is not scientific but if you are honest with yourself, it could give you some direction in how to be tougher under stress.

# Coping Response Inventory

| **1** | **2** | **3** |
|---|---|---|
| **Rarely like me** | **More often than not like me** | **Usually like me** |

_____ 1. When problems arise, my closest associates are included immediately in efforts to solve the problem, rather than keeping it all to myself.

_____ 2. When feeling more pressure, I do not typically avoid people to "get myself together."

_____ 3. I have little difficulty coming up with new and untried solutions to problems in my life.

_____ 4. When problems arise, I compromise with the other person involved.

_____ 5. I am typically free of worry.

_____ 6. It is easy to show my feelings and put them into words with other people.

_____ 7. When I am involved in a conflict with my partner, I stay patient and tolerant.

_____ 8. I meet challenges in a logical way and think clearly even when emotionally upset.

_____ 9. I do not try to keep the peace at all costs in my marriage.

_____ 10. I think before reacting.

_____ 11. My reaction to a lot of pressure is to tackle the problem rather than getting discouraged.

_____ 12. When "the heat is on," people around me still see me as composed and under control.

_____ 13. If my feelings become very unpleasant during a problem, I still put them aside enough to stay focused on solutions.

_____ 14. I listen to my partner, considering his or her views, but have definite opinions of my own.

_____ 15. I try to have close personal relationships with people.

_____ 16. I am comfortable taking charge of a situation, but can also let others take charge if that would be more constructive.

_____ 17. Typically, I do not avoid issues I know (or think) will involve some conflict.

_____ 18. I do not easily feel defeated when things are not working out the way I wanted or thought they should.

_____ 19. When difficulties arise, I do not tell myself over and over that I "should" have done something differently or better.

_____ 20. I consider the facts rather than jumping to conclusions based on some assumptions.

_____ 21. When people I care about are angry or depressed, my moods are affected, but not to an extreme.

_____ **TOTAL SCORE**

A score of 63 is perfect, meaning you cope with stress very well (and it also means maybe you aren't being very honest with yourself!). A score of 42 means you may occasionally do some things that do not help with stress, or there may be some areas needing urgent attention. Any scores under 3 on any given item are worthy of your attention. The lower the score, the more work is needed. Pick out any of these items that you could work on and make it a priority. Where in the coping cycle do your responses usually happen? Come back to this inventory as often as needed to keep you on track and focused.

Let's check in and see how the Flanagans are doing at this point. One of the most important items for them was item #6. Russ answered "rarely like me," and not only did he not express feelings, but we discovered together that he did not even have a vocabulary for them! Even with lots of help, he was unable to describe his emotions and had developed a coping style of ignoring any emotional discomfort. This became a big problem, since he would allow his emotions to build over time without resolving them. Instead of then blowing up, he went into deeper verbal withdrawal. This made it impossible for them to talk about their conflict about parenting Jack. I strongly urged him to do the best he could to talk at those times. I assigned Mary to "teach" him feeling words.

♥ After completing the above inventory, do what the Flanagans did and review any tendencies that contribute to relationship conflicts. Share your answers with your partner. Choose at least one item that you are going to work on when stress occurs. If you seem unable to do things differently, agree to tell your partner as it happens so she can help you at that very moment.

## BASIC PERSONAL NEEDS AND STRESS

There are some fundamental emotional, psychological, and spiritual needs you are born with, regardless of who you are. If they are unmet, you feel stressed and interact differently in your marriage. All your emotions are connected to these needs, and symptoms will develop when we think they are unmet. If you do not address an unmet need successfully, it starts to affect your heart. Attitudes and relationship habits start to deteriorate.

As you listen to the concerns and issues you have with your partner, consider how they are a reflection of one or more of these personal needs. It will give you strong clues about what makes him tick. Then you can help your partner sort things out if there is a need not being met. Your marriage may be the reason a need is unsatisfied, but it may also be that you or your partner entered the relationship with an unresolved issue. Until you know which, you will continue to be confused and without direction.

Most negative coping behaviors and the emotions that go with them stem from one or more of these needs.

The four basic needs we all have are:

1. *Have some kind of life meaning on a day-to-day basis*

   Without meaning and a sense of purpose every day, most people just end up looking to "creature comforts" to get by. Comfort food, constant video games, and physical pleasures are some examples. Or we can become sullen, bored, or constantly dissatisfied. Stress drives us deeper into these behaviors until they don't work anymore. Then we crack. Whatever your response is to this need, see it for what it really is. Deal with it. Figure out a new way to make sense of your world. The fact is, God has a purpose in creating you.[9] He has created you to need a deep sense of meaning in your daily life by giving you a deep sense of eternity in your heart.[10]

2. *Have authentic relationship with self, others, and God*

   Some people have grown up with a distorted view of themselves based on unhealthy past relationships. They might feel shame easily, cling to someone else too much, or be hermitlike. If you are not fully comfortable being inside your own skin, you may not have learned how to nurture yourself. Part of this is coming to terms with your relation-ship with God and your own mortality. Your biggest issue might just be that you do not have strong, healthy relationships with others. This could even include your spouse. It is critical that you resolve any issues you have about yourself, figure out your relationship to God, and develop enough healthy relationships with other people. Otherwise, many of your relationship behaviors will confuse you and those around you. Internally, you will be a ball of knots much of the time.

### 3. *Safety and security*

We all depend on our environment to have a certain level of pre-dictability. Some of us have to have too much of that. That is usually the result of some bad past experiences. We need to feel physically and psychologically safe. It's important that we can fully be ourselves. Otherwise, we become gun-shy in certain situations and become anx-ious. Worry is another big part of it. Some people have developed a habit of worry because of what they expect from their world. Your reac-tions in this area, as with all of these needs, are either based on past experiences, current experiences, or a combination of both. You must identify what is going on to begin with, then understand whether there is anything currently going on that threatens this need.

### 4. *Sense of justice about life*

Life is too cruel to bear if we do not find a way to make sense of it. Life is just not fair. Gina had her daughter taken away by the court, which gave full custody to the father. She was convinced the decision was completely unjust and unwarranted. Maybe it was and maybe it wasn't. After two years of struggling with this heartbreak, she broke down and insisted that "It isn't fair!" I looked at her and finally told her she had to learn to accept it. Life just isn't fair. God actually promised us that life on this Earth will not be fair. He will deal with injustices later.[11]

Much of the world believes revenge is often the answer. It's in all the violent movies we watch. But that never really helps. All it does is build your appetite for immediate justice, which is not always available. Anger and frustration tend to be the main result of this need being unresolved. Sometimes your spouse isn't fair and you get angry. It is human to become frustrated or disappointed. But the heart of a shatter-proof marriage remembers the three elements during these times. Expect injustice in your marriage. Work with it.

When you and your partner have problems, does discouragement or despair get in the way? What about feeling safe to be yourself and speak up? Maybe one of you believes you will be persecuted if you relax and are yourself. Is shame or dependency causing problems? If so, either some needs are unmet in the relationship, or there are past issues from other relationships that have never been resolved. If you are symptomatic in any way, try to discern if any of these basic needs are involved.

> *Review these needs, then talk together about which of them reveal your greatest weakness(es). Develop a strategy of working together as a team when the need comes up.*

So what has become of the Flanagans? During the course of our sessions, it became clear that Mary was almost obsessed with the concept of justice. It turns out she had been poorly treated and taken advantage of in her previous marriage. She had always had a temperament of directness and seeing things as either black or white. She was able to talk about this tendency openly and was encouraged to catch herself when she was being too reactive with Jack when she thought he was getting away with something.

> *Discuss the kinds of symptoms you normally get when under stress. As those are occurring, identify what you need to do differently to manage those symptoms better. Then*

*discuss how your partner can work with you so that it does not negatively affect your relationship.*

Now, any of the symptoms mentioned so far can be an indication of a more serious individual problem. You should give individual attention to issues like mood disorders and depression, substance abuse, addictive behaviors, or deep-seated personality problems. Be careful not to confuse these things with marital stress. If symptoms continue to be confusing or exceptionally persistent, I recommend you consult with a therapist to help you sort it all out.

## DIFFERENT PERSONAL STYLES AND STRESS

We all know that personality clashes can help spice things up a bit—or they can be extremely destructive. Personality and temperament differences cause lots of habitual conflict between marriage partners. It is way beyond the scope of this book to get into personality theory and temperament types, but let's take a quick look at one theory to help you determine if this is something worth further exploration for you.

### Your Temperament Helps Shape Your Marriage

Way back around 1920, Carl Jung theorized that we all have a preferred style for how we "function." Therefore we can be "typed" according to it.[12] There are four personality styles based on this theory. These styles are a great introduction to considering personality differences in our marital stress.[13]

1. The first is "extroversion versus introversion." Conflicts can arise when an introvert wants space, alone time, and emotional distance, or when an extrovert won't "shut up."

2. The second style looks at whether you are innovative or more practical. Can you both work together to put together a new barbecue, or do you fight about whether to read the directions? These two styles represent the biggest reason people misunderstand and begin pointing fingers at each other. The

fact is, you are just different and need to validate that in each other.

3. The third style is whether you are a thinker or a feeler. Women tend to be leaning toward the feeling side of things (big surprise, right?). Some women see men as being heartless just from using their preferred style, while men see women as illogical and too emotional! Don't make the mistake of misunderstanding your partner's temperament for something else. If your wife needs to cry, let her!

4. The final style is whether you are concrete and want solutions immediately or would rather have more information to consider. Do we always follow a plan, or are we going to fly by the seat of our pants?

Learn to recognize when you are simply having a clash in temperament style. Then you won't waste so much energy arguing! There are tons of reading material on personalities and temperaments. The point is, if you sometimes clash with your partner even when things are going well, you should consider how you are just different. You have to learn how to work *with* that, not against it. Accept each other, remember? This is another place that the three elements become critical in your marriage.

It is fascinating to look at the kinds of words people use based on their style. Word choice can be revealing about what style someone has, and also help you make sense of miscommunication. For example, the more practical person would use words like *settled, fixed, get the show on the road,* and *deadlines.* The innovative person will often talk about *letting things happen, make changes as you go, what's the hurry.*

♥ Talk with your partner about how you think and express things very differently (or the same). Identify ways this can help you communicate more clearly with each other in the future. Review your progress weekly for several weeks to make sure you are heading in the right direction.

The Flanagan couple found that they were both thinkers, being quite rational about most things. You remember Russ—he had no words in his vocabulary for feelings. But he did tend to want to keep his options open and maintain maximum flexibility as long as possible. Mary, on the other hand, wanted closure and wanted it now. Both of them had a tendency to think the worst of each other in this area. In essence, they did not accommodate each other's different temperaments.

I encouraged them to understand how different they were and how neither approach was necessarily right or wrong. Being people with great hearts, willing to look at themselves honestly and make needed changes, they learned quickly from this and made adjustments. They applied the three elements to get past this source of conflict.

> During a disagreement, stop and notice the kinds of words you and your partner are using to convey your ideas. Write some of the key words or phrases down (or they will elude you as fast as you say them). Talk about how you and your partner are different in how you think and feel about your surroundings.

If all this does is make matters worse, your personality and temperamental differences may in fact be an important reason for your conflict. I have only scratched the surface with this one theory about temperament; if this stimulates your interest you may want to begin learning more about personality and temperament. If the conflicts are too severe, consult a therapist for additional help. A good therapist will save you a lot of time and grief as you sort through these differences.

## CLOSENESS NEEDS AND STRESS

Before Mary Flanagan even married Russ, she recognized that some of the closeness between Russ and Jack was unhealthy. Plus she was the "odd man out," being a new, nonfamily member on the scene. These three very different people all had very different ideas about being close within this newly formed family. Furthermore, they all went about it in extremely different ways. This one issue brought out the very worst in all of them.

A lot of family research has examined the relationship between flexibility, how connected people feel, and communication. Believe it or not, it turns out that feeling the right amount of connection is the most important of the three.

*KEY ATTITUDE:*

**A meaningful connection with your partner is worth consistent effort.**

How close and connected people are, and the way they go about it, is the source of a lot of conflict in marriages. Everyone has a unique view of what he or she wants in this area. Maintaining the proper balance of closeness and distance with your mate is vital to your marriage.

For example, I sometimes tell people they need to learn the skill of distancing themselves from their partner in certain situations as a way of coping with a tough time. That can be a lot more constructive and productive than getting all upset. If your partner can't tolerate a little more distance, there is probably some kind of personal insecurity going on.

People find their own special ways to connect with others in the household. What is important is that they do this in a manner that works best for everyone. Most families tend to see communication and closeness as directly related to how well things work in the family.[14] The more connection there is, the better things are, right? I wish it were that simple, but it just isn't the case. The fact is, too much *or* too little closeness becomes problematic. Communication does *not* directly relate to better family functioning. In other words, blaming everything on "communication problems" is missing the target! The real issue is whether people are feeling connected at the level they like. And this does not mean that more closeness is necessarily the answer. Sometimes it's less!

Marriage partners tend to feel stress when any of these—communication, flexibility, and connection—do not seem to be at the right level. But research suggests that connection is more important than the others. Look at your daily "agendas" for getting the right connection level and make sure you are not working on two opposing agendas. Getting personal needs met is more likely to happen if you are working well together and feeling the amount and *kind* of connection you like.

When Russ and Mary Flanagan were at odds about Jack, both reported feeling distance from each other. They both saw this as a problem, and it actually helped further motivate them to find out the real problem between them and resolve it. They were not reinforcing their caring for each other at those times, so this was encouraged. Whether they could talk things through yet or come to an agreement, feeling that bond had to come first.

Like the Flanagans, talk about how you can reinforce your connection with each other even when things aren't going well. Identify at least three ways you can show your support of each other as marriage partners, regardless of what the disagreement might be.

What helps you feel connected the way you like with your partner? How is that the same or different from your spouse's answer? Discuss ways to accomplish both, meeting in the middle if necessary.

Regardless of how much closeness or distance you want, *some* meaningful connection is necessary if you want a healthy marriage. Most couples neglect this, so their needs in this important area are often in conflict.

Here is where I often suggest a little homework assignment for couples that is so little that most people don't even bother doing it. It seems almost too easy and too simple. But it is incredibly powerful and keeps many problems from ever hatching. I call it "daily connection time." If you think you are too busy for this, you have your priorities all wrong. Having a daily connection time means you take *at least* five minutes a day (it could sometimes be two hours) to sit down without any distractions of any kind, take a deep breath, and get "tuned in" to each other. Whatever you have to do to accomplish this, you do. Get tuned in to your partner's feelings, thoughts, moods, and concerns of the day. Ask your partner whatever you have to in order to achieve that. Focus on your partner entirely for part of this time. If any of his "stuff" at the moment involves you, make sure you address it. That way, problems do not build up all week or all month.

The second part of daily connection time is that you have to be prepared to share openly in the same manner. If your partner isn't asking, or isn't asking the right question, be in touch with yourself enough to share these things anyway. If you make this a daily habit, it will pay big dividends and ward off lots of problems. This will enable you to be on the same page every day, receive the personal support you may need, and eliminate the chance of issues building up.

Schedule a daily connection time with your partner and take responsibility for seeing that it happens. Try this for one solid week. Then discuss what benefits, if any, you see from the experience.

## INTENSE EMOTIONS AND STRESS

As I've mentioned before, there are times in marriage therapy when you can cut the tension with a knife. After taking a logical, objective approach to sorting through the issues, there is still an undercurrent of emotion that defies understanding. Most couples who experience this lose themselves in the moment and have no idea what to do with this when it happens. For many years as a marriage therapist, I didn't either!

Couples sometimes think they have resolved an issue, but the emotional undercurrent doesn't go away. This can go on for several days (or therapy sessions) or even years at home. I have learned through the years that this emotional undercurrent actually represents the barometric climate of what's really going on in the relationship. This creates an entire climate from long-standing unresolved issues. What it usually means is that the real issue has not been addressed openly. I will address this much more in the chapter on power struggles, but in the area of stress management it is worth mentioning. Managing stress means paying attention to signs that indicate something is just not right.

*... This emotional undercurrent actually represents the barometric climate of what's really going on in the relationship.*

When you get your senses trained to recognize this condition, a simple way to get to the root is to ask what is really going on. I usually say, "I'm just not understanding what is going on here, and have learned to listen to my gut." We then discuss some of the inconsistencies and things going on that don't seem to fit the situation. Maybe a partner's reaction to something is much stronger than the situation merits, or someone still acts angry even after something was supposedly resolved. You can learn this skill in your marriage with practice.

This happened with a fifteen-year-old girl, Chelsea, who said she thought her dad was acting selfishly. In the counseling session, the two talked things out and the dad admitted he had been selfish for the last few months. When they were driving home, he had Chelsea in tears, telling her it was not her place to say something like that to "someone in authority," as he put it. I could tell in the session that he was still very tense. Unfortunately, he would not admit his true feelings at the time the discussion was going on. Mom and Chelsea both had reported previously that Dad was quite high-strung and his emotions were often a destructive force at home. Emotions were running high once again, and later Chelsea said she knew what was going to happen when they left the session. Unfortunately, she was right. One of the ways this father could begin to understand his marital problems was to look at the stress between him and his daughter.

When the emotional barometer is high in your marriage, two things need to happen. Both partners need to make sure they are in control of their emotions; then they need to talk about them openly. Once again, this will not happen if you are not developing the three Key Elements.

There is often a more central issue at stake when the emotional barometer is high. Perhaps an issue that has been brewing for years in dozens of different ways has left you disappointed in one big way. You could be feeling that your partner just doesn't really care about you because of some things that happened ten years ago. Instead of tackling that directly, you bicker over all kinds of little things. You go to therapy saying you need help with "communication," when the real issue remains unspoken.

A simple way to check for this in your marriage is to ask yourself what primary need continues to frustrate or disappoint you. Or beyond all the specifics of your bickering, what do you *really* want that you aren't getting? Respect? Support? Getting to this core issue empowers you to bypass lots of silly and unnecessary arguing.

Exchange ideas about how you know when your partner's emotional energy has risen to a level that is typically not good. Review how you have been handling this as a couple and come up with a new approach for the next time it happens.

## OTHER SUGGESTIONS FOR
## STRESS MANAGEMENT

There are some general principles that are common to successful coping.[15] Just identifying the source of stress is important. I may be upset with you for being late when the real problem is I am upset over money problems. An individual's stress is still a marital issue, since it does affect the marriage relationship. My wife's stress is automatically *our* problem. Instead of blaming, focus on solutions (see the next chapter).

Partners must stay tolerant and caring even under pressure. Communication needs to stay open and partners should stay connected; leaving or withdrawing is only constructive if it is necessary to contain anger. Once you manage the anger, then address the issue. Recognize that poor coping strategies tend to mask the real issue, making solutions almost impossible.

It is important for you to recognize that your partner needs certain things from you to get through a crisis.[16] Show your partner emotional support and encouragement, offering advice only if that is what he or she wants. If you aren't sure what your partner wants, *ask*. Husbands tend to be "fixers" even when wives just want them to listen.

Crisis workers have found that the person in crisis needs to feel valued.[17] If you are not 100 percent sure how your partner feels valued, find out so you can provide this in a way he or she needs, not in the way you need. Partners who just have a tough time with stress in general should admit this freely, be careful not to blame their mate, and learn some personal stress-management techniques.

Here are just a few final suggestions you may find helpful:

**Say good-bye to your fantasy partner.** Most of us are in love with an *idea* of who we want someone to be (at least a little bit), not the person. Stop long enough to see the difference and keep your desires reality-based. History is full of people who became stressed and in conflict because their partner wasn't living up to their fantasy notion.

*Remember the good times.* You got with your partner originally for some reason you may have forgotten. When things get really bad in marriage, couples often forget why they liked being together in the first place. Reminisce about the good times and plan ways to recapture those times. Even the smallest step in this direction can ignite the spark needed to make big changes.

*Manage your time.* If your schedule is too full, it's too full! I know that isn't the most profound thing you've ever heard, but it's amazing how we can lose sight of this one point. I saw one couple who had been together for seventeen years—and had been unhappy around each other *the whole time.* To cope, they got busy with everything other than their relationship. I assured them that if they would just invest time and energy into each other they would see dramatic results. Both acknowledged I was right, yet never did change their routine enough even to try it. What were they so afraid of? I never did find out.

*Balance your time together.* Managing the time you do make for each other is important. Be creative! Likewise, having healthy and positive time apart is valuable. Couples who can never be apart (or feel separate) are going to smother each other. Sometimes the best way to help your marriage is spending *less* time together. Don't use this as an excuse to get your partner to let you just do whatever you want all the time, though. If your schedules are really busy, take a minute at least a couple of times a month to review how you spend time together and apart.

*Watch your daily routine.* Make your daily routine work for you, not the other way around. This includes ruts, like watching TV every night, and also feeling so obligated to certain things that you can never change the routine. Distribute responsibilities fairly to ease the demand on any one person. Make sure that your routine allows enough opportunity for relaxation, together time, and alone time.

*Keep an eye on outside pressures.* Sometimes one of you is having a tough time with something individually, whether it is work-related, a friendship, or maybe a physical problem, like fatigue. You both may know about this stress but underestimate its impact on what is going on between you. If that is happening, think of concrete and specific ways to keep the stress from interfering with your relationship so much. Instead of blaming, show understanding. Instead of being defensive, take responsibility for needing to manage the stress.

*Understand stage-of-life pressures.* Your marriage will go through some normal stages the longer you are together. At first, you may very well have little money and are scraping to get by. Then you have kids and have no time to read the newspaper, let alone time to go out and have fun like you used to do. Maybe you hate your job and are wondering if it is even the kind of work you want to be doing. The same thing happens with kids not being the right "fit" for the school they go to.[18] You can become preoccupied with those issues. Whatever the challenge of the moment, be sure to keep in mind the things that help you feel close and connected in your marriage.

*Have fun.* If you are not having fun in your marriage, life begins to feel like one big chore. This does not have to cost money! I fell into this rut at one point in my marriage. We were both working a lot and got lazy about how we spent our time. To shake up the routine, I suggested we go out (get out of the house and familiar surroundings) every Thursday night. Why Thursday? Fewer crowds and it broke up the week for us. We had to take turns surprising the other with some activity that was outside the norm. A new restaurant, a walk in the park followed by an ice-cream cone, a trip to the bookstore to browse and have coffee together. It was instantly wonderful! We found we did not even have to stick with this schedule for long because we naturally started thinking this way. Back when our kids were little, we planned late-night candlelit dinners at home.

*Take care of unfinished business.* Get issues out in the open and make

*Stress left unmanaged weakens your heart. This erodes your marital foundation.*

things right. If you don't, times of special stress have a way of exposing these issues and your weaknesses. You may have learned to "live with" the fact that your partner chooses to ignore you. But when the stresses mount, you are more likely to get angry about feeling so alone. That may lead to major arguments, which turn into resentments if they keep happening. Then this piles on more stress! Stress left unmanaged weakens your heart. This erodes your marital foundation.

## KEY ATTITUDE: Live in the present.

How does it feel when someone keeps bringing up what you did in the past, even if you have tried to change? You feel like you are in a box and your partner will not allow you to be different today. Plus, you can't change what has already happened. I listen to long-standing arguments almost daily from couples who keep bickering over things that happened a year ago. They never get around to talking about *today*. If you just talk about what you are going to do differently today, suddenly a lot of these issues become relatively simple. Let it go. As unsophisticated as it sounds, there is one principle that resolves a lot of things—"get over it." You can't do anything about what has already happened, but you *can* do it differently *today*.

**Keep setting goals.** This is so important I have dedicated an entire chapter to it. We all need things to look forward to. During a disagreement we should know what we want to happen instead of the problem. But we need to have goals, large and small, just to make life fulfilling. One friend of mine has a "state of the marriage" talk with his wife every year. They review their lives together and all the goals they have. There are all kinds of things they want to do. It injects excitement into their marriage. Okay, he is a therapist, too. Why not follow the personal example of a therapist with a good marriage? I do.

So what else did the Flanagans need to do to manage the marital and family stress better? Well, they had to keep an eye on outside pressures. They were shopping for a new house in the country after living in the city all their lives. They had to sell two houses, and they would all have to adjust to a very different lifestyle and routine. Stage-of-life pressures were also huge for this new family. A new marriage, a new stepfamily, already existing issues between Russ and his son, plus each partner was entering a second marriage: all of these posed unique challenges. Russ and Mary were both very good about acknowledging these very legitimate challenges, keeping them on their "radar screens," and addressing them as needed.

> Discuss with your partner all the sources and types of stress that exist in your life. Write them down so you can keep track of them. Develop appropriate strategies to deal with each of them separately, so you do not blame each other for things inappropriately. Do a periodic review of your overall stress management plan (decide now how often this should be).

As you begin to look at the stress in your life and in your marriage, approaching it with a loving heart and strength of character will pave the way to making needed adjustments (Elements #1 and #2). It can take some effort and time to sort through the ideas in this chapter. Admitting that stress may be influencing your own behavior is not always easy. It requires openness and a desire to want things to be better, even if it means laying aside your agenda or sense of upset in the relationship. That's the essence of Element #3. You have to want solutions and be willing to look at anything necessary to pave the way for them.

Examine how your stress challenges your ability to be selfless, humble, devoted, and persevering. There is no shame in admitting that stress has weakened you. In fact, it's liberating! It frees you to adopt better coping strategies and shows once again what you are made of. Make sure nothing is keeping you from pursuing lasting solutions wholeheartedly. You see, if you really believe in God, you believe that every day can be good, no matter what has happened. You believe that God can renew you and your partner, starting right now.[19] So instead of being consumed with discouragement, you examine the stress in your life with optimism. You have a spirit of seeking real solutions, not quitting. This is far better than blaming your partner for problems caused by stress.

Learn what it takes to "keep your tank full"—both individually and in the marriage—and then keep your eye on the gas gauge often enough to keep from running out.

## MAIN CHAPTER ATTITUDES

✓ Be proactive under stress instead of reactive.
✓ Always manage your daily routine to minimize stress.
✓ Know your deeper needs and be open about them.
✓ A meaningful connection with your partner is worth consistent effort.
✓ Live in the present.

### ATTITUDES IN ACTION

1. **Attitude: Be proactive under stress instead of reactive.**

   a) Identify the main causes of stress in your marriage (do together), including how they affect married life, and develop strategies to cope more effectively with them.

   Each partner is to make two short lists. The first list contains things that describe your most pronounced personal qualities when under stress, both good and bad. For example, one item might be hot-tempered and another could be very giving. The second list contains descriptions of what you want to be like under stress. Compare the lists and discuss what needs to happen to achieve the second list.

   b) Reviewing materials in this chapter, particularly the Coping Styles

Inventory, identify specific coping behaviors used by either partner that are not helpful. Decide on more helpful coping strategies.

2. **Attitude: Always manage your daily routine to minimize stress.**

   Talk about how you see your usual daily routine in terms of minimizing stress. Give your routine a letter grade (from A to F). If it is anything under an A, commit to some changes that will bring the grade up.

3. **Attitude: Know your deeper needs and be open about them.**

   Each partner should identify which of the four basic needs covered in this chapter he or she is the most sensitive to and discuss:

   **a)** How you both see this need getting expressed in the marriage (like symptoms, attitudes, or expressed needs).

   **b)** Any other needs either partner has in the marriage.

   **c)** How these needs either create, or are otherwise influenced by, stress in your life. Develop a plan to meet these identified needs.

4. **Attitude: A meaningful connection with your partner is worth consistent effort.**

   **a)** As a couple, discuss what it takes for you to feel connected the way you like with your partner. In addition, describe what makes you feel close to your partner. Compare similarities and differences in your answers. Agree on an approach that provides the right balance of closeness and distance (individuality) for each of you.

   **b)** If you haven't already done so by now, commit to a "daily connection time" as discussed in this chapter. Remember, this is a time to "tune in" to your partner. Discuss what connection time is to be sure you both understand the point of it and how to go about using this time.

5. **Attitude: Live in the present.**

   Identify any negative experiences in your marriage that seem to keep affecting how you react today. Discuss with your partner how you both can begin to make today different in a positive way.

# 12

# Set Goals and Watch Things Change

*Winning isn't everything,*
*but wanting to win is.*

Vince Lombardi

*I*n shatterproof marriages, couples resolve problems by turning them into goals for change. This is an art and can be learned. Either most people don't know what is wrong, or they focus way too much on their complaint. You can step out of this quickly by learning three simple steps.

**KEY ATTITUDE:**
**Always be goal-oriented.**

Being a "solution finder" starts with an honest desire for solutions. At some point, you have to stop dwelling on the problem and consider what you are going to do about it. You have to switch your agenda from focusing on the negative and think about a positive direction *after the problem is gone*. Jesus even went so far as to say that you are blessed if you are a peacemaker.[1]

This chapter focuses on how to do this in your marriage. Most of us look at all that is wrong when we have problems in our marriage. This happens especially if the problems won't go away. There is plenty of research showing that when people begin visualizing what things will look like *after* the problem is gone, solutions are more likely to happen. But the one thing that is always missing in all these studies is having the spirit of finding solutions for the *relationship*, not just for your personal agenda. You can go through certain processes to set goals—and I teach them here—but it is critical you use this method with an attitude of genuine, heartfelt desire to do your part in making things right. This chapter is the core of Element #3. I provided the other chapters within this element to make your efforts even more effective to convert problems into solutions.

It's funny how the field of psychotherapy has evolved over the last hundred years. Everyone knows about Sigmund Freud and the famous "Freudian slip." Our subconscious and our dreams never betray us. We might call someone the wrong name because we were thinking of someone else. So he tells us that must have been a "Freudian slip."

In more recent years, an approach called "solution-focused therapy" emerged. This approach helps people find more practical solutions for here-and-now issues. The emphasis is on what behaviors need to happen for you to find solutions. If you are like me, this sounds a lot better than going through some painful process of rehashing past memories.

## Key Attitude:
**Examine the condition of your heart regularly.**

An important ingredient to successful goal-setting in marriage is that both partners have to be willing and ready to be forward-looking enough to let go of the problem once you decide to start looking for solutions. If one partner is unwilling to really let go of the problem, this is the problem and should become the primary goal to be discussed. The Bible puts it this way. It tells us to make sure that no root of bitterness springs up and causes trouble in our life.[2] You have to stop and deal with this; otherwise, you are wasting your time.

This is easy to identify if it happens and is actually even easier to address. Every time you talk about what would make the problem go away, if your partner keeps focusing on the complaint, he is resisting any kind of solution. Calmly call time-out, confront this politely, and refuse to continue unless he is ready to consider fixing the problem. Don't get sidetracked here. If this is happening, it is not complicated. Either you are talking in positive terms about what a solution will look like, or you aren't.

If your partner is not letting go of "problem-thinking," the biggest mistake you could make is to try harder. This lets your partner off the hook! You are not holding him responsible for his negative thinking and this gives the impression that you should continue defending yourself. This sets up your discussion to be an adversarial one.

Experience and research prove that solution-focused approaches work. At some point in any situation we all have to be willing to do what will be helpful, whether we feel like it or not. We have to let go of our feelings and bad attitudes, making an honest effort to solve the problem. Be true to the three key elements of a shatterproof marriage. This is crunch time!

## GOAL-SETTING WORKS ONLY IF GOALS ARE MATCHED TO THE RIGHT PROBLEM

Another thing that can sabotage your efforts is to set great goals for the wrong issues. As we have seen, labeling everything a "communication" problem often misses the mark. A great goal, yes, but not the problem. You could set better communication as your goal and make great progress, then wonder why the original problem is not better.

To illustrate, consider the mother who brought in her fifteen-year-old son because of "school problems." Mother reported that her son's grades were poor and he was getting into trouble at school frequently. She completely focused on how horrible these things were with him, but neglected to talk about how she was at the point of "falling apart." If she continued to ignore this aspect of the problem, she would have missed a lot of what needed attention. Her stress was actually part of the reason her son was not doing so well.

Joslyn did the same thing in her marriage. She had a personal history of being involved in a local church and took her faith in God seriously. Yet she had become a chronic complainer and was harsh with John every day. When I asked her how this fit in with her spiritual convictions, she looked at me and said, "You are so right. I've completely lost sight of my relationship with God." She began putting her focus on strengthening her relationship with God instead of blaming John.

Change will probably be an up and down process. No matter how bad the problem gets, you must remember the only hope you have is if you do not give up. If you have a bad week, get right back to the techniques in this chapter and work on even small ways to point yourself in the right direction again. This is where you have to believe all things are possible and have some endurance.

Problem behaviors often do not disappear forever. That is normal. Expect them to come back at least occasionally. When they do, don't overreact to them, but continue building on the foundation you have been building. Also be sure you do not get overwhelmed with all the ideas and tools shared in this book. Just pick a couple at a time to focus on.

**KEY ATTITUDE:**
**Admit and acknowledge the problems in your marriage, and work on them.**

Identifying and converting problems into positive goals is maybe the hardest part of working out problems. The better you are at it, the more efficient your problem-solving efforts will be. Expect to struggle a bit. It starts with being honest about what your problems are. If one of you starts to give up, *that* must become the primary problem.

The Flanagans were no different when they began marriage counseling. Their initial complaints included having the classic "communication problems," too much arguing, and a power struggle over how they should parent Jack. Jack's whining and manipulative behaviors were big focal points, even more than the couple's inability to work together. Although quite intelligent, they were very confused about what exactly the problem was.

♥ Like the Flanagans, the place to start is the beginning (that isn't too profound, is it?). Begin thinking of the main areas in your marriage where you want to see improvements. Compare notes with your partner.

Setting goals is, by nature, a fluid process and is ongoing. You are free to add or take goals off your list as needed. I recommend that you write down your answers to the exercises. Either make copies of them, write in the book, or sketch them out on your own paper. Save your work and review it in six months. An annual or semiannual review can become a tradition in your relationship. Remember: you only get out of it what you put into it. Investing in your relationship in this way will pay huge dividends. Plus, if you and your partner are focusing on this material, *that* probably represents a change that can set in motion lots of good things. Just the willingness to do this work sets you apart from many couples.

> Just the willingness to do this work sets you apart from many couples.

## THE POWER OF TINY GOALS

A great way to get your focus off the negative is to make some tiny, positive requests of each other. This is based on tons of research showing that positive behaviors set the tone for all the right things to be happening in your marriage.[3] This is a simple thing, but not easy if you are caught up in negativity. Make sure you do this little exercise. It helps you to start thinking in goal-oriented terms. In fact, this whole chapter is one of the components of the communication model I share in the next chapter. Jesus told His followers that it is more blessed to give than to receive.[4] This is a perfect way to start.

These requests should be things that you would like from your partner that would make you feel special and valued. But they have to be stated in positive terms, be concrete and specific, and as small as you can make them. This forces you to verbalize what you really want from your partner. If you cannot do this, you shouldn't expect your partner to read your mind.

Here are a few examples to show what I mean:

1. Write me a little note in the morning.

2. Touch my shoulder when you talk to me.

3. Show me you are listening by waiting for me to finish.

I had to do this assignment in my training program, only I had to come up with twenty-five items. After two weeks of adding to my list, I came up with number twenty-five, and it turned out to be the most important one to me. Sometimes you can't think of the small things that make a difference to you. If you think about it, all the small stuff during an average day is what makes or breaks how we feel. Doing small, nice things for each other creates goodwill and feels good.

♥ Exchange your lists (described above) once completed and agree to do one or two things from your partner's list every day. Come up with at least fifteen items.

There are a couple of pitfalls with this little exercise. Couples often wait for the other person to go first before doing anything. If your partner does not do anything on the list, it can tempt you to be stubborn. Also, your partner may keep doing only some of the things and not anything else from your list. That's okay—don't dwell on things like that. Be thankful for any effort your partner makes and focus on being a good partner yourself. If your partner is just not being cooperative with this exercise, sit down and talk about what is really going on (in a humble way).

In the midst of all their problems, the Flanagans were willing and able to remember small things like this in their daily routine. Russ liked it when Mary spoke to him in soft tones and told him how much she cared. Mary liked it when Russ verbalized his marriage commitment in front of Jack. It took effort since they were struggling, but it ended up making a world of difference.

## THREE EASY STEPS TO CONVERT
## PROBLEMS INTO SOLUTIONS

Okay, now you are ready to start finding solutions to your issues. This is, in my opinion, the most important single thing I do in marriage counseling. Do a good job here, and all the other techniques you might use in your marriage work that much better. I suggest you go through this section fairly quickly, then come back and spend some time working more thoughtfully through these three simple steps.

### STEP 1: Identify Workable Problem Areas

The first step in working out solutions is to decide exactly what the problem seems to be in your eyes. This can be done by having each partner organize his or her thoughts on the Working Problems List (found in this section). This is a master list of the main problem or concern areas. In other words, if these areas changed, you would be happy and feel like things are much better. Just state these things in the terms you understand best. For now, start with the big things.

The best way to do it is by listing issues according to category, like all the communication-related problems together and all the intimacy-related issues together. This puts more order and logic to the process. Some common problem areas expressed by couples appear here to give you an idea of how this works.

Headings are the "main problems," and the "problem *behaviors*" appear under them. You and your partner can actually learn to think this way, and this approach then becomes second nature to you.

## Example of Problems List

| Communication | Disrespect | Poor Intimacy |
|---|---|---|
| Poor listening | Disregard my opinions | Not affectionate |
| Interrupting | Name-calling | Rarely have sex |
| Arguing | Rude to me in public | Don't share feelings |

Under each problem area (such as communication, disrespect, poor intimacy), identify actual *behaviors* you see when the problem is happening. Remember: all attitudes or feelings have behaviors attached to them. I have listed some examples above so you get the idea. One good way to begin identifying specific *behaviors* you want changed is to look at the sequence of events, blow by blow, that creates a given problem. Who does what when the problem is happening?

It's important to reduce all problems down to specific behaviors. Once the behaviors change, the problem goes away. If you do not state problems in behavioral terms, this process will not work.

If you need some help figuring out what your concerns really are, read the Condensed Life Principles Inventory and the Marriage Evaluation Questionnaire found in Appendices A and B. These tools will help you evaluate some of your attitudes in some of the areas many couples find helpful. Organize your main concerns on the Working Problems List in this section.

Among other things, the Flanagans were able to identify a few personal attitudes and behaviors that needed to change. Mary tended to insist on doing things her way (number fifteen on the Marriage Evaluation Questionnaire in Appendix B), and both were able to identify behaviors that made their teamwork difficult (number five, Marriage Evaluation Questionnaire). Russ withdrew and Mary became too direct. Listening to each other (number nine, Condensed Life Principles Inventory in Appendix A), they realized, involves more than being quiet. It means you really understand the other person's point of view.

After some discussion, we identified these main problem areas, then decided what behaviors needed to change. That gave order to the process and helped us put some confusing things into more concrete terms.

*Once you have identified the main problem areas that are of concern to you, write them down on the Working Problems List that follows. Try to boil things down to two or three main concerns. Then list a few behaviors under each that seem to create the problem. Use the questionnaires in the appendices to help you with this if needed, as the Flanagans did.*

After you complete your problem list, then convert them into goals. For now, take the time needed to be thorough and accurate with your list.

## Working Problems List

MAIN PROBLEM 1: *(Flanagans put "Inability to compromise")*.

Problem *behaviors*   a. *(Flanagans put "Demanding your way without hearing what I want to do")*.

        b. _____

        c. _____

        d. _____

MAIN PROBLEM 2:

Problem *behaviors*   a. _____

        b. _____

        c. _____

        d. _____

## STEP 2: Convert Problems into Goals

The next step in setting goals is for you and your partner to take each problem in your lists and look at the flip side: when the problem stops, what will be happening *instead*? Answer that question for each problem behavior. It's natural to lose your focus quickly if a clear answer does not come to mind. Be careful: stay with the question until you start getting some concrete and positive answers.

*This* is what a solution-focused approach—and having a spirit of seeking solutions—is all about. Ultimately, you want this to be the way you think naturally. It requires you to keep bad feelings and attitudes in check. If you are not thinking this way already, you are not living consistently with the three Key Elements. Let go of negative, self-centered thinking and allow yourself to think in terms of what you want *instead* of the problem.

A well-known therapist by the name of Steve de Shazer came up with an extremely helpful question to complete this step. He called it the miracle question, and it is so simple it seems almost unimportant. The question goes something like this, "Imagine if you went to sleep tonight and woke up tomorrow, and a miracle happens. Suddenly your problems are gone, just like that! How will you and your friends know that the miracle has happened? What exactly will be different?"[5] Be specific and use your imagination. Who will be doing what, where, and when, if the problem is gone? What behaviors would you need for that to be a reality?

All you are doing here is being clearer about what you *want* instead of what you don't want. So if arguing is the problem, you might want "to discuss conflicts calmly." However, this is still too general. The word "calmly" could mean different things to different people. Identify what "calmly" looks like. Voice tones, body language, slowness of speech, listening behaviors, and the list goes on. Many times we are doing things we are unaware of and being this specific can make all the difference.

*Once you meet your objectives, you achieve your main goal.*

This is the reason you have listed *behaviors* under the problems. You convert negative behaviors into positive objectives. Once you meet your objectives, you achieve your main goal. The goals and objectives in Step 2 should correspond to the main problems and sub-problems in Step 1. Consider each, one by one, and convert each to a goal by asking yourself the miracle question above. Sometimes this process goes very quickly and sometimes it is tedious and takes a lot of work. Either way, stick with it. If you do, solving your issues will be so much easier in the long run.

Write down your goals and objectives in the following table. Be sure each goal and objective corresponds to each problem and negative behavior listed earlier.

| Goals & Objectives | WEEK | | | |
|---|---|---|---|---|
| Example: | 0 | 1 | 2 | 3 |
| Main Goal 1: Flanagans put "Compromise when we can't agree." | 6 | 7 | | |
| Objective (a specific behavior): Flanagans put "Listen to my ideas, then review all ideas together before making a decision." | 4 | 8 | | |
| **Main Goal 1:** | | | | |
| Objective: | | | | |
| Objective: | | | | |
| Objective: | | | | |
| **Main Goal 2:** | | | | |
| Objective: | | | | |
| Objective: | | | | |
| Objective: | | | | |

After you have done this, review the following criteria for setting good goals. Make sure all goals and objectives meet the criteria. You may have to go back and make changes.

## All Goals Should Include Certain Ingredients

Theorists have written volumes about the ingredients of effective goals, but here are some of the most important ones.[6] There are just seven of them here. Make sure all your goals and objectives include all these ingredients.

1. **Small goals work best.** The smaller the better. Change happens one second at a time. In fact, changing too fast is overwhelming, so "going slow" can actually work to your advantage.[7] This is why you have smaller objectives. Do not underestimate the importance of this one ingredient.

2. **Goals must be stated in positive terms.** Say what you want *instead* of your complaint. For example, instead of blowing up when an agreement is broken, you may want your partner to *stay respectful when upset* about this. This is *instead* of blowing up, and is positive.

3. **Goals must be measurable.** This should include when, where, who, and how often, and they must be stated as behaviors you can see. A quick acid test is to ask yourself how easy it will be to know you have accomplished it. *Every* goal can be put into measurable, behavioral terms.

4. **The solution should replace the problem.** For the most part, the solution is often the opposite of the problem. Visualizing a new behavior is a big first step in being mentally ready to eliminate the old behavior. This can help you get out of vicious cycles and endless discussions.[8] This is also a great way to mentally "rehearse" the good behavior in stressful situations.[9] It's like mental practice.

   It can also help to think of a behavior that is impossible to do at the same time as the problem behavior.[10] It would be like trying to sing while swimming underwater! As simplistic as it sounds, this principle works!

5. **Everyone wins.** Remember: a problem for one partner *automatically* makes it a problem for the other partner. Formulation of a good goal means there are no losers when you achieve it, and both benefit when the goal is reached.

6. **Solutions will be exceptions to the problem.** Do your goals represent examples of when the problem does not happen *or is not as bad?* This "exception to the rule" is often the difference that can make all the difference.[11]

7. **Verbally commit to making positive change.** Tell each other—out loud—you are going to start focusing on what will *fix* the problem, and not the problem. Do a heart check if feelings and attitudes are getting in the way. Remember the three Key Elements.

Mary Flanagan did not do so well when it came to setting goals. She did not focus on the *desired* changes she wanted to see in Jack. When she was challenged with having to think about what Jack will act like *when the problem is gone*, she and Russ had an entirely different kind of conversation.

What she wanted was actually the same thing Russ did. This process helped her realize it. Russ did not realize this either, so both had to work on exploring what common ground they did have. Discovering what you do agree on, actually, is another extremely important skill. Start with asking each other if there is anything you *do* agree on—this will make the discussion so much easier.

♥ Review all the problem areas you want to see improved. As Mary Flanagan had to learn, ask yourself if you have converted your concerns into positive goals and objectives that are measurable behaviors. And do they include all the ingredients of effective goals? If not, review this section again and rework your goals and objectives until they do.

## STEP 3: Measure Your Progress

A simple and powerful way to measure your progress for each goal and objective is to give them number grades each week. This may sound stupid, and some people don't want to come up with a number. But trust me, this works.

A "10" means your goal or objective has been fully reached, and a "1" means you are nowhere near reaching your goal. Write the number in the box next to each goal for whatever week you are in. Follow the example given.

If change is ever going to happen, first you have to *expect* it to happen.[12] Couples, like individuals, tend to create "self-fulfilling prophecies" about whether desired changes happen. If you focus on the negatives of the problem and how it "never seems to go away," then the problem will not go away! Scaling your progress with number grades holds your feet to the fire, gives you direction, and provides encouragement. If you don't keep track of small changes in the right direction, you will quickly forget about the goals you set. It is critical you use Step 3 even if putting a number to things in your relationship feels weird.

> ## *K*EY *A*TTITUDE:
> **Change *always* starts one minute, one thought, or one behavior at a time.**

Don't be fooled into thinking that one small change here and there won't make much difference. I have seen quick and big progress that started with the smallest change.

And don't underestimate the potency of this little grading technique. I had a couple come to me for marriage counseling that rated their marriage at an 8. For most of us, this would be pretty good! But they had high standards. Pinning them down to what they needed to get to a 10 was the only way I knew how to help them. After four sessions they reported being at a 10 and were very happy. This approach can also help you know just how dissatisfied you really are (or not), and also find out the same about your partner. If you are at an 8 and your partner is at a 3, well, you can see how this would be a big problem. You had better sit up and pay attention to what your spouse is saying.

Using this technique with the Flanagans proved to be especially useful. First, it forced them to be more specific than they ever had been about all the behaviors concerning either one of them about Jack.

Second, it trained them to notice even the smallest of improvements. This gave them more hope and enabled them to keep doing some of the right things. One such behavior was Jack feeling sorry for himself. He would mope around until he got the attention he wanted from his dad. Russ and Mary began working cooperatively to ignore this when it happened. In just one week's time their rating of this problem went from a 4 to a 5.

Scaling with numbers teaches you to be patient and persistent. Don't panic if change isn't immediate. Chip away at the problems, taking it a day at a time. If you drift from this technique, or the problem gets worse instead of better, it just means your idea of what would make things better was mistaken. Sometimes your objectives have to be revised several times before you find what works.

Sit down and scale the progress of each goal and objective listed, the same way the Flanagans did.

After a week has passed, review progress and re-scale each goal and objective in week two. Do this each week for several weeks if necessary. Each week, ask what behavior it will take to move up one number on the scale.

Discuss any goal or objective that is not progressing as well as expected. This is crunch time. Identify the kind of heart most needed at this point and get your attitude in line with someone of deep character. See if and what either of you can do differently. Should you reach a stalemate, discuss honestly what you can do about it, up to and including giving in or enduring a situation that you can't change.

There you have it. These three simple steps can work wonders in your marriage. Learn them and practice them.

## ADDITIONAL TIPS FOR SETTING GOALS

Everyone makes assumptions about his or her marriage partner and our relationships show it. If you assume your wife wants to get her way, your relationship will surely reflect defensiveness and you will both trigger reactions from the other. There are some assumptions therapists make about people that make their therapy more effective.[13] You and your partner can learn a lot from them and, if put into practice, your relationship will go much more smoothly. In addition to the three Key Elements, apply them especially during the goal-setting process. This will go a long way in facilitating a cooperative spirit.

### Talk Your Partner's Language

Marriage partners have a preset idea about how things are and how they are supposed to be. Find out the motives of your partner, what her belief system is about an issue, and how she talks about it. Talk to her on that level. Help her see the same in you, coaching her how to talk your language as well.

### Your Partner Is Doing the Best He Can

Parents, for example, who restrict their kids from being with certain friends are just doing the best they know how in keeping their kids from negative peer pressure. We need to credit people for doing the best they can at the time. Give your partner a break! Even destructive behaviors are a form of coping, and usually a symptom of something going on inside. Have some mercy and try to understand your partner's world.

### Behavior Is Not the Person

You have to separate what someone does from the person himself. You might be saying, "But doesn't his behavior reveal who he really is?" Yes and no. Your behavior does reveal your character, but it does not equate to the entirety of who you are. There is much more to all of us than any one (or even more than one) behavior. Even if I have a problem with lying to you, there are a lot of other qualities I was born with that are great. To practice this principle, ask your partner if you show acceptance of him as a person when you are upset.

## Key Attitude:
**Desire solutions in which you both win instead of complaining or finger-pointing.**

Giving your partner choices facilitates solutions. Everyone, even kids, needs to feel as though he can make choices about his life. You don't go around making every choice for your two-year-old, such as whether he likes beans or corn better. Your partner has to feel like he is an active participant in solutions. Ask questions like, "Do you agree it makes sense to do things this way?" Ask your partner if he or she feels like you respect his or her personal preferences and choices most of the time. If the answer is not always, take some time to explore this further.

## Key Attitude:
**Count your marital blessings and be an encourager to your partner.**

Don't lose touch with why you got married in the first place. You married each other to share life and make each other's life better. Do you remember specific things you used to like about each other? Find ways to encourage each other and be a positive influence in your marriage.

### Your Partner Is Capable of Solutions

People often ask me how I can do therapy all day. A big reason is because I believe that everyone has strengths and experiences that make solutions and problem-solving possible. You may not know how to ride a bicycle yet, but you do know how to balance yourself in other ways, move your legs in a circular fashion, hold on to handles, try new things, etc. Learning to ride the bike is just a matter of putting all these abilities and attitudes together in a new and sometimes better way. Don't we all learn more quickly when others act as if we "have what it takes" to be successful? Instill this belief in your partner. A pleasant discussion to have over dessert would be complimenting each other on all the qualities that make your partner a competent person. You might be surprised at the impact this has.

Francine had grown very angry with Tim, her husband of more than thirty years. He had let her down during all those years and she managed to keep a smile anyway. When he finally surrendered and said he was willing to do anything in his power to make things right, all she could do was belittle his efforts and discount the value of anything he did. A solution—any solution—was impossible. Folks, if you don't let it go, it won't go away! Sounds like another profound quote by Yogi Berra, doesn't it? If you are too young to remember him, I mean it doesn't take a brain surgeon to understand the importance of letting go of the problem.

In the case of the Flanagans, they successfully implemented two important assumptions with each other. Russ and Mary each needed to respect that their partner was honestly making the best choice they knew how to make when parenting situations arose. When they stopped to better understand each other's way of thinking, it made them both more sympathetic with the other person's experience. As a direct result, they established lines of communication that never existed before. Rather than fighting each other over these things like before, they "buried the hatchet" and began approaching each other with an earnest desire for things to be good again.

The second assumption was that each needed to believe they had some choices in responding as a parent. Once they understood this, both were much more willing to throw out several possible ways to deal with Jack as well as listen to each other's ideas. This eliminated the need to resist the other person. Once this happened, they were quick to realize the solution needed was pretty simple—and that they agreed with each other about it!

This, folks, is another perfect example of Element #3 at work! Along with the right personal character and an unconditional love, the spirit of converting problems into solutions produced a kind of synergy in their marriage. It even felt somewhat miraculous to them, and it will for you as well when you experience it. Suddenly, things just start to "click." Learning to convert problems into solutions can be learned. But you have to *want* this skill.

Review the above assumptions and ask yourself if you have truly made all of them about your partner. Once you have viewed your partner in the best possible light, proceed with showing that to your partner in your approach. Review these as a couple, identifying how you are showing these assumptions to each other.

The process of setting goals fits right in with the next chapter, which addresses conflict and communication. Converting conflicts into a direction for desired change is an art that all good communicators possess. Talking about things in the right way resolves a lot of problems.

A summary of suggested exercises appears here. Just working through these exercises could take a couple of weeks. No matter. Take your time and work at your own pace. If you master the three simple steps in this chapter, you may not need many of the things I share in the remainder of the book. Why? Because just bringing all three elements to the forefront of your marriage often is enough! Just be careful not to get overconfident. You could still need some additional tools.

## MAIN CHAPTER ATTITUDES

✓ Always be goal-oriented.
✓ Examine the condition of your heart regularly.
✓ Admit and acknowledge the problems in your marriage, and work on them.

✓ Change *always* starts one minute, one thought, or one behavior at a time.

✓ Desire solutions in which you both win instead of complaining or finger-pointing.

✓ Count your marital blessings and be an encourager to your partner.

## ATTITUDES IN ACTION

1. **Attitude: Always be goal-oriented.**

    Discuss with your partner whether you (as a couple) get off track in your efforts to set goals. Identify when this happens and what seems to be the reason. Make adjustments accordingly.

2. **Attitude: Examine the condition of your heart regularly.**

    As you try to put these principles into practice, discuss each chamber of the loving heart: selfless, humble, devoted, enduring. Does either one of you need to strengthen your heart in any of these areas to set goals more effectively?

3. **Attitude: Admit and acknowledge the problems in your marriage, and work on them.**

    If you have not already done so, do Step 1 and complete the "Working Problems List." Use the Condensed Life Principles Inventory and the Marriage Evaluation Questionnaire from Appendices A and B (if necessary). This is typically something you do together.

4. **Attitude: Change *always* starts one minute, one thought, or one behavior at a time.**

    Do Step 3. Rate your current level of satisfaction for each goal and objective using the 1 to 10 scaling technique. Consider what it will take to raise the score by one notch (a behavior), then work on doing that until the score improves.

**5. Attitude: Desire solutions in which you both win instead of complaining or finger-pointing.**

Do Step 2. Convert the "Working Problems List" into goals and objectives using the "Goals and Objectives" format provided. Ask each other the "miracle question" discussed in this chapter.

**6. Attitude: Count your marital blessings and be an encourager to your partner.**

Discuss the Additional Tips for Setting Goals at the end of this chapter. Then talk about all the things that were *ever* good in your marriage. Listen for—and brainstorm—ways you might need to change your approach with your partner in order to get back to your first love with each other.

# 13

# Communication
# Essentials 101

*The greatest compliment that was ever*
*paid me was when someone asked me what*
*I thought, and attended to my answer.*

Henry David Thoreau

he way you talk to others is one of the biggest windows to where your heart really is.

A careless or reckless tongue causes great damage. The Bible says that if you mind what you say, you direct the rest of your life. It's just like a big ship that is controlled by a small rudder.[1] You can (and should) apologize, but your partner may need some time to heal from remarks you have made. I see people regularly who are surprised their partner needs time to get over things that were said. Don't underestimate the power of the tongue. On the other hand, there is always hope in your marriage relationship as long as the two of you can talk. An old proverb tells us that "a soothing tongue is a tree of life, but perversion in it crushes the spirit."[2]

Communication is the bridge linking needs and desires with another person. Conflict is inevitable, and a certain amount of it is actually healthy. Some couples have almost no conflict but still find themselves in my office for marriage therapy. Conflict is okay and yes, even desired; it's *how* we have conflict that becomes a problem.

This chapter takes a close look at the minimum requirements for acceptable communication. This includes fair-fighting rules and a discussion of your particular reaction cycle. The chapter closes with a summary of some of the destructive communication patterns many people develop in their marriage. If you are reminded about them, you can watch for them and avoid many of the problems common to all of us. The next chapter takes a close look at a simple but powerful communication model I use every day in my counseling practice. If you master this model, I guarantee that you will be communicating more effectively.

Have you ever met someone who prided himself on being a great communicator—even a great debater? Some people even go so far as to say you will never win an argument with them. They are just "too good." In any love relationship, that is a horrible trait to have. The materials in this chapter will give you some great communication techniques, but even more importantly, using them correctly requires a *spirit* that wants harmony, peace, and reconciliation. Actually, the goal-setting process you learned in the previous chapter is one slice of the communication pie. In my opinion, it's the most important slice, but the rest of the pie is still very important. One of the specific properties of Element #3, a spirit of converting problems into solutions, is good communication with the right spirit. In fact, good communication is mostly about having the right spirit. I share some great tools here, but using them with success requires an honest *desire* for success.

The more skilled we are in communicating, the more power we have in our relationships to influence others. Many arguments occur not because people disagree so much, but because they *think* they disagree. How many times have you thought you expressed yourself clearly, only to find out your partner heard something totally different? This is often because what someone says has a totally different meaning to the other person, perhaps triggered by the memory of some kind of past experience.[3] But Jesus told us to look past wrongdoing by another person and start with a clean slate, no matter how many times you have been wronged.[4]

For example, if I ask my son if he has considered "this way" of doing something, he remembers five years ago when I criticized him about something unrelated and blows up. So on the surface, it looks as if my communication was perfect and he just reacted "out of the blue." This happens to all of us sometimes. If you do not see this situation for what it is, though, and talk it through, tensions mount. A lot of marital misunderstandings are the result of this dynamic.

Being unaware of what it is you need to express is another common barrier. There are things we are naturally more tuned in to than others.[5] We have a lower awareness level with communication styles that differ from ours. Some people don't tune in to feelings or emotions very much. But many people do, so it is something we must pay attention to regardless of our style. Be ready to recognize your communication limitations, since this will show you where you need the most work.

> **KEY ATTITUDE:**
> **It's important to understand how your partner experiences things.**

Another barrier to communication is when people do not affirm each other. Effective communication makes it easy for people to see themselves (their self-image) in a way that makes them feel respected and worthy. This is an important part of feeling understood.

If my friends keep inviting me to go to the library and I see myself as an avid outdoorsman, chances are I will begin communicating differently with my friends. I might lose some of my enthusiasm when I talk with them and share less openly with them, thinking they don't understand or know me very well. I need them to affirm some things about me to show they can "tune in" to my world. So they could say, "We know you would rather be fishing today, but we discovered an entire section at the library on fly-fishing. Why don't you come with us, and maybe you could show us how you fish with some of the books."

This shows they are sensitive to who I am, even if they want to do something else. Husbands and wives often need to work at this, since their interests are often different.

## MINIMUM STANDARDS FOR SUCCESSFUL COMMUNICATION

Before we look at a simple communication model, we need to define what communication behaviors meet minimum acceptable standards. In other words, these behaviors are the *least* we should expect in order to have effective communication. The fact is, you are the only person responsible for what you say and how you say it. If you have developed destructive or unhelpful communication habits, you must do two things. First, react responsibly. Second, be accountable to fight fair.

You can be stubborn and insist that your partner should have no problem with the way you communicate. But that isn't very sensitive, is it? Relating to another human being always requires us to adapt the way we communicate *just for them*. Always. The other person may need to make some changes, too, but your first thought should always be to consider carefully how you are coming across to the other person.

**KEY ATTITUDE:**
**Be goal-oriented and devoted to communication growth, enduring failures.**

I often give couples "Fair-Fighting Rules" so they can hold themselves accountable to some basic acceptable behaviors at home. Some couples continue violating them, then come back in and want me to fix their "communication" problems!

If you are unable to control your behavior enough to follow these

principles, you are defeated before you start. I can't—and no one else can—
be your self-control. At some point, you have to be accountable. If you cannot follow these guidelines, something else is going on with you. Rather than
fighting with your partner, figure out what that is and how you *can* follow
them. You should put your relationship discussions on hold until you can com-
pose yourself. If you cannot control yourself, you are like a "city broken into
and without walls."[6] It's a surefire way to ruin your own marriage. I will share
some great tools here to help you with this, but you have to *want* to be under
control. If you look to God, His love will give you the motivation and desire
to change.[7]

You may need to manage your own stress before you can hope for an effective conversation with your mate. If so, at least admit it and reschedule your
discussion until you can control yourself. The most important thing is that
you commit yourself to doing the right thing and refuse to give up. If you
blow it, admit your mistake, pick yourself back up, and try again. Before you
read further, you may want to review the three Key Elements again so they
are fresh on your mind.

## Minimum Standard #1: React Responsibly

This is not a chapter on anger management. But understanding how anger
works and learning a couple of things about it can go a long way. Spend some
time reviewing the Reaction Cycle below and plug your name in with different situations that come up with your partner.

Learning your cycle is like running a movie in slow
motion and looking closely at each frame. Each frame is
almost exactly the same as the one before, but just different enough to be important. Describe your behavior in detail at each frame. The term for this is
"freezing the frame." Then look at what triggered
the behavior *right before* it happened. Change your
interpretation of what is happening, or simply change
your behavior. Take written notes describing some of

> *When you
> learn your reaction
> cycle, you can intercept
> your anger at
> several points of
> the cycle.*

the frames, training yourself to recognize them quickly when they happen. When you learn your reaction cycle, you can intercept your anger at several points of the cycle.

For example, if you and your spouse always get into an argument when you get home from work and you don't know why, use the freeze-frame technique. When you first walk in, you are very quiet and want your partner to leave you alone. Your husband has been off all day and just can't wait to talk. He keeps "bugging" you (that's part of how you are interpreting it). At first, you show some patience, but that doesn't last too long. You ask your husband to leave you alone and so he gets all hurt and defensive (part of how he is interpreting things). At this point, either one of you can choose to change your interpretation OR your behavior.

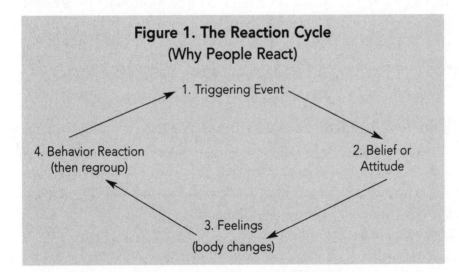

**Figure 1. The Reaction Cycle
(Why People React)**

1. Triggering Event

4. Behavior Reaction
(then regroup)

2. Belief or
Attitude

3. Feelings
(body changes)

1. **Triggering Event.** Identify exactly what triggers the first negative reaction from you. Believe it or not, many people skip this part and miss some important information. What triggers you might just surprise you!

2. **Belief or Attitude.** What are your thoughts or beliefs about the triggering event? Be specific. Then think of every possible view of

the triggering event. This should even include ways that sound unacceptable to you. Change your thinking in any way necessary to lower your anger or at least slow it down. Solutions often seem completely unacceptable at first, then we realize our thinking was all messed up the whole time.

3. **Feelings (and body changes).** Notice the very first signs of anger within your body and emotionally. Note: these are *caused* by your belief or attitude. That is the exact moment to make a change. Learn the early signs of your emotions (like anger), including what physical changes are happening within your body. Train yourself to use certain emotions and body changes (i.e., breathing harder) as reminders to react more deliberately.

4. **Behavior Reaction.** Change a behavior. Identify unhelpful behavior habits (typical reactions you have) and replace them with more helpful ones. There are times when doing absolutely nothing in response represents a new behavior for you. Don't limit yourself with narrow-minded thinking. Even little changes in your behavior could end up making a big difference.

If tempted to do something unhelpful, find a way—in advance—to slow down your response. Decide what the alternate response should be ahead of time. Get back to fair-fighting rules if you have violated any of them. Learn from your mistakes.

Russ Flanagan was convinced (his belief) that Mary just wanted to control things all the time. While she had this tendency in her personality, it really wasn't the kind of heart she had. Parenting discussions would trigger this belief, and then his tendency was to shut down. He could feel his body tensing at this point. Russ learned to recognize when this was happening and challenge this internal response. It made a huge difference.

Mary was convinced that Russ and Jack had some kind of unspoken conspiracy against her, so when a parenting issue came up, she found herself wanting to talk faster and louder. Mary recognized this was not helping and learned that finding new responses at those exact moments was critical.

*Following the example of the Flanagans, take a real issue in your marriage and plug it into the Reaction Cycle. Talk about what you can learn about your cycle and how you can channel it more constructively.*

## KEY ATTITUDE:
### Practice leads to growth.

Anything learned can be unlearned. Old habits are hard to break, though, so you and your partner need to be patient with each other. Practice new habits for a while before hoping they come naturally. Train yourself to use triggering events, your belief about them, and feelings to remind you that this is where you get into trouble. Let that become a new triggering event for you!

Practice is usually not much fun (remember having to sit down at the piano as a kid on a sunny Saturday afternoon?). But remember what we talked about in earlier chapters: there are no good shortcuts to growth. Burn this attitude into your brain. If you have not already done so, you may wish to answer the Communication Self-Evaluation questions found in Appendix C and discuss answers with your partner.

## Minimum Standard #2: Fight Fair

In addition to the following guidelines, there is a Communication Self-Evaluation found in Appendix C. This enables you to explore your communication habits in a more detailed way.

When you have disagreements, you should hold yourself accountable to standards of good behavior. The love passage we looked at in Element #2 says that we are all to "not act unbecomingly."[8] Admit it. Everyone knows what constitutes reasonable, courteous behavior. Or do they? I actually had a husband tell me once he did not see anything wrong with calling his wife names. He said sometimes she deserved it!

At some point, you may wish to go through those questions and discuss your answers with your partner. Now let's look at the absolute *minimum* behavior standards when you disagree with your partner. Learn these inside and out—they will serve you extremely well.

## FAIR-FIGHTING RULES

1. Accept responsibility for your anger without blaming someone else for it.

2. Slow down! At the first sign that anger is beginning to escalate, agree ahead of time to slow down, and have an agreed-upon way to be able to take a deep breath before becoming rude.

3. Accept responsibility for managing your anger, always communicating constructively, or learning how if needed.

4. Make no excuses for being rude, disrespectful, using negative body language, or being harsh.

5. If you can't control your anger, identify a way to intercept it, such as excusing yourself from the situation. Make an agreement on how you should do this.

6. Schedule a time to come back to the issue if you need a cooling-off time.

7. Name-calling, cursing, accusations, and insults are forbidden. These are all signs you are not under control or have a bad attitude.

8. Let the other person finish talking without interrupting. It is the listener's responsibility to convince the talker that real listening is taking place.

9. Use "I" statements to take ownership for the way you feel, think, or interpret what you are upset about. Say, "I think" or "I feel."

10. Acknowledge you could be wrong in how you see things by saying, "I could be wrong, but this is how I see things."

11. End every disagreement with discussion about how you think you can solve it. In other words, what would people actually DO to solve the problem (not what do they *stop* doing).

12. Raised voices are rarely helpful; agree ahead of time to slow the discussion down or take a time-out if voices are getting loud.

13. Mind reading or assuming is unacceptable. Do not insist you know what the other person is thinking or what his or her motivation is.

14. If you are interpreting the other person's actions negatively, describe to him/her what behavior leads you to that conclusion, then *ask* if you are right or not. This includes unpleasant body language or tones of voice.

15. If someone is being rude or using negative body language, call time-out, point out the behavior, and ask what that behavior means. Then, if necessary, ask the other person to modify that behavior for a better conversation.

16. Keep discussions in the present; try to find solutions to past frustrations so that today is a new day with improved interactions. Then let go of the resentments.

17. It's okay to be skeptical because of a repeated behavior by someone, but it's not okay to just expect bad behavior or be unforgiving. Give the benefit of the doubt.

18. There is a time and place to address issues. Be willing to face issues by talking about them. Also recognize that issues often do not get resolved when discussion is heated.

19. An issue important to one person is automatically an important issue for those who are in a relationship with that person. Be willing to discuss anything that concerns your partner.

20. Your partner may be basing feelings on incorrect information, but you should always listen to and respect them. Then you can discuss or correct the information, not the feelings.

Place a check mark next to the item(s) you see yourself doing. Create some kind of strategy to change your behavior. Visualize it and rehearse it in your mind. Take three minutes a day to review this list, and whenever you have a bad argument or interaction, review what you should have done differently. Review your progress each week with your partner.

Identify at least one fair-fighting rule that you tend to violate. Tell your partner how he/she can help you to control your behavior. Hold yourself accountable the next time an argument happens (whether your partner helps or not).

These rules are all very important, but there are a few that merit special attention.

## Your anger is all your fault.

Did you know that no one can "make" you angry? The Bible says that anger lives in the heart of fools.[9] You can choose to react to life calmly. Your partner might do something outrageous, and it could be a pretty good "cause" to feel anger, but *how* you express it is entirely your deal.

An illustration I often give is if you and I went to the nearest mall, and I asked you to pick fifty different people—men, women, and children of all ages and races—and slap them as hard as you could. How many different responses would you get? Just one? No! Some old ladies would cry and be confused. Some big, burly man might hit you back, thinking he isn't going to take that from the likes of you. A child might have such fear he runs and hides. Others would actually wonder what *they* did wrong. The reason you would get different responses is that we all process (interpret) events around us in our own way. Who is in control of that, you or the other person?

If you're still not convinced, let's take road rage. Many of us have gone through periods of getting angry on the highway at "all those other" stupid drivers. I can honestly say that I have grown to be pretty tolerant of other drivers, but not without a lot of effort over the years. How did I do that? By changing the way I *think* about the way people drive. When I get in the car now, I fully *expect* other drivers to cut me off. Why wouldn't I? It comes with the territory of driving nowadays! Rather than getting more competitive, I choose to let them in and not give it a second thought. I have taken away their power to influence my anger.

You can apply this to virtually any situation, no matter how bad it is. Remember the prisoners of the Nazi prison camps—some of them chose not to hate or be angry with their captors despite atrocities of epic proportions. Don't ever fall into the trap of saying, or even thinking, your partner is to blame for your anger. It is how you *interpret* your partner's behavior that results in anger.

Tell your partner about a time when you thought he made you angry. Then explore how you could adjust your interpretation of his behavior to take more responsibility for your anger. Discuss how you will express yourself differently at such a time.

## When all else fails, slow down!

The second fair-fighting rule is to slow down your response. I can't say enough about this one either. God tells us that whoever is slow to anger is better than the strongest of people.[10] It takes more courage and strength to hold your anger than it does to lash out. This one principle is powerful and can change the way you interact together.

The first cardinal rule for working with domestic violence is for people to learn how to slow down their reaction time. There are hundreds of ways you can slow things down. Talk more slowly, excuse yourself for two minutes, count to ten, take deep breaths, be a better listener, ask your partner to slow down, and so on. The point is, if things are escalating, learn to recognize it early and intercept it. Don't feed the problem by escalating yourself. Slow things down in a way that works for you.

## Know how to be angry and respectful at the same time.

Rule number three is close to it: manage your anger. There are a lot of folks out there that did not know you could be angry yet respectful. I have to tell you, it's absolutely possible! Being angry does not mean you have to be loud. Or out of control. Or rude. Or accusing. You can learn to express what you are angry about calmly, with a low voice, in a caring and courteous manner. If your partner does not believe you are angry, that is your partner's problem. It is never necessary or acceptable to be disrespectful when angry.

> ♥ Identify one of your first responses (internal or external) at the very beginning of getting angry. Choose a substitute response and try it the next time a frustrating situation arises. If you forget, rehearse it in your mind every day until it happens again.

**KEY ATTITUDE:**
Be accountable for behaving with respect and common courtesy at all times.

Use of common courtesy is an incredibly important principle to follow. The more comfortable we get with someone, the more we think we can behave poorly. It's hard to be "on good behavior" twenty-four hours a day, seven days a week, isn't it? We all have our "moments" in which we do not behave in a way that we want outsiders to see. Being rude is just not okay. Imagine some of the little rude behaviors you have used with your partner, then try to imagine doing them during your wedding ceremony. I have never met anyone who doesn't know what polite behavior is. I don't have to elaborate about it here. If this is going on in your marriage, talk to your partner about it and commit to this one change. Staying polite even when upset goes a long way in helping you get along.

*Imagine some of the little rude behaviors you have used with your partner, then try to imagine doing them during your wedding ceremony.*

Talk about what common courtesies both of you have stopped doing for each other. Even if it feels weird, start doing them again. Plan to talk in a few days about whether it made any difference in how you felt.

## Be careful with your assumptions about your partner.

Expecting your spouse to be a mind reader is common for couples. We can't help but anticipate what someone is thinking or feeling when we get to know them well. That is fine, but be careful how much you do it and don't get cocky. As soon as you are sure you know what someone is thinking, you find out you really don't. If your partner reads your mind and presumes too much, you may or may not be able to identify at first that is what she is doing. Does it ever feel like your partner is responding to you in a way that boxes you in? Like she is not giving you the benefit of the doubt or just "knows" what your intention was? Think about whether this happens in your relationship. If and when it does, call attention to it. Double-check your information with your spouse—you might be surprised.

Unfortunately for them, Russ and Mary Flanagan were actively doing all the things wrong just discussed. They were sure they knew what the other person was thinking, and were convinced their partner had an "agenda" every time parenting came up. Mary became overly direct and harsh as she spoke with Russ. You could literally see them bouncing off each other almost like pinballs. She would bring up a topic and he either interrupted or withdrew. The conversations went way too fast, going from one comeback to the next. I showed them what they were doing to each other as a couple and they learned to watch for these specific behaviors. Then they were in a better position to make big changes.

♥ Ask your partner how (not if) he thinks you act like you are reading his mind at times. Find out specifically what leads him to believe you are doing this. Hint: it's usually some kind of assumption you are making, and many people don't even realize it's happening.

With an issue you and your partner have disagreed about, write down all the assumptions you make about what he is thinking, his intentions, his behavior, and so on. It's highly unlikely you did not make any. In your next disagreement, be painfully clear about all the assumptions and beliefs you have about your partner.

## COMMUNICATION PATTERNS TO AVOID

People often develop ongoing communication patterns that are destructive, either as individuals or as a family group.[11] Most of the time, these patterns have crept in subtly and we are not even aware of them. Let's review several here.

## Disconfirming Talk

We can fail to "confirm" someone or we can actually "disconfirm" him. A good place to start being a good communicator is to show affirmation for people. Individually, there are at least three ways a person can disconfirm someone, which is a guaranteed way to destroy good communication channels.

First, we can be indifferent to our partner. This happens when we act like he doesn't exist or his behavior is barely noticeable. You can do this selectively, only with certain issues. Being unaffected or unaware of things most people would notice characterizes this type of disconfirming.

The second way to disconfirm someone is to be "impervious" to him. Either we act—or are—unable to understand what he is trying to say. In other words, you are clueless. After a while, he just gives up trying to get you to understand. I saw one woman with multiple sclerosis whose husband acted impervious to her need for reassurance from him. This became very distressing to her. Unfortunately, she did not communicate her need very clearly, plus she did all the talking instead of asking him questions about whether she could count on him. It took two sessions just to discover that she was afraid he would not take care of her if her condition worsened. I had to listen very closely to hear that message from her—he didn't stand a chance of understanding, so he became impervious to her. She lost hope because she was unable to get him to focus on her fear. This story illustrates how the problem of being impervious can be the fault of either (or both) partner.

Third, we can disconfirm someone by disqualifying the truth of someone's message. It's a first-class deflection technique. You're upset with me for using a harsh tone of voice with you, so I defend myself by blaming someone or something else. Or you catch your partner gambling household money after agreeing not to do this, and his defense is to talk about how you aren't any fun anymore. It's as if the response somehow takes any legitimacy out of your issue, even if it is a factual situation that cannot be denied.[12]

## KEY ATTITUDE:
### Develop a heart that wants to be a good communicator.

The biggest trap the Flanagans kept falling into was not tuning in to each other. In fact, they were rather impervious to how the other person was really thinking. This was incredibly frustrating to them both. Their frustration kept mounting, making them even more uninterested in how the other was thinking. After I gave them extra help by directing them both to consider more closely what the other was thinking, they recognized how they needed to be careful to keep listening.

Ask your partner if he or she feels listened to most of the time. If not, discuss why not and what it will take to fix this. This is not a time to argue, but to listen to each other!

So the bottom line is, you need to take personal responsibility for making your partner comfortable in your discussions. If he can't be pleased in this area, ask him specifically what kinds of communication behavior will satisfy him. Then if he still is not pleased, it is his problem, not yours. But if your partner perceives you are disconfirming him, you should be quick to want to know it so you can make adjustments. Partners who do not have this attitude have a real heart problem, in which case reviewing the four parts of a loving heart should help pinpoint the real problem.

Usually when one partner feels disqualified by the other, this kindles lots of emotions like anger, hurt, and fear. The partner goes into defense mode, setting the couple up for the early onset of power struggles. If you don't feel counted in your relationship, figure out what kind of relationship pattern this creates. When you feel discounted, how do you act, then how does your partner act, and so on? Once you see what you are doing to each other, you can see how silly you both are being and can commit to changing this cycle.

*Ask your partner if he feels comfortable and heard when he talks to you (ouch, this could take some humility!). Under NO circumstances are you to argue back. This is not a time to disagree but to show a real openness to your partner. Ask how you can do a better job in the future.*

There are as many patterns as there are people. A few more here should help you to begin thinking about what kind of pattern(s) characterizes your marriage:

## Narcissistic Talk

This pattern is characterized by at least one of the members being focused mostly on himself or herself. One friend told me of a coworker who was so narcissistic she would change the subject as soon as you talked about something she knew nothing about, or something that did not hold any interest for her. Another example is a father who gets angry with his son for making a bad football play. He is really upset because he wants his son to be a hero and isn't taking the son's feelings into consideration. Listen for how much give and take there is in your communication with your spouse. Is it always about you?

## Ghost Talk

Some people relate to certain people in their lives as if they are ghosts from the past. I always used to hate it when I was young and dating and my date cut the relationship short because of some past hang-up. These haunted conversations tend to be extremely confusing, because often what someone says is not at all what you might expect. You want to talk about your wife's spending habits and her response is to talk about the way you treat her, based on some rejection she experienced in a past relationship.

## Fantasy Talk

As I mentioned before, partners often are in love with the *idea* of their partner, not always who their partner really is. Resentments can set in because your wife isn't the goddess you imagined when you got married, and you keep comparing her to that. You can detect this communication style when you express a lot of unhappiness or criticism toward your partner.

## Sham Talk

In this communication pattern, people are doing or not doing things based on unrealistic expectations. The son who becomes a doctor because he thinks his dad won't care about him anymore if he doesn't is an example. There is an undercurrent of misunderstanding as expressed in tension, frustration, and superficiality—anything to avoid direct discussions. Any semblance of deep conversation, at least about certain things, is a sham. The way out of it is to stop holding things in and being willing to address any and all issues.

## Control Talk

Typically, this communication pattern has one of two extremes: someone is in charge and someone is not. Simple questions like, "Where do you want to eat?" become frustrating issues. Sometimes a partner rarely has an opinion and the other partner usually ends up making the decision. People take on roles with each other based on this polarity and we can see it in the way they talk to each other. The one in control tends to become a bit presumptuous and too assertive. The other partner gives in too much. One way to challenge this pattern is to reverse roles just for fun. Have your husband do the cooking all week while you handle paying the bills.

The Flanagans were beginning to slip into a pattern of trying to control each other's behavior in their discussions about Jack. Language was forceful or very defensive. They recognized this was happening, and fortunately made the first counseling appointment to avoid further damage from this kind of communication. At that time, they just did not have the tools or the understanding of each other (being newlyweds) to intercept what was happening.

♥ Discuss whether you see any of the above—or any other— unhelpful patterns of communication in your marriage. The Flanagans were humble enough to look at themselves honestly and examine any attitudes that needed adjusting. Agree to some changes you can both make to improve things—either with your attitude or your behavior.

In severely disturbed marriages, these patterns (and some that I haven't mentioned) are just more extreme. When issues continue being unresolved, some couples adjust by coexisting instead of working things out. Or they might make one partner the focus of all the frustration. If you just take a step back and look at the *kind* of communication that goes on, you see that the pattern masks or distorts the real issues. This is where all kinds of unspoken messages creep in, which tend to be crazy-making.

Good communication does not solve all problems. Just because you learn some good tools does not mean there will no longer be struggles. That isn't real life. Sometimes all we can do is express ourselves fully and honestly, listen to each other, and begin the search for solutions.

Remember that above all, it is possible to have conflict and to stay respect-ful. If you are not experiencing this in your marriage, one or both of you has learned some very bad habits. But it is possible. Good communication requires you to act "as if" you feel caring and respectful, even if you don't. Don't assume you know what the other person is thinking, feeling, or even saying. At some point, you have to give your partner the chance to correct your perception, and then you have to trust him to be sincere and truthful. If you can't do that, you have a much bigger problem on your hands.

Healthy communication takes self-control, period. If your partner is unwill-ing to acknowledge using bad communication habits or will not work on them, the real problem is one of the heart. Element #3 is not present. Even if it's hard, this element leads you to be slow to speak and quick to hear. A lot of the communication dangers discussed in this chapter are eliminated by the simple presence of Element #3. Examine yourself, especially when you become the most upset. Are you bringing the right spirit into your conversation?

Every time destructive communication behaviors are used, it becomes a defining moment for both of you. It's a test of your character. Just remembering to hold on to all three Key Elements when times get tough has the effect of shatterproofing your marriage.

## MAIN CHAPTER ATTITUDES

- ✓ It's important to understand how your partner experiences things.
- ✓ Be goal-oriented and devoted to communication growth, enduring failures.
- ✓ Practice leads to growth.
- ✓ Be accountable for behaving with respect and common courtesy at all times.
- ✓ Develop a heart that wants to be a good communicator.

## ATTITUDES IN ACTION

**1. Attitude: It's important to understand how your partner experiences things.**

Take turns asking each other what, if anything, you think your partner could understand better about you.

**2. Attitude: Be goal-oriented and devoted to communication growth, enduring failures.**

As problematic communication behaviors occur, review your communication habits using all the materials in this chapter. Continue setting communication goals and commit to working on them together consistently.

**3. Attitude: Practice leads to growth.**

Practice a new response to a nonhelpful reaction you would normally have to something. Use the Reaction Cycle to help you identify what the new response should be. Practice the new response until it is a new habit.

**4. Attitude: Be accountable for behaving with respect and common courtesy at all times.**

Identify together at least three fair-fighting rules that need to be improved. After disagreements, review progress (or lack of it). Recommit yourselves as needed.

**5. Attitude: Develop a heart that wants to be a good communicator.**

Using the four chambers of a loving heart as a guide, identify your biggest challenge with being a healthy communicator. Discuss with your partner ways that you need to develop stronger character to be a more consistent, healthy communicator.

# 14

# Communication Essentials 201

*The greatest problem in communication is the illusion that it has been accomplished.*

George Bernard Shaw

Our communication is only as good as the connection between people. If the speaker is unclear to the listener, or if the listener has faulty antenna, the intent of the message is not accomplished. Most people tend not to be all that cautious about making sure the message is sent *and* received as intended. The Bible instructs all of us to be "quick to hear, slow to speak and slow to anger."[1] When people disagree, the worst thing they can do is go too fast and assume their communication is being transmitted well. Oftentimes, fixing this one aspect of your communication opens the door to all kinds of good things.

We now turn to a simple but powerful communication model that will revolutionize the way you talk to your partner. The reason it is in a chapter all by itself is because it is simply that important. Take your time with this model. Make it yours. Own it. Practice it until it is second nature to you. If you do, and remember the three Key Elements as you do, I guarantee your marital communication will become strong. This model, although simple to learn, will challenge you to the core. It forces you to keep your agendas and emotions in check. The Bible says to "let your speech always be with grace, seasoned, as it were, with salt. . . ."[2] This is primarily talking about speaking the truth of God, so how much more should we do this in everyday conversation? If you remember the main property of Element #3, the *spirit* of converting problems into solutions, this model will change your communication forever. I guarantee it. But you must use this tool with a sincere desire for solutions, not just for venting frustrations.

This model teaches you to express yourself clearly in the important ways to get your point across. It also teaches you to listen correctly. It can feel a little tedious at first; hang in there because it will pay huge dividends.

## A Simple Communication Model

Communicating effectively is a learned behavior. The core of this section is the Healthy Communication Pyramid, which can be easily memorized by using it over and over. It's easy to learn and much more difficult to master because feelings get in the way. In addition, most people have developed some bad communication habits.

The large bold print—items 1 to 3—are the most important parts for you to memorize.

**KEY ATTITUDE:**

**Be accountable to using good relationship tools with all the right attitudes.**

This model is a great tool. But remember the three essential elements. This model will fall flat on its face if you have bad attitudes.

A description of each section follows the pyramid to help you understand how it works. It will not feel particularly natural using the model, but spend time practicing with the exercises provided in this chapter. This model is the guts of the communication training I do, so spend some time here.

Expect this model to challenge you in at least two ways. First, it will challenge you to behave differently, which is always going to require some extra effort for a while.

Second, it will challenge many of your attitudes. You won't be able to just react anymore. It forces you to control your emotions and behaviors. Commit now to practice this tool until it is working effectively for you.

## Figure 2. Healthy Communication Pyramid

Start at the bottom and work your way up to achieve healthy communication.

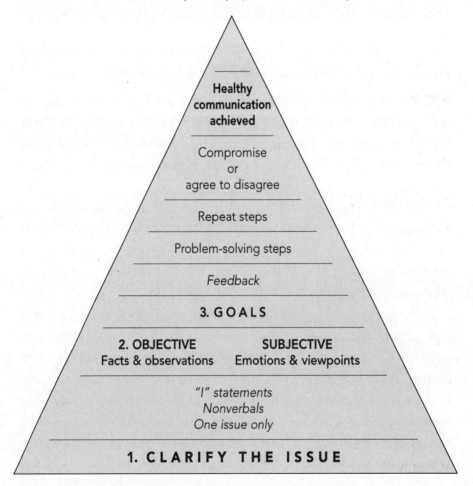

# 1. CLARIFY THE ISSUE

Many issues would be resolved quickly if you could just agree on what the real issue is and stay on it. I have yet to see a couple who has been arguing a lot who doesn't switch subjects.

As part of learning this model, I tell a couple to start talking about their concern. Let's just say it is how much time they spend together. The wife points out how her husband is never home and works too much. He responds to this with how she spends so much money he has to work a lot. She then responds with how all the responsibilities at home are falling on her. Now we have three issues, and a full-blown three-ring circus! It happens—literally—in thirty seconds or less in my office. And that's under a controlled environment!

Be clear about what the issue is, then stay on it. A sure symptom of getting off the issue is when you are feeling confused in the conversation. Call time-out and ask, "Now what is the issue here?"

We can only talk about one issue at a time effectively. Did you hear that? Usually, several issues relate closely to each other, as in the above example. As hard as it is, keep the focus narrow and only on the one issue.

## Nonverbals, "I" Statements

Much, if not the majority, of communication is nonverbal. A father just has to look at his child a certain way to get a message across. Your wife can give you "the look" and you know it's time to be quiet. Or she can give you "that other look" and you know she wants to be frisky.

If your partner is using negative nonverbal communication, politely call time-out and describe in detail the *observable behavior*. It is not enough to say your wife has a disapproving look on her face. What makes it look disapproving? A slight curl on one side of the mouth, a raised eyebrow, a change in the tension level in her voice perhaps. Be specific here! Tell her what those behaviors look like to you, then wait for her to confirm or dispute your perception. If she disputes it, ask for an explanation for those behaviors that at least makes some sense. You have to be prepared to admit you might have misinterpreted the nonverbal behaviors, and she has to be prepared to admit she might have done them in a negative manner.

**KEY ATTITUDE:**
**All behavior is a form of communication and sometimes should change to be more like that of Jesus.**

♥ Invite your partner to tell you what nonverbal communication behaviors you use the most, both good and bad. Ask him or her to point out the negative ones to you when they happen so you can either express yourself verbally instead or modify the behavior.

One young man got angry and frustrated every time he got around his mother. He couldn't figure out what the problem was. After years of confusion, he realized she was communicating nonverbally in some ways that made him very uncomfortable. He began to realize she was using tones of voice that seemed to be disapproving, certain facial expressions that appeared rejecting, and even silence at times that others could interpret negatively.

One day, she did it again, so the son shared with her his observations of these behaviors, describing them in detail. He told her how he was interpreting the behaviors and asked her if he was correct about what they meant. She quickly said no, apologized for the misunderstanding (which had gone on for thirty years!), and never communicated that way again! Why did that work so well? First, she was exposed—or busted—for negative behaviors. It forced her to communicate verbally if she had something to say. Plus, she was probably not even aware she was doing it at least half the time. If your partner just has a way of getting under your skin, become an expert at describing any and all nonverbal behaviors that make you uncomfortable. Then tell your partner what it is about those behaviors that doesn't feel right.

You may have heard the communication rule that you should always use "I" statements, but most people do not understand why. Using "I" statements forces you to take ownership for the way you are interpreting the events around you. You could say, "When you didn't call me, it *seemed* (your interpretation) to me like you were blowing me off. Am I wrong?" This always gives your partner a chance to correct your interpretation. It shows humility and lessens the chance of an argument. Remember, you don't know everything at all times! God wants you not to think more highly of yourself than you should, and to think with sound judgment.[3]

> Talk about ways you can share unpleasant things with each other in a more diplomatic manner, taking more responsibility for your feelings and interpretations. Focus on your nonverbal communication and the use of "I" statements.

## 2. OBJECTIVE AND SUBJECTIVE

### Objective

This part of the Communication Pyramid includes facts, observations, and concrete examples that help to further clarify the issue. The more specific you are with factual information about the issue, the clearer your discussion will be. Stick with observable behaviors here, not your interpretations of them. Give at least one recent example of what you want to talk about. Use "I" statements such as, "I saw you come home last night" or "I noticed you appeared upset last night when you raised your voice and walked out." Make sure your partner agrees with the basic facts before you go further. If he never agrees, this is where your communication is breaking down, so decide how you can still talk about your concern. Sometimes people can't even agree on a recent example that took place. If that happens, you have to talk about possible future situations instead of arguing about whether something happened.

## Subjective

This includes your feelings and thoughts about the issue. What does the issue feel like when the problem happens? This should describe your emotions, like feeling angry, hurt, rejected, scared, and so on. Describing everything as "frustrating" is just not enough. Elaborate enough here to help your partner really understand how you feel. If you don't express your emotions, the problem may never go away because he just doesn't understand how it affects your feelings. He won't be able to appreciate what you are going through. Try to use more than one word to describe your feelings.

Your thoughts are your opinion, your viewpoint, how you are interpreting the issue when it happens, or why the issue is important to you. Communication often breaks down when you assume you have conveyed your thoughts, but your partner could not repeat them back to you in a million years. As I have already said, research has shown that our thoughts produce our feelings.[4] You are fully in control of what you choose to think, so your feelings are ultimately your responsibility. Express your thoughts and feelings like this, "I could be wrong, but when you walk out I *think* you must not care, and that's when I *feel* really hurt, rejected, and angry."

Note: Underneath anger there are almost always other feelings and lots of thoughts or opinions. You may not always express them verbally, so it is important to make this kind of communication a habit.

## 3. GOALS

Do you remember the chapter on setting goals? If you read that chapter and have developed those skills, you already know how to do this part of the model! You have already learned how to take complaints and convert them into things you want instead. Expressing your goals is how you should finish every presentation of a problem issue. Tell your partner what you are willing to do in order to contribute to the solution. I urge people to play "Let's Make a Deal" here. If you will do something to make a solution possible, I will do something in exchange. It's a simple but powerful habit.

A word of caution: don't fall into the trap of Machiavellian Manipulation. This is where you believe "that others don't know what's best for them, that it's a good idea to put pressure on others if you want them to do something, that breaking promises and using white lies are often useful . . ."[5] You may be a talented talker who can usually work the conversation to your favor, but the healthiest communication involves genuine teamwork and cooperation by both people. Honor and respect your partner. Don't proceed as if you have all the answers.

> ♥ With a real issue, discuss how you can "make a deal," in which each of you gives something the other person wants in return for something the other wants.

## Feedback

Truly listening is the other half of effective communication. Jesus had so much trouble getting people to listen that He spoke to them in riddles. His reason was that "while seeing they do not see, and while hearing they do not hear, nor do they understand."[6] That way, people who really *wanted* to understand still would. Wanting to understand is seen in how much you listen carefully. There are a few tips here to help you listen this way.

Once you have fully expressed what you need to say about the issue (and both of you are following fair-fighting rules), the listener should say what he heard in his own words. Be sure he summarizes everything you said from the model. If the listener misses any important part, it is the original speaker's job to point it out (using common courtesies). Don't get ahead of yourselves by commenting just yet with your response. The feedback stage is another major point at which a lot of communication goes wrong.

**KEY ATTITUDE:**
**Be a good listener.**
It has been known for a long time that in addition to hearing what your partner said, you also need to validate him.[7] This means that if you stood where he stood, knowing what he knows, you express your understanding about how he sees things the way he does (even if you disagree!). Once your partner gives feedback and validation, then it is his turn to respond to what you said. Follow the same rules with the response.

♥ Commit to one or two new listening behaviors, telling your spouse what they are.

The Flanagans, while they were capable of communicating reasonably well, found that they were not doing it as well as they thought. Communicating in an intimate relationship is a whole different animal than at work or in the grocery store. They never did (before therapy) really articulate what they were thinking or feeling about the issue of parenting Jack. They certainly were not listening closely to each other. Once they practiced the communication pyramid at home, both acknowledged the many mistakes they were making. It took quite a bit of humility and a willingness to let down their defensive walls. But once they did, they began hearing each *for the first time ever.* It was all made possible by following the three Key Elements.

♥ Identify the part(s) of the Healthy Communication Pyramid that you need to work on the most. Tell each other how you see your attitudes or behavior needing to change. Like the Flanagans, admit to each other the mistakes YOU make (not your partner).

## STEPS TO PROBLEM-SOLVING

If your partner proposes a solution and you can't agree on it, realistically what can you do? What could anyone do? Brainstorming all the possible solutions—whether good or bad—and picking one is sometimes all we can do. When you are at this point, brainstorm ways you can make a deal in which both partners get *part* of what they want. Otherwise, one or both of you will be insisting on your own way. This is contrary to the Key Elements.

So if a teenager wants to have money to buy the things he wants and the parents want some kind of limit on "foolish" spending, one solution is to give the teenager a limited monthly allowance. Once the money is gone, it's gone. This gives the teen freedom to make spending choices, but there is a definite limit on how much money is available for foolish spending. Use a two-winner strategy at all times. This just means the goal you are seeking, and the way you are going about it, allows both people to come out with something they want.

A final thought: don't allow yourselves to slip into the habit of talking about your goals in negative terms, as in, "I just want the arguing to stop." Remember to talk about what will happen *instead* of arguing. Again, this is the very essence of Element #3. Catch the first sign of bad communication and nip it in the bud. If someone begins to raise his voice, stop the conversation until everyone can calm down. Refuse to participate in conversations in which people are disrespectful, rude, and inconsiderate, or violate the rules of good communication. Make an advance commitment with each other about this.

## MAIN CHAPTER ATTITUDES

✓ Be accountable to using good relationship tools with all the right attitudes.

✓ All behavior is a form of communication and sometimes should change to be more like that of Jesus.

✓ Be a good listener.

## ATTITUDES IN ACTION

1. **Attitude: Be accountable to using good relationship tools with all the right attitudes.**

   Each partner should take turns finishing the statements below. Follow the Healthy Communication Pyramid closely to practice. Be sure the listener gives feedback as described earlier in the chapter. These statements represent an issue from the Communication Pyramid.

   a. I want to be close to you when . . .

   b. I want to be away from you when . . .

   c. Something I don't like talking to you about is . . .

   d. A time when you didn't seem to hear me was . . .

   e. What I like best about you is . . .

   f. What I dislike most about you is . . .

   g. I think we would enjoy each other more if . . .

2. **Attitude: All behavior is a form of communication and sometimes should change to be more like that of Jesus.**

   Using the materials provided in this chapter, have both marriage partners identify specific communication behaviors that need to be improved. Add these to the "goals and objectives" list located in Chapter 12.

3. **Attitude: Be a good listener.**

   Ask your partner to tell you how good you are at listening, inviting suggestions to be a better listener.

   Once you have established some relationship goals as outlined in Chapter 12, discuss the progress with each of them using the Healthy Communication Pyramid.

# 15

# Getting Out of Gridlock: The Basics

*We must all hang together, or most assuredly we shall all hang separately.*

Benjamin Franklin

Shatterproof marriages aren't immune to power struggles; the spouses just know how to dissolve them before they go very far.

Allowing yourself to get sucked into a power struggle is not much different from hanging yourself. If you stop and think about it, a power struggle happens because you have become stubborn with your position on something. You might be really convinced that bad things will happen if you budge. But I just don't know of too many things that are as bad as the product of a long-standing power struggle. God warns us to be very careful not to develop a stubbornness that refuses to give in, saying this just stores up "wrath" for ourselves on the day of judgment.[1] He is talking about being unwilling to give up our ungodly ways, but that is exactly what we are doing when we allow ourselves to engage in a power struggle with our spouse.

For one thing, when you bring all three Key Elements into your marriage, power struggles are impossible to begin with. Essentially, power struggles result when one or both partners has allowed at least one element to be taken out of the mix. We're human, but you can fix this if it happens. The final property of Element #3, the *spirit* of converting problems into solutions, includes learning how to simplify your understanding of a power struggle so you can dissolve it effectively. You will rise above the situation and look for ways to dissolve the conflict.

Power struggles develop when people are unable to work through personal fear and anger, certain rigid attitudes, or habits. These emotions are like a reckless driver coming down the street. Only these emotions drive right through the middle of your relationship.

I define the term "power struggle" loosely as any marital interaction that is stuck and unresponsive to simple commonsense changes. This would include, then, a variety of root problems ranging from grief and loss to resentments to control problems. At least one person is stuck in the way he is responding to a situation, which gets the other person stuck. If both people are individually stuck, the relationship can look like a train wreck.

We can all be stubborn. However, staying stubborn is usually costly to you. It starts with rigid thinking, resulting in rigid behavior, which ultimately leads to destructive relationship patterns. As we have learned from the Reaction Cycle, changing one small thing about your interaction (or your behavior) can potentially cause a chain of events that unlocks the door to solutions.

In this chapter, we will look at four primary "power points"—ways that couples can and do find themselves stuck. These power points can feel like you are working through a minefield, so learning how to navigate them can make life a whole lot easier. This chapter concludes by reviewing some of the main types of power struggles I see with couples, offering suggestions for unlocking the stalemate.

Certainly, poor relationship skills can prevent people from solving issues, and this can turn into long-term struggles. But if you are using the tools presented so far and are still finding yourself in an undercurrent of tension, something else is going on. Let's review the four power points.

# THE FOUR POWER POINTS

## Power Point 1: Getting Stuck in Anger

If you continue to become angry over the same things, review the Reaction Cycle to see where exactly you are having the problem. Identify reaction habits that need to change and take responsibility for your reactions. The Bible tells us that if we are angry, we should still not "sin." That simply means don't be destructive with it and don't let it blow out of proportion to the rest of life. Is the issue you are so angry about really as big as you have made it? We are also instructed not to let the sun go down on our anger. Resolve it today, at least enough of it to have peace with your partner. Maybe the issue is still there, but you have made peace with your partner.[2]

*Behaving differently seems unacceptable at the time, but continuing to behave within the power struggle is more unacceptable.*

If you just have an anger problem, or a stress problem, see that for what it is and do what you need to about it. Check your heart to see if you are truly being selfless, humble, devoted, and persevering. Look at how the three Key Elements can help you.

Your continued anger will drive your partner deeper and deeper into a position of resistance. You polarize each other, almost leaving your partner with no choice in how he responds to you. If you are honest, you have to admit that you choose behavior in the power struggle to counter that of your partner's. The behavior of both partners is usually destructive and needs to change. Behaving differently seems unacceptable at the time, but continuing to behave within the power struggle is *more* unacceptable. If you don't know what the alternative behavior "should" be, just pick one. When it gets to that point, almost anything is better. Just pick a behavior that is different and positive.

**If you or your partner is bitter, that is the only issue you should be addressing until it is resolved.** Continuing to be angry for a long time just amounts to indulging your self-centered preoccupation with your wants and expectations. If any of us indulges our anger long enough, it turns into bitterness. Bitterness is a huge problem and devours everything in its path. You can't reason with it; revenge is the only thing it wants and it brings all efforts to fix problems to a complete halt. You are wasting your time and energy to try to live up to your partner's bitter expectations. You will never be able to do enough to satisfy his demands. If you try to jump through enough hoops to please your bitter partner, it will eventually swallow you up. You will become a reactionary, feeling and responding like a trapped and wounded animal.

I commend marriage partners who make a valiant effort to satisfy the bitterness of their spouse. But at some point, my recommendation is that they refuse to play the game anymore. If you don't, you are just giving your partner the needed opportunity to keep venting anger and bitterness. It is honestly no different than throwing gasoline on a fire.

Back when I was young, I went camping with some friends of mine. I decided to make myself some lunch while they were all out on the lake boating. Stupid me (I was young, what can I say?), I decided to get the fire going by squirting gasoline on the fire. If you have never done that before, let me tell you that the fire follows the stream of gasoline all the way to the source just like a burning fuse. As I watched the fire gulp up the gasoline all the way to the can in my hands, I realized it was time to drop the can and run! I hid behind the tree, and when the fire reached the can it burned itself out. Don't fuel the bitterness of your partner by acting as if you hope to satisfy his anger. Drop the can.

You quit playing the bitterness game by refusing to engage when your partner starts to indulge his bitterness. Quietly excuse yourself and refuse to interact. I've had people tell me their spouse won't let them disengage. She will follow him through the house and stand in front of the door. This is a serious problem if it happens, and you have to figure it out. First, make sure you are not just trying to escape conflict. If it is truly a case of a bitter spouse, it is imperative you find a way to disengage when he or she is trying to fuel the anger.

**KEY ATTITUDE:**
**Take ownership and**
**responsibility for your**
**own anger.**

I have covered this already, but many people have to hear it over and over. If you are resentful or bitter, take responsibility to do something about it.

The Flanagans were pretty smart about this power point. Mary was finding herself becoming more and more angry, and it was the first few months of their marriage. Both partners were quick to see how dangerous this was and sought help immediately when they were unable to sort things out. They will be the first to tell you that a marriage should not have anger driving day-to-day events.

> If either one of you is bitter, what can the other person honestly do to make things right? Then will you let go of your anger? Discuss this and develop an action plan. If you both do your part and one of you is still angry, take responsibility to stop blaming and look deeper at some internal changes you need to make. Be like the Flanagans—let go of your anger.

If your partner is bitter and it comes out as a fit of rage, it will serve you well to be familiar with the cycle of abuse. The first stage is the tension-building stage. Things are building up. Regardless of your efforts to soothe the person, he becomes more critical, irritable, or distant. This can go on for days.

Then it moves into the abuse stage. This is where the person erupts verbally or physically, or both, directing irrational anger in your direction. If you are on the receiving end of this, it could leave you feeling guilty, hurt, and confused. The triggering event is often relatively trivial.

The third stage is remorse and apologies. With his tension released, he can think more clearly and becomes apologetic. Truly abusive people have become skilled in charming their victims at this stage to counteract the consequence of their behavior. The victim finds herself (or himself) "trained" to accept his apologies, paving the way for the next time. Then the cycle starts over.

Not all people who exhibit abusive behaviors are "abusers" or "batterers." I don't like labels. But it is still a serious problem. I had one husband in therapy because his wife was leaving him. He had a history of temper flare-ups in which he would scream and curse. His blowups clearly met the criteria for abusive behavior. After making a huge issue of it, his wife definitely had him admitting it fit the definition of abusive. Unfortunately, she wanted him to admit he was "an abuser" needing extensive domestic violence counseling. He made the changes needed and she would not accept them.

She was so bitter that for divorce purposes, she wanted others to see him as innately bad and unable to be any different. I found just the opposite. He made several significant changes in how he managed his anger and stress in general. If your partner is exhibiting verbally abusive behaviors, focus on the behaviors themselves. Give him or her a chance to change if he or she admits the problem. At the same time, *do not* continue engaging in interactions that are abusive. Put your partner on notice that you are unwilling to play that game.

## Power Point 2: Habitual Reactions

There are attitude, thought, and reaction patterns that make up a lot of your personality. If you carry any of them to an extreme, they will typically lead to problems in your life. They can lock you into a rigid reaction cycle that often turns into a power struggle with your mate. Whatever rigid attitudes or behaviors exist in your life, be willing to challenge them in the name of growth, character, and marital commitment. The famous love passage from the Bible we covered under Element #2 addresses this. It says that when we were children, we used to speak and think like children.[3] When you get married, it's past time to let go of old attitudes and reactions, using maturity and flexibility.

Common reactions (see Appendix D) tend to create problems if they happen with any regularity. Reviewing these may help you identify specific reactions (internal or external) that need your attention.

It only takes one or two of these to create some big problems for you if carried to any kind of extreme. Russ Flanagan kept things to himself when he was upset (item #6 from Common Reactions, Appendix D). Mary lived her life thinking that approval from others comes from doing things the right way (item #8). She grew up with this outlook. So when young Jack showed even normal growing pains, she reacted strongly. Russ then became quiet, "siding" with Jack in subtle ways, like exchanging winks when Mary was upset. What started dissolving their power struggle over parenting was when they both started looking first at their own tendency to react.

These reactions, when they occur over and over, turn into unspoken "rules" that we seem to have to follow in certain situations. Many of these rules just reflect "how we do things" and determine how you or your spouse responds to a given stress. They become habitual and automatic. They end up being predictable behaviors and interaction patterns that keep you locked into certain responses. They are not easy to change. The most dramatic change a family unit can experience is when they question how they normally do things or reevaluate their values.[4]

Likewise, individuals within marriage develop unspoken rules about their relationship, who they are, and how they do things. You spend much of your life organizing your experiences so they make sense to you. Most of the time we do this well, but none of us does it perfectly. What happens is that we have some life rules working well for us, based on good past experiences.

Then we have at least a few rules that don't work so well. Those develop after having some kind of negative experience. These rules are based partially on myths or faulty memories of what really happened between us and another family member.[5] If you have children of your own you know just how true this is. Your child has perceptions of you that are hard to change, even with lots of talking and changed behavior.

Several years ago I saw a fifty-two-year-old woman who remembered some painful things that happened at the age of five with her mother. She still saw herself—in middle age—as a little girl who should be ashamed to speak up or ever be angry. Fortunately, her mother was still alive, so I suggested she talk to her about these memories, speaking up for herself if necessary. Once she did, she realized she had been living out this myth about herself and was able to change the rule, "It's never okay to speak up for yourself."

Theresa did the same thing in her marriage, only in a different way. She came from a large family, and all of her family members had major personal problems ranging from alcoholism to being in jail. Theresa found herself taking care of everyone and learned to feel good about herself only when she was doing this. Raul, her husband, had his own drug problems. She came to me because she was having trouble breaking the cycle of taking care of him even though it made her angry to do so.

What rules govern the way you live? Most people do not take the time to explore this, and if you have trouble with power struggles, I can guarantee that you have some rules (spoken or unspoken) about life that are not serving you well. You can bet that if either you or your spouse has a destructive rule, it is affecting the other, which then affects the other, and so on. In actuality, much of the work of marriage and family therapists is identifying these rules and helping couples approach problems with a different set of rules. This brings us right into the next power point requiring attention.

♥ *Discuss any of the common reactions you have in certain situations that seem destructive either to you or your partner. Explore how you got this way and how you see it in your marriage. While your partner might be able to help, take responsibility to monitor this reaction and keep it within manageable limits.*

## Power Point 3: Self-Defeating Thoughts

Since we are talking so much about our habits, most of our thoughts are also a matter of habit. Most of them are subconscious or automatic. Noticing pain in your leg while you are reading a book involves quite a bit of subconscious thought.

You are undoubtedly using some rigid thought patterns if you are in a power struggle. It might go something like this, *Here we go again. She's going to nag me until the cows come home. She never leaves me alone and is such a loser when she gets like this.* Now you might not be sitting there actually thinking those thoughts, but if I pressed, you might realize this is exactly what you think. Another example is when your partner just seems to take everything personally. Past conditioning leads him to think in certain ways at certain times. If you say hello to a store clerk, suddenly he is jealous and wishes you wouldn't be so friendly. What are the real thoughts behind that reaction? That is what you have to find out.

The Bible says we should be transformed every day by the renewing of our minds.[6] This cannot happen unless you are examining your thought habits and contrasting them with Christian teaching. Folks, that just doesn't happen naturally and automatically. It must be deliberate on your part. Even putting a Bible verse on your bathroom mirror is a start.

Cognitive-behavioral therapy is a huge branch of the mental health literature. This approach has been around for years, helping people get to the bottom of these thought patterns and how those thoughts lead to certain behaviors. One of the most helpful books on the subject is *Feeling Good* by David Burns. It has influenced the methods of a lot of therapists, including my methods. He teaches a systematic way to journal your thoughts on paper, then play devil's advocate with yourself to replace faulty thoughts with more useful ones.

## KEY ATTITUDE:
**The way you think may not be fully realistic and may need to change in big ways.**

From my experience, there are a handful of thinking tendencies people have that get them into trouble. If any of these describe you, identify the specific thought(s) reinforcing the tendency and replace it with one more based in reality. Faulty thinking simply amounts to exaggerating or stretching the truth about something. It's extreme thinking. Consequently, it is often a partial truth and you should modify it to be a complete truth. This is the "belief" stage of the Reaction Cycle, and the "subjective" part of the Healthy Communication Pyramid from Chapter 14.

## SELF-DEFEATING THOUGHT TYPES

MAGICIAN—This habit makes assumptions about what you know, even without the facts. You think you know what someone else thinks, feels, intends, or is going to do or say next. This often reveals your own insecurity about waiting for the facts and impedes your ability to be a good listener. Nonverbal behaviors of your partner are a breeding ground for this. This could include expecting the worst from a person or situation. An example of this might be this subconscious thought, *Since you would rather go out with your friends tonight, I know you're fooling around on me.*

MELODRAMATIC—You exaggerate the truth about events or experiences by making things much more important than they really are. Sometimes the way you feel emotionally is enough proof for your conclusion and represents an exaggeration of the facts. You interpret negative events in the worst possible light (an outgrowth of a pessimistic personality style) and see them as proof that it will never change. You overreact to triggering events, which is usually based on painful past experiences. You may be tense, driven, or overly serious in certain situations. Keeping things in perspective is difficult. The conclusions you draw are usually without hope and make positive change impossible. The melodramatic style expresses a lot of anxiety in stressful situations, making mountains out of molehills. An example of this might be the subconscious thought, *Since I was disciplined at work today, it means I will never* [an extreme exaggeration] *move up in my profession.*

CYNICAL—This habit sees the negative side of everything, even positive things. Fairness is often a central issue in which you point out the unfairness of a situation. Disappointment or conflict do not produce efforts to fix the problem, but rather this habit uses whining, complaining, skepticism, and even anger. A cynical thinking style quickly fuels the fires of resentment and bitterness. Finding the silver lining in a situation is rare. Responses in a marital relationship tend to be harsh and unforgiving.

One stepmother I was seeing became rather cynical when her nine-year-old stepdaughter had a streak of sneaking things into her room and lying about it. The stepmother went from thinking the girl was a "good girl" to someone who "used to be" a good girl. A cynical thinking style has a rigid outlook that makes positive change difficult. An example of this could be, *It was nice that my husband paid attention to me on my birthday, but he will just go back to his own selfish habits tomorrow.*

EXAGGERATED CONCLUSIONS—When you exaggerate the significance of an event, you make connections that should never be made. You draw conclusions about it that are not very logical. It is an "if, then" statement you make to yourself that should never be made. If I get laid off, then I am a loser and will never get a job again. *If my husband comes home late even after I told him I don't like it, then he just doesn't care about me.* This extreme style of thinking makes connections where they should not be made.

INSECURE—Events are seen as evidence that you are unworthy or maybe even at fault. You take things too personally. You may think you absolutely have to do things a certain way or you are no good. You could be quick to take the blame for what is occurring and have thoughts telling you that pleasing your partner is the only priority. You think you have more influence over other people and situations than you do, equating much of your self-worth with things outside of yourself (like what you own, who you are friends with, how you influence the response of your partner). An example of this subconscious thought is, *He's mad at me, so I must have done something wrong again.*

BOXING IN—This thinking style attributes unchanging qualities to yourself or your partner. Thinking your husband is an "abuser" based on some behaviors keeps him boxed in and unable ever to be anything different. That's just what he is. Your husband thinks you treat his child from another marriage unfairly, so you can't even discipline the child without receiving this accusation. You are put into a box that you can never get out of. You may find this same pattern connected to certain kinds of problems. An example of this might be the thought, *Being honest always ends up in an argument. It doesn't pay to talk openly about problems.* You have just boxed yourself in to the situation and have given yourself no way out.

The Flanagans were stuck in several of these bad thinking styles, but especially the Magician. They were just sure they knew what the other person was thinking at all times. When challenged, they ended up finding that they agreed on far more than they believed. It's poor communication and poor thinking that allows you to assume you know things that you have not openly confirmed.

When a power struggle locks you in, stop and examine what kinds of thoughts you have about the situation. You must replace rigid thinking with more flexible thinking that puts everything into better perspective.

Identify the thought style above that most characterizes you. Discuss the situations that trigger this type of thinking and describe how it then influences your response. The next time you or your partner sees that response, agree to stop and consider whether you have slipped into this destructive habit.

## Power Point 4: Past Conditioning

Every family—and marriage—has no doubt developed some predictable ways it responds to certain situations. Much of this comes from our family when we were kids. Every family has its own way of expressing expectations, emotions, and conflict with its members. These things help determine what role everyone takes at home. Unspoken rules develop, which gives your family its personality. Predictable patterns develop from the unspoken rules discussed earlier. Unless we stop to see what they are, we automatically pass them down to the next generation. Some of them may not be so good.

**𝒦EY 𝒜TTITUDE: Face the truth about how your childhood experiences may affect you now.**

Through the many years of doing marriage and family therapy, I have discovered some questions that help folks get a deeper understanding about past family influences. This can be fun, it can be painful, or both. Reflecting on these questions as a couple can be a tremendously rewarding experience as you share things about yourselves you probably don't know about each other. More importantly, seeing how some past experiences are not so helpful is an eye-opener for many people.

You may be stuck in the middle of a power struggle because doing things another way is unthinkable to you. If so, where in the world did your way of doing things come from? The more you know, the more power you have to be different. For example, it has been found that discussing the influence of your cultural background on how you do things now is useful. This often reveals invaluable information.[7]

One young man came to me for help with problems he was having with his fiancée. He was from South America and his family of twelve came to the United States when he was fourteen because of political pressures. None of them spoke English at the time they immigrated. He had a master's degree in engineering and had managed to become quite successful. His outlook on life—including personal relationships—was very intense and extreme. Everything he did, he did with high expectations and tenacity, not unlike what his whole family had to be like in order to survive in the United States. Understanding this, I directed him to take a closer look at how this impacted his approach to problems with his fiancée. It did not take long for him to see that he could not apply the same intensity with her that he had grown accustomed to in other parts of his life.

Following are some questions to help you explore the influence of your childhood on your marriage. This list is by no means exhaustive and should only help you begin this journey. If you see how any of these are contributing to clashes with your partner, it is helpful just to see that it is not evil intent but something very normal going on between you. You can affirm your appreciation and acceptance of each other, then work together to make some adjustments that will work better. Keep the three Key Elements of a shatterproof marriage in mind as you consider your normal way of doing things. Element #3, the right spirit, paves the way to learn about how your past conditioning may need to change.

Just skim through these and mark a handful that jump out at you. Talk about those with your partner.

## INFLUENCES OF PAST FAMILY QUESTIONNAIRE

1. Are there any ways your marriage is different from previous generations that you do not want to change? How could you make your marriage even more like that?

2. Are there ways your marriage is similar to previous generations that are not helpful? Who needs to do what for this to begin changing? Begin setting specific goals.

3. Who in your extended family knows of your personal or marital problem(s), and how have their views influenced you and/or your marriage?

4. Who sided with whom during disagreements when you were a child, and why? How did that affect the way you think or react?

5. Describe marital responses to crisis so that a stranger would be able to understand your marriage relationship better. Is that a picture you want to keep?

6. Imagine assigning one job title to each marriage partner within the marriage. What would that title be, and how does that fit in with your childhood experiences?

7. What are the five biggest expectations in your marriage? How do they compare to your childhood family, and are they helpful?

8. Is either marriage partner in charge more than the other, and is that always what you both want? How did you decide who is in charge, and how would that have worked in your childhood family?

9. How did members show approval in your family growing up? How do you show approval now to each other in your marriage?

10. What would you say to your partner if you could get across any message you wanted? Write down your answers and agree to listen to each other's answer wholeheartedly. Did people listen to each other when you were growing up?

11. Did issues ever go unresolved in your family growing up? Do you have any now and, if so, how do you need to do things differently to change this pattern?

12. How did members show affection in your family growing up? Has that had a positive or negative influence on your marriage? What should be different in your marriage and what will that require of you to be possible?

13. More than anything else, what did your family seem to value the most growing up (i.e., honesty, achievements, being responsible, etc.)? Is that helping now?

14. Growing up, did anyone in the family feel blamed for things? If so, how did that influence the way you do things now?

15. Was your family very expressive with emotions growing up? How is that the same or different from your partner, and does that contribute in any way to getting stuck sometimes?

16. Were your opinions valued at home while you were growing up? What about now?

17. Did your family allow you to make mistakes as a kid without feeling ashamed? Is that ever an issue in your marriage for either of you?

18. Did everyone in your family apologize when they were wrong as you were growing up? Are apologies part of the way you do things in your marriage?

19. Were problems discussed openly at home as a child, and how do you see that style in your marriage?

20. How have your most pleasant and most unpleasant memories shaped who you are today?

21. Did anyone on your side of the family have any personal problems, like alcohol or drug abuse, arrests, bad temper, depression, anxiety, sexual abuse, and so on, and how did that affect the family—and you?

22. Was everyone in your family growing up loyal to each other? How did they show it?

23. How did your parents discipline you, and how did that help form either personal strengths or weaknesses?

24. What were the big events or circumstances through the years that affected your family the most? How does that influence how you think or behave in your marriage today?

25. What makes your growing-up family unique (such as interracial marriage, large number of children, highly educated parents, etc.), and how can that be evident in the way you go about married life?

26. What were the biggest disappointments in your childhood family— either yours or someone else's in the family? How have those disappointments helped to shape your approach to marriage?

Exploring persistent family patterns can help you understand some important things about your marriage. It's harder to keep doing unhelpful things once you are aware of them. This opens the door to needed change.[8] It also enables you to see how power struggles may be normal responses given the family history. You might come up with new ideas to disrupt the reaction cycle at any or all the stages. Just getting your thoughts started in the right direction often sets in motion a positive chain of events.

The biggest thing the Flanagans discovered about the influence of their childhood families is that Russ's mother was extremely accommodating and Mary's parents were stern and not particularly warm. This predisposed them both to have somewhat opposite relationship styles. Instead of continuing to fight for their respective style, they recognized no style is perfect and learned to appreciate how they complemented each other. They actually *looked* for ways the other person's approach could be helpful. Once they did this, talking about how they were *not* helping was much easier.

> Choose the question above that influences your marriage the most in a negative way. Decide that the pattern stops with you and come up with specific behaviors to do differently when it comes up. Like the Flanagans, take ownership for your reactions instead of blaming your partner.

You should keep asking, *How can this question help me see unspoken rules or patterns that keep my marriage in a power struggle?* Try to identify attitudes or behavior habits that started in your past. If you discover one, trace it back to its beginning to gain the best understanding. In addition to giving you some direction, allow your new understanding to reinforce what you *don't* want to change.[9] This gives you encouragement and helps you focus also on what you are doing right. Then you can do more of it.

**KEY ATTITUDE:**
**Be humble, enduring, devoted, and selfless enough to disengage from a power struggle.**

There are lots of possible factors that might lead to a power struggle or get you back into one after you thought things were going well. If people stay frustrated long enough about something, they are more likely to dig their heels in even deeper.

For example, you or your partner might be experiencing some kind of social pressure, for example, through a problem with a coworker. You come home in a bad mood every day and argue with your partner. Or one of you might have a personal weakness that causes a relationship conflict, like drinking too much. The more conflict it produces in the marriage, the more drinking goes on, and vice versa.[10]

You must get to the root of the issue. Sometimes you have to decide what you most value: the relationship or your behavior. What kind of heart you have determines what you will do at those defining moments. Now that you know about the four chambers of a loving heart, approach *all* power struggles with utmost humility, devotion, endurance, and selflessness. If necessary, give back more than you receive. If you do, and apply a few good techniques, you will be amazed at the result.

A few behaviors tend to keep couples in power struggles more than other behaviors. A partner who dominates the discussion makes change very difficult. Children who create chaos or are disruptive during serious parenting discussions can defeat the process and be very disruptive to the marriage.[11] One discussion worth having with your spouse is to share what behaviors you think are more likely to lead to a power struggle between you.

## Avoid scapegoating your spouse.

One tendency common even to the healthiest of families is scapegoating, which means that all of the problems of the group are blamed on one person.[12] Tension and frustration are what drives scapegoating, which almost

always has roots in unmet expectations. Strong expectations, such as needing intimacy from your spouse
or fear of rejection, are hard to change or challenge.

Unfortunately, as reasonable and logical as our
expectation might seem, we often find a lower
expectation is what works. If three-year-old Tommy
is "a real handful" and you have unresolved issues in
your marriage, it's easy to scapegoat Tommy and neglect a deeper issue. After a few short years of this,
Tommy is like a sponge who takes in all the negative emo-
tion of the family. He even learns to think that is his job! And chances are,
he has developed some behaviors that feed right into this view of him. If
scapegoating is going on in your marriage, realize it is terribly destructive.
Back off! Look for solutions, not blame.

> *Tension
> and frustration
> are what drives
> scapegoating, which
> almost always has
> roots in unmet
> expectations.*

## KEY ATTITUDE:
**Always honestly consider
what changes *you* need to
make in your marriage.**

No one person is ever the cause of
all marital problems. Even serious
acting-out behaviors by one partner
have an interactional, evolutionary
dimension to them. In other words, sometimes the "innocent" partner could
have done something differently along the way, but did not. Dividing up the
exact amount of guilt for each partner is clearly not the point. Accept
mutual responsibility for a problem in your marriage. Sometimes what you
need to change is to *stop* cooperating with bad behavior from your partner.
If he is unreasonable and blames you mercilessly for something, giving in is
not helping.

Scapegoating exists because of extreme emotions, attitudes, and reactions.
This is a character issue—it reflects a heart that has become weak and atrophied. In the midst of a power struggle, getting to the core of what motivates
each partner is vital. Then you can begin dealing with the *real* issue.

Once you identify the major concern for each person, use the other tools shared in earlier chapters to convert these concerns into positive goals. Whatever blocks you, expose it for what it is. Let's close this discussion by reviewing a few of the common situations couples find themselves in. I do not give you complicated strategies for solving these, but instead share a few simple ideas. Remember that with the right attitude and belief system, power struggles can melt away.

## THEMES OF COMMON POWER STRUGGLES

Understanding the theme of your struggle allows you to begin thinking in solution-oriented terms. In addition, I share some simple strategies with each theme to point you in the right direction. If these seem too complicated in your life, it's because they are! If both of you fix the attitudes in your heart, these situations will not be overwhelming.

### Control

Partners with an overconcern for controlling the outcome of a situation cannot tolerate any uncertainty or ambiguity. To be honest, there is often the appearance of arrogance, with an exaggerated sense of your own powers or abilities. If you were able to control a situation completely, your assumption is that everything would be okay. This is unrealistic because life—and your partner—just isn't that way. People sometimes become preoccupied with control when their self-esteem is low. Being the one in power gives them a false sense of their own value or importance.

The best way to find control is to let go of it. Real control is an elusive concept, particularly in human relationships and external circumstances. If you are in a power struggle of control, reexamine your expectations in the situation. Learn to trust that people, and life, have a way of turning out okay with or without your influence.

Sharon, a client of mine, learned all this the hard way. She had married young, at twenty, and had two young children. Her husband decided he did not want to be married anymore after fourteen years of marriage, so he moved out. This understandably threw her into a state of depression. Unfortunately, she would not do one of the main homework assignments I kept giving her, which was to journal what was going through her mind while she felt her depression "brewing." After a daylong brew, she would experience a depression crisis, cutting on her arms and feeling suicidal. This finally resulted in forcing her to go to a hospital emergency room because this condition continued to worsen. She was kept overnight, then deemed okay to send home the next day.

Sharon came into my office the next week (this happened on Friday night) and said she did not want to do the journaling because putting her irrational thoughts down on paper somehow made her lack of control *real*. This time, I insisted she journal if she "truly wanted to be in control of her life." Admitting weakness was the first step for her to regain control. After just a few days of facing her real thoughts, she was able to see what she was doing to herself and immediately began to recover from her depression.

Sharon's expectation (belief) was that she could have no weakness in life. It is beyond this discussion to explain this further, but the theme of her struggle was maintaining absolute control. She lived this way in her marriage, too, always creating the illusion everything was just fine and she was in control. If her husband were to challenge this notion, she would meet his efforts with staunch resistance, and thus a power struggle. This finally led to their divorce.

The lesson? Get more control by giving it up! Sometimes you have to let go of your safety net and see what happens. Even if the result is not good, is it really the end of the world?

## Retaliation

This theme occurs when a marriage partner feels extremely wronged. It is usually associated with feeling powerless to make things better and a general intolerance of the other person. At times, it can border on hatred toward the other person. Someone in a retaliatory mode may struggle with a concern over being made to look foolish and feeling a need to "save face" by retaliating.

If you are in a power struggle centering on retaliation, it is especially important to remember who you are and who you want to be. This is how my wife trained our children to think about situations with their friends, or even in our own family. You have to be "the bigger person" sometimes, or at least be bigger than what a bad situation is. Instead of retaliation, if you think consequences are in order, find socially acceptable ways to give consequences.

For example, if your partner has wronged you, one consequence might be that you want to spend more time away from your partner than normal. It isn't out of a spirit of meanness; it is your way of communicating to your partner that there are consequences for what he did. There are lots of socially acceptable and natural consequences that can replace retaliation.

## Threatened Values

We can find ourselves in the middle of a power struggle that we cannot get away from. A good example is when parents have opposite or opposing parenting philosophies. Something this important tends to be very difficult to work with because we think there is no other way to consider parenting. It violates our conscience to think any other way.

There are actually very few situations in life that are downright destructive if we let up on our position. Notice I did not say compromise our values. We can continue to stand by our values but accept the fact we cannot always live them out fully in a given situation. The fact is, it is impossible to "make" anyone do anything.

If your spouse refuses to parent the way you do, avoid a power struggle by refusing to go to the opposite extreme. Another strategy that can potentially work wonders is to stop resisting it altogether. Do it your partner's way. Impossible, you say? It *is* possible, and if there is "fallout" from doing it his or her way, calmly look at that together and ask your partner how *he* or *she* proposes dealing with it. This strategy completely eliminates the power struggle.

## Fear

The things people fear the most are a loss of personal identity and a sense of well-being or safety. Fear is an extremely powerful motivator. Fascist regimes, like the one built by Adolf Hitler, relied heavily on instilling fear in people. In intimate relationships, I hear people every week talk about how they have "lost themselves" in the relationship. If you do not address fear decisively, a power struggle is likely. If fear is driving a lot of things in your marriage, there are several things you can do about it.

Above everything else, you must reestablish and maintain your autonomy and sense of individuality. Having a personal life outside your marriage and family is a must. This can include simple things like reading books, pursuing a hobby, or having lunch with a friend. You have to know who you are and live a life consistent with it.

Second, learn and exercise how to be assertive in your marriage in healthy ways. Speak up for yourself, verbalize your fears, and expect your partner to participate in helping you feel better. However, be careful to identify any irrational fears that have nothing to do with your partner. There will be times when you have to act as if you are not fearful, even if you are. Don't reinforce your fears with fearful behaviors, thus creating the very situation you fear.

Third, know what kinds of personal boundaries are healthy and require your partner to respect those boundaries. This will serve to provide you with the sense of security that you need. As with all these themes, identify the real problem and set reachable goals to solve it.

## Loneliness

At their core, power struggles with loneliness often have some kind of cold war of isolation, or a series of desperate attempts at more intimacy. Your partner may not be responding as you would like, or you may not be doing a very good job of communicating your need, or both. Persistence is required in marriage and I see too many people give up easily.

As in the case of Sharon above, one of the reasons her depression began to lift was the realization she was not as alone as she thought. Don't let your feelings run away with you and convince you that you are completely alone.

To get out of a loneliness power struggle, get back to being vulnerable with your partner. This is the only healthy way to behave anyway. Accept him for who he is and try to find ways to share life together based on what you *can* do instead of focusing on your disappointments. Be smarter about how you try to discuss the problem by being more creative with your questions. Use the tools in this book to elicit more meaningful conversation.

## Major Wounds

Partners who have been hurt, either repeatedly or deeply one time, can find themselves slipping into "automatic pilot" of self-protection. The harder their mate tries to get close, the harder the injured partner retreats. Trust concerns are usually strong, and the other partner has to keep proving himself. This can set in motion an escalating set of back-and-forth responses. The wounded partner insists on reassurance and proof, the other partner tries until he gets frustrated, the hurt one gets more upset, and so on.

Couples who are in a power struggle of hurt need to communicate clearly and calmly about the trust issues going on. It is critical that you create a nurturing environment of reassurance, with some clear commitments to the kind of changes needed to prevent what hurt the person to begin with.

## Projection

The final power struggle we will discuss is when one or both partners project on to each other frustration or unhappiness that has nothing to do with that person. There are a lot of things that can cause this, such as a mood disorder, lack of personal inner peace, a physical problem that produces pain or stress, to name a few. This kind of power struggle is highly confusing since the cause is something unrelated.

By far, the first and most important thing for couples to do in this kind of vicious cycle is to acknowledge that projection is even going on. One of you (if not both) is reacting much too strongly and inappropriately to whatever the issue is at hand. Then you should redirect the frustration where it truly belongs. To illustrate, a couple came in because of constant bickering. She complained that he was unkind and rude to her on a regular basis. After exploring this over a few sessions, it finally became clear that he had become very disappointed that the family did not allow him to take night classes. This made him unhappy and irritable in ways he did not even realize, and he was projecting this mood on to his wife. Once he realized what he was doing, he redirected some attention to resolving this within his own mind. And of course, you know the rest of the story. No more unkind words and no more arguing. This situation had been festering for a couple of years, and disengaging from the ensuing power struggle was literally that quick and easy.

There are numerous power struggle themes common to many couples. Within any of these, there will be specific recurring topic areas. This would be whatever it is that you are actually struggling with each other about. The number of possible topic areas are as numerous as there are people. However, there are often just one or two main things that continue to come up over and over. You can fill in the blank here, but a small sampling of them follow. Identifying your theme can help you pinpoint the problem and begin the goal-setting process.

- ✓ Achievement
- ✓ Being good enough
- ✓ Be responsible
- ✓ Fairness
- ✓ Making others happy

- ✓ It's every man for himself
- ✓ Be smart
- ✓ Do whatever you want
- ✓ Don't feel (emotions)
- ✓ Grow up and behave

♥ Explore with your partner what kind of power struggle you are in or would be most prone to. Promise each other you will not be so inflexible that you will keep the other person locked in a power struggle. Swallow your pride here if you must.

You may be thinking that these themes only become the focus of attention in a power struggle. In actuality, whatever you value, whatever is important to you, these are the things that get "played out" in your life. It can be so subtle you don't notice. But I guarantee that when you were growing up, if push came to shove, your family had some kind of theme that characterized it and made it unique from every other family. It might not have been something negative at all. But as we have continued to say, anything carried to an extreme becomes a problem.

Tom illustrates this point perfectly. He was a divorced man in his thirties, reasonably successful in his job, and was at the tail end of recovering from his divorce when I met him. He complained of a low-grade depression (called dysthymia) that he thought he had had since his teen years. His complaints focused on layoff rumors at work and having been physically sick for several weeks. As he put it, he had been "chewing bad mental cud" the last several weeks. Tom was unable to be more specific than that about his problem. What was clear is that he was heading into a major depression.

In the second session he reported his depression had improved. Instead, he was getting very anxious, describing a constant feeling of "fight or flight." He felt like running, but also felt compelled to fight through his feelings. As we kept exploring his family history and the origins of some of his beliefs and troubling emotions, Tom deteriorated instead of getting better. To make a long story short, Tom had to go to an inpatient therapy program because he quickly reached the point of not being able to cope with daily life.

Before his admission, Tom was exploring his feelings about what it was like growing up. He said his parents had few expectations of him, but then, it was almost impossible for him to know whether they approved of him. He described his mother as someone preoccupied with feeling secure psychologically. There was an undercurrent of fear, coupled with an overall uncertainty about meeting the approval of his parents, as Tom grew up. He coped with this by being a highly accomplished swimmer, and got a scholarship to a prestigious small college.

After his discharge from the hospital, Tom said he became completely overwhelmed because emotions were never shown at home as a kid, and he never learned how to be in touch with his own feelings. When we began to explore them, he felt overwhelmed again. Unfortunately, this all happened after his marriage had already fallen apart. Otherwise, who knows what might have been possible? If he had pursued Element #3 in his life before the marriage ended, he would have learned what he needed to about the power struggles they had, and the rest would have been up to his wife. Would she have stepped up and provided the personal character, unconditional love, and spirit for finding solutions needed? We'll never know now. But for Tom, his motto became, "It's better late than never." He determined to live the rest of his life bringing all three elements of a shatterproof marriage into any new relationship.

If you find yourself in a power struggle, don't make the same mistake Tom made. Face your feelings with courage. Remember this is an important defining moment. It's a test of your character. It forces you to consider whether you love unconditionally, and whether you are living true to your professed belief in God. And finally, it challenges you to take an honest look at the spirit you have about you in your marriage. Set aside your upset or your agenda enough to transform problems into solutions. Don't put it off. Every day you hold back is costing you.

Act now.

## Main Chapter Attitudes

✓ Take ownership and responsibility for your own anger.
✓ The way you think may not be fully realistic and may need to change in big ways.
✓ Face the truth about how your childhood experiences may affect you now.
✓ Be humble, enduring, devoted, and selfless enough to disengage from a power struggle.
✓ Always honestly consider what changes *you* need to make in your marriage.

## ATTITUDES IN ACTION

1. **Attitude: Take ownership and responsibility for your own anger.**

   Openly share any sources of anger that have been building for a long time. What prevents them from being resolved?

2. **Attitude: The way you think may not be fully realistic and may need to change in big ways.**

   Determine whether either of you tends to get stuck with your approach to things. Come up with practical strategies to challenge your thinking when it is needed the most.

3. **Attitude: Face the truth about how your childhood experiences may affect you.**

   Spend some time talking about your childhood family using the questions provided in this chapter. Explore if, and how, this contributes to your tendency to be stubborn with certain issues.

4. **Attitude: Be humble, enduring, devoted, and selfless enough to disengage from a power struggle.**

   As a couple, identify which power point needs the most attention in your relationship. Outline the sequence of behaviors (who does what and when) that result in a power struggle. Be specific and write down these behaviors so you can begin to see the cycle visually.

5. **Attitude: Always honestly consider what changes *you* need to make in your marriage.**

   Identify one or two themes that you do—or could—find yourselves in a power struggle over. What change(s) would be necessary for this to get resolved instead of becoming a power struggle? Most importantly, what can *you* do differently that will make a positive contribution to the situation?

# 16

# Summary and Conclusion

*Disappointment to a noble soul is
what cold water is to burning metal; it strengthens,
tempers, intensifies, but never destroys it.*

Eliza Tabor

This book has been about disappointment and victory. Victory *anyway*. Victory before, during, and after whatever life can throw at you. What you do with disappointment says a ton about who you are and is "the" question to answer if you want a shatterproof marriage.

We were able to follow the progress of a real couple who showed how the ideas in this book really work. They were not particularly spiritually minded people, but instinctively understood what kind of attitude they needed to work through marital problems. The Flanagan power struggle quickly evolved into one of control and threatened values over parenting. Specifically, the recurring conflict was about Jack needing to grow up and behave, and also be responsible.

A power struggle is about the worst condition your marriage can get in, short of a huge and sudden crisis. Many situations are unfortunately not as "clean" and straightforward as illustrated in these pages. You may already be wondering what to do if your power struggle involves more than one theme, for example. I have found myself in more than one counseling situation in which I stayed confused about what was going on for several sessions.

Russ and Mary Flanagan understood that each time a parenting situation came up at home represented a defining moment. They looked at their own hearts and brought strength of character to the table. Their basic beliefs about themselves and life itself laid the groundwork for solutions. The ultimate humility of their hearts was perhaps the biggest strength each of them had. They were willing to lay down their swords, so to speak, and honestly consider other ways to think and behave. Had either one of them lacked humility, their story would most likely have ended very differently.

The Flanagans were quick to take the practical relationship tools at their disposal and apply them. They considered the stresses in their life, such as a new marriage, a new stepfamily, and buying a new home in the country. They talked openly with each other about these stresses, managing them as needed. They explored ways they communicated well and ways that were not so helpful. They made personal changes as they learned to talk about their concerns differently. Both realized the need to get off the negative and focus on making things different in the future. With help, they learned to talk to each other about how to convert complaints into workable goals. The hope and encouragement this provided just gave them more energy to work hard in a positive direction. Finally, the Flanagans showed us all that power struggles are more about heart and less about knowing exactly how to solve everything. Marriage is not an exact science—one size does not fit all. There are clearly some skills and behaviors that work. But larger principles of character are what drive them. And your beliefs drive your character.

Yet here's the most interesting part: the Flanagans did not really have any kind of relationship with God. They made great strides with right attitudes combined with right skills. But they are still potentially vulnerable to situations that try their character to the limit. I don't know if they are "exceptional people" or not. Their ultimate moment of truth may not yet have come.

There are a lot of other factors that might make it seem impossible for your marriage to work, despite all the good advice and tools. Sometimes your partner just won't cooperate or be reasonable. Some partners are happy for years until one day, their mate seems to change who he is and become someone else. It happens. Other partners grow older and more mature, then realize the choice they made in a life partner was one they regret. Life can stretch your character to the limit—and beyond—getting a stranglehold on you and making you into someone even you don't like. Just as we all have different pain tolerances, we have different "relationship tolerances." What's yours? If you are at this point, seek professional help. Don't wait until it is too late. And by all means, don't look to your therapist for "the" miracle.

Although I wrote this book with a strong Christian perspective, it has not been my intention to preach pat answers to you. My hope is that at times you felt inspired, at times you felt a conviction to make a personal change, and at times you saw ideas that really made a difference to your approach at home. As nice as it would be, I can't answer every question for you. But I do know that having attitudes like those of Jesus are what carry people through incredibly trying—even heroic—situations. He told us that the world will know we follow Him by the way we love each other.[1] If you are married, that is the first place people should be able to look.

To meet the challenge of all your defining moments and to be an exceptional survivor of life's challenges, you have to be willing to dig deep. Then when you have dug as deeply as you can go, *let go* and give the rest to God. Your partner may not be a willing participant in this journey. Remember: you can't control someone else. You will have enough challenge holding yourself accountable to the ideas in this book. I do. Guard your heart with all diligence. Don't let your partner—or anyone else—rob you of that. That is something you *can* control, and the payoff will be worth it.

If you do not really believe in God, you can still live in a way that will strengthen your marriage by pursuing the three Key Elements in this book. But you're really missing out on the blessings and power Jesus gives. If you do believe in God, asking yourself what Jesus would do—and doing everything necessary to learn what that is—will provide an unfailing compass as you navigate the waters of marriage. The New Testament of the Bible shows us all what the three elements for a shatterproof marriage should look like. This will spill into every other part of your life as well.

Here is a summary of the main attitudes presented in this book. Pursuing these attitudes will help you develop the properties of the core elements. They reflect all walks of life, as we have seen, but all are rooted in the attitudes of Jesus. You might be thinking it's a lot to live up to, and besides, it will be impossible, so why try? Remember that the love passage found in I Corinthians 13 summarizes them. Learn what it really means to have love that is selfless, humble, devoted, and enduring. The following attitudes simply reflect these four main character traits. Then you will find that all these other attitudes are just a natural part of loving the way Jesus has loved us. Put your trust in God and make His nature your goal. Even doing this imperfectly will result in a marriage that nothing can destroy. Practice putting these attitudes into action, going back to exercises throughout this book as often as needed. Use them over and over. Pay attention every day to whether you have these attitudes or not. Don't be like a fad dieter. Choose to make it a lifestyle change starting today. Expect failures. These attitudes will carry you through all of them.

## SUMMARY OF ATTITUDES
## SUPPORTING THE THREE ELEMENTS

1. See opportunity in adversity and expect positive things.

2. All things are possible.

3. Be willing to face the pain.

4. It's important to look at yourself honestly.

5. Giving to others is more important than serving yourself.

6. Be aware and in control of your emotions.

7. Do the helpful thing even if you don't feel like it.

8. Do whatever it takes to address issues, challenging yourself to behave differently if needed.

9. Admit your weaknesses as a matter of habit. Choose to make this your value!

10. Value the things that will last beyond your lifetime.

11. Work on personality growth whenever and wherever needed.

12. Invest the effort to learn from past experiences.

13. Be open to changing your expectations.

14. Develop a clear sense of your obligations to your marriage and live up to them.

15. Be honest about how real your belief in God is.

16. Give up any sense of entitlement that is selfish.

17. Be willing to admit what your behavior is really saying.

18. Be open to changing your values.

19. Base happiness on the things that are lasting.

20. Base your marriage commitment on things that last.

21. Love unconditionally.

22. Desire to examine the condition of your heart regularly.

23. Have a "work ethic" to strengthen your character.

24. Always look for ways to live your life—and marriage—with true character.

25. Choose to love selflessly.

26. Know the difference between wants and true needs.

27. Choose today to be selfless the way Jesus was.

28. Commit to a lifelong process of becoming a selfless person.

29. Be humble enough to accept your partner for who he or she is.

30. Always keep your ego in check.

31. Always be ready to admit wrongdoing and apologize.

32. Have the humility of Jesus in all situations.

33. Be devoted to being a good marriage partner.

34. Be devoted to complete openness and truthfulness.

35. Learn how God thinks and desire to think that way.

36. Be devoted to doing things God's way.

37. Want to do what's right in God's eyes.

38. Desire to learn what makes you want to give up in order to make changes.

39. Be enduring in your love for others, giving the benefit of the doubt.

40. Do what it takes to build your faith in God.

41. Have a "work ethic" to strengthen your endurance.

42. Be proactive under stress instead of reactive.

43. Always manage your daily routine to minimize stress.

44. Know your deeper needs and be open about them.

45. A meaningful connection with your partner is worth consistent effort.

46. Live in the present.

47. Always be goal-oriented.

48. Examine the condition of your heart regularly.

49. Admit and acknowledge the problems in your marriage, and work on them.

50. Change always starts one minute, one thought, or one behavior at a time.

51. Desire solutions in which you both win instead of complaining or finger-pointing.

52. Count your marital blessings and be an encourager to your partner.

53. It's important to understand how your partner experiences things.

54. Be goal-oriented and devoted to communication growth, enduring failures.

55. Practice leads to growth.

56. Be accountable for behaving with respect and common courtesy at all times.

57. Develop a heart that wants to be a good communicator.

58. Be accountable to using good relationship tools with all the right attitudes.

59. All behavior is a form of communication and sometimes should change to be more like that of Jesus.

60. Be a good listener.

61. Take ownership and responsibility for your own anger.

62. The way you think may not be fully realistic and may need to change in big ways.

63. Face the truth about how your childhood experiences may affect you now.

64. Be humble, enduring, devoted, and selfless enough to disengage from a power struggle.

65. Always honestly consider what changes *you* need to make in your marriage.

66. Take ownership and responsibility for your own reactions.

If all I have done is give you a template to start with, God working in your heart will do the rest. The template shows you what really needs to happen and points the way. The tools and "attitudes in action" have helped many people. I recommend you use this book as a reference to keep coming back to the suggestions. But ultimately, *how* and *whether* you get there is up to you. I sincerely pray that God will work in you through this material and bless you with a shatterproof marriage.

In marriage, as in life, to have a loving heart of character is to be prepared for anything. Don't take this book—or any other book, for that matter—and think it's going to be the answer to all your problems. In our society of self-help books and programs showing you how to walk on hot coals, it's easy to become confused, overwhelmed, and feel incapable of rising to the challenge. In the 2005 movie *Batman Begins,* there is a line that resonates for each and every one of us: "It's not who you are deep down, but what you do that defines you." I would change that line a bit, however. I think it should have been, "It's who you are deep down—and what you are made of—that guides what you do, and *this* is what defines you." This book has really—simply—been about appetites. Whatever you practice thinking about, that is what you develop an appetite for.

Right before finishing this book, I visited with a sixteen-year-old boy in my office who was yelling at his mother a lot, which was out of character for him. After talking for a while, it was clear that he had become anxious and felt pressured in school. Small in stature, he worked hard on his soccer skills and was about to move up to the varsity team. But he kept comparing himself to bigger kids, more popular players. He began to realize he had taken his eyes off his relationship with God and was losing his sense of self-confidence. My advice was to read one encouraging quote, ideally a Bible verse, every day, and concentrate on remembering it all day long. In other words, feed his appetite for God's presence and starve his appetite for status. They work hand in hand and both are necessary. You have to starve the ferocious dog, but also be feeding the good-tempered one if you want the good one to dominate. Just doing one of these won't work. My sixteen-year-old client, by the way, reported in just one week a significant change for the better.

Each and every day from here on out is full of defining moments. They exist for you and me both. I know what I'm trying to do in my marriage. What are you going to do in yours?

# APPENDIX A

## $\mathcal{C}$ondensed Life Principles Inventory

Rate yourself and your partner using the scale below, with 1 being "not at all like me or my partner" and 10 being "very much like me or my partner." Then consider how these impact your marriage, good or bad. Include in the Working Problems List (page 240) as needed.

**Not at all like me/partner**         **Very much like me/partner**

| 1 | 2 | 3 | 4 | 5 | 6 | 7 | 8 | 9 | 10 |

Me | Partner

\_\_\_\_\_ | \_\_\_\_\_ 1. **As if**—I am willing to do what is best or most productive even when I don't feel like it. I act "as if" I want to do this, especially in tough situations.

\_\_\_\_\_ | \_\_\_\_\_ 2. **Positives**—My tendency is to focus on positives and solutions even in tough situations. I make the best of these situations and see opportunity in problems to set new goals.

\_\_\_\_\_ | \_\_\_\_\_ 3. **Present**—I do not dwell in the past or get preoccupied with future plans at the expense of living in the present. I am satisfied with what I have and this enables me to forgive.

_____ | _____     4. **Humility**—Concerns, opinions, and desires of others are at least as important as my own. I am a gracious loser, can give in and let others influence me, accept criticism, and am honest with myself and others.

_____ | _____     5. **Growth**—I am willing to consider other views and ways of doing things. I am willing to face uncomfortable feelings. I am not simply a creature of habit but am growing as a person, willing to change, and others find me approachable.

_____ | _____     6. **Giving**—Others see me as generous with my things and also my time. I am willing to be inconvenienced and sacrifice for others.

_____ | _____     7. **Tolerant**—I have learned to be patient and manage my own irritability. I accept my partner for who he/she is.

_____ | _____     8. **Courteous**—I am basically polite and considerate of my spouse, using common courtesies that I would typically use with strangers.

_____ | _____     9. **Listening**—I do not interrupt too much, convincing others I want to know what it is that concerns them.

_____ | _____     10. **Attentive**—I pay attention to those things my partner wants from me and follow through with requests made of me.

You can do the math here. The best (and impossible) score is 100.

# Appendix B

## Marriage Evaluation Questionnaire

1. What was the main thing(s) your partner provided to you early in your relationship? Is that still what you want?

2. How has the marriage disappointed you the most—what need has not been met?

3. What behaviors by your partner would eliminate that disappointment?

4. Are you willing and able to control your behaviors enough (i.e., communication ground rules) to work on solutions?

5. What do you do to contribute to a negative cycle of interaction with your partner? Are you willing and able to change those behaviors long enough to work on solutions?

6. What are the "bottom-line" requirements for you in the marriage? These should be behaviors you want to see from your partner.

7. Do you communicate what you'd like from your partner clearly, slowly, and in a way that asks for a specific response? Would your partner agree with your answer?

8. Define what "for better or for worse" in your marriage vows means to you, and where you "draw the line" in how far you go with those vows.

9. On a 1 to 10 scale, rate the importance of romantic love to you in marriage (versus other types of love and other reasons to be committed), if 10 means it's the top priority and 1 means it's unimportant.

10. Rate your commitment level to the marriage on a 1 to 10 scale, with 10 meaning absolute commitment. What do you base your commitment on?

11. Do you accept your partner, including faults, and forgive him/her for past disappointments?

12. Do you need to be a better marriage partner and, if so, what specifically do you need to *do* differently?

13. What are the personal strengths of you and your partner, and how can you begin building solutions around those strengths?

14. What *does* work well between you, and how can you bring more of this into your lives together?

15. Are you humble enough not to insist on your own way (unless it is a bottom line from #6) and think first about how you can please your partner with your issues?

# APPENDIX C

Complete this privately before discussing it. Answer "yes" if it applies to the way you think you communicate *much of the time*, or answer "no" if it doesn't apply *most of the time*. An attitude of openness and humility will go a long way with this exercise.

## Communication Self-Evaluation

| Yes | No | |
|-----|-----|-----|
| _____ | _____ | 1. Do you have difficulty listening closely when the topic doesn't interest you? |
| _____ | _____ | 2. When the subject of discussion might lead to a need for you to change in some way, do you tend to either get defensive or withdraw? |
| _____ | _____ | 3. Do you approach conflict as though someone has to be a winner and someone has to be a loser? |
| _____ | _____ | 4. When you detect unpleasant body language or voice tones, do you react in ways that are not helpful? |
| _____ | _____ | 5. When you hear certain words or topics you don't like, do you react in unhelpful ways? |

_____ | _____    6. Do you tend to be opinionated or have your mind made up before discussing certain things?

_____ | _____    7. Do you anticipate in advance what someone is going to say about certain topics?

_____ | _____    8. Do you find yourself using the word "you" a lot when you are upset with someone?

_____ | _____    9. Do you ask leading questions that control what the answer will be?

_____ | _____    10. When someone has expressed his/her position on an issue, do you look for "holes in the argument" to disqualify the position?

_____ | _____    11. When you have a disagreement do you ask "why" questions, such as why he/she did or felt something?

_____ | _____    12. Do you interrupt when you have a disagreement?

_____ | _____    13. When problems arise, do you complain about all the problems from the past?

_____ | _____    14. In presenting opinions, do you offer lengthy explanations before making sure you're being understood?

_____ | _____    15. Do you tell others you know what they _meant_, even if they didn't actually say it?

_____ | _____    16. Do you tell others you know what they are thinking or feeling, even if they haven't said so?

_____ | _____    17. Do you expect others to just "know" what you want, feel, or think?

_____ | _____    18. Do you have trouble either knowing what the issue is or staying on one issue during disagreements?

_____ | _____ 19. When explaining yourself in a disagreement, do you do more blaming than actually explaining why it is so important to you?

_____ | _____ 20. Is it hard for you to know the difference between your thoughts and feelings?

_____ | _____ 21. When upset, do you blame the other person for how you are feeling?

_____ | _____ 22. Do you have trouble knowing your true feelings?

_____ | _____ 23. When making your point are most of your comments complaints?

_____ | _____ 24. Do other people accuse you of not listening well?

_____ | _____ 25. When things bother you, do you keep it to yourself or let them build up?

_____ | _____ 26. Is discussing daily events, interests, thoughts, or feelings uncomfortable for you?

_____ | _____ 27. Do others tell you that your tone of voice tends to be negative?

_____ | _____ 28. Is it hard for you to be warm and affectionate?

_____ | _____ 29. Do you tend to say things better left unsaid?

_____ | _____ 30. Do your moods get the better of you?

_____ | _____ 31. Do you become irritable because of how you manage stress?

_____ | _____ 32. When it feels as if you're not getting your needs met, does your frustration take over in negative ways?

_____ | _____ 33. Do you tend to interrupt others when they are talking?

_____ | _____    34. Are there certain topics you find almost impossible to
                      discuss because of how you feel?

_____ | _____    35. Do you avoid disagreeing with someone because of
                      what might happen?

_____ | _____    36. Do you try to just "control" your feelings of anger
                      because a problem just won't go away?

_____ | _____    37. Do you have trouble admitting it when you have been
                      wrong, and apologizing?

_____ | _____    38. Do you tend to use terminal language (absolute terms
                      like "always" or "never") when upset?

_____ | _____    39. Do you respond to a complaint by making one of
                      your own?

_____ | _____    40. Are you quick-tempered?

Once completed, commit to working on all "yes" answers regardless of how others are treating you. Also place a check mark next to the top three items in which you would like your marriage partner to improve. Talk to each other about them.

# APPENDIX D

## Common Reactions

> **KEY ATTITUDE:**
> **Take ownership and responsibility for your own reactions.**

Use these items to help you identify reactions that are typical of you. They will give you direction for areas you need to work on personally.

Following are some common reactions I have encountered in my more than two decades of doing therapy. If you think or react this way *most* of the time, put a check mark next to the item. Any of these you do frequently is likely to cause problems in your life. Talk to your partner about your answers and set some goals for improvement.

1. When disagreements come up, people usually end up getting hostile.

2. Don't do anything to embarrass the family.

3. Success equals how good you are at doing things.

4. When you mess up, you're on your own.

5. Mistakes are not to be tolerated.

6. When upset, I usually don't say much.

7. Yelling is how I handle frustration or anger.

8. Approval from others only comes from doing or performing right.

9. I don't deserve affection or attention.

10. I deserve to be punished most of the time or receive little from others.

11. Punishment always follows imperfect performance.

12. Receiving approval is impossible to predict.

13. There is always something close by that threatens safety.

14. No one would want me, I'm inferior.

15. Others belong but I'm different and always will be.

16. My looks contribute to my not belonging.

17. There is no excuse when I mess up.

18. My opinions don't count.

19. I am a failure.

20. I should be ashamed for who I am.

21. Living right should produce an easy life.

22. Why try, life can never change or be better.

23. No one is ever to be trusted or counted on.

24. Having or showing feelings, especially certain ones, is unacceptable.

25. I must never look foolish—ever.

26. My thoughts and feelings prove whether something is real or true.

27. Conflict must be avoided.

28. Good things in life never last.

29. Being irresponsible is never acceptable.

30. Always being responsible is unacceptable.

31. Being productive at all times is essential.

32. Rarely being productive is just fine.

33. The very existence of injustice cannot be tolerated.

34. Being honest with others usually results in being rejected.

35. I must always control my situation completely.

36. Problems in my life must all be my fault.

37. Problems in my life are practically never my fault.

38. I have to find ways to prove I am an acceptable person.

39. I can do what I want, when I want.

40. I am not allowed to please myself, only others.

41. Nothing I do is really good enough.

42. I am totally alone.

43. I do not need anyone.

44. It is not worth risking being rejected.

45. Love comes from measuring up to some standard.

46. I must never be alone.

47. I must never let people see the real me.

48. Some long-standing resentments are okay.

49. Sometimes people need to get even.

50. I will change only when someone else does.

51. Doing something is only right if it feels comfortable.

52. Others should just know what I need.

53. I am responsible for the happiness/feelings of others.

54. I am never responsible for how I may affect someone else.

55. Others are responsible for my happiness or reactions.

56. Forgiveness by, or to, others must be completely deserved.

57. Submitting to or being influenced by others is a sign of weakness.

58. There must be no uncertainties in life.

59. What "the group" thinks determines what is okay.

60. The sincerity of others should constantly be tested to see if it's real.

61. Showing weakness is unacceptable.

62. It's impossible to be my own person if I ever depend on others.

63. I must always be needed by someone.

64. Others have been the cause of me not reaching my goals.

65. Joking about problems is unacceptable.

66. Talking about problems is stupid.

67. Always being close to someone is really important but probably not likely to happen.

68. I must look self-confident no matter what.

69. I have to be perfect and prove my superiority.

70. If someone messes with me they are going to get it right back.

# NOTES

Bible references are taken from the New American Standard version.

## INTRODUCTION

[1] Harris Interactive (February 26, 2003). *The religious and other beliefs of Americans 2003*. Retrieved November 3, 2007 from http://www.harrisinteractive.com/harris_poll/index.asp?PID=359.

[2] Adherents.com (last modified August 7, 2007). *Major religions of the world ranked by number of adherents*. Retrieved http://www.adherents.com/Religions_By_Adherents.html.

## CHAPTER 1

[1] Hanline, M. F. & S. E. Daley (1992). "Working with the strengths of black families." *Child Welfare*, 61(8): 536–544.

[2] James 1:17

[3] Seigel, Bernie S. (1998). *Love, Medicine and Miracles*, 29. New York: HarperCollins.

[4] Ibid., page needed?

[5] Wolin, S. J. & S. Wolin (1994). *The Resilient Self: How Survivors of Troubled Families Rise Above Adversity*, 67–203. New York: Villard Books.

[6] Romans 2:14–15

[7] Daley, Jason (2004). "Out of the void: Coombs vs. the avalanche." *Outside Magazine*, September 2004. Retrieved March 24, 2006 from Outside Online, http://outside.away.com/outside/features/200409/top_survival_stories_1.html.

[8] Numbers 14:11

[9] Mark 9:17–23

## CHAPTER 2

[1] Matthew 6:21

[2] Proverbs 23:7

[3] Burns, David D. (1980). *Feeling Good: The New Mood Therapy*, 10–12. New York: Signet.

[4] Matthew 22:36–40

[5] Romans 7:4

[6] Taylor, Humphrey (2003). *The religious and other beliefs of Americans 2003*. In Harris Interactive, Harris Poll #11, February 26, 2003. Retrieved March 13, 2006 from http://www.harrisinteractive.com/harris_poll/Index.asp?PID=359.

[7] I Corinthians 13

[8] Romans 8:1ff.

[9] Proverbs 10:18

[10] Philippians 2:3

[11] Romans 6:16

[12] Stuart, R. B. (1980). *Helping Couples Change*, 52, 193. New York: Guilford Press.

[13] James 1:22

[14] Romans 7:13ff.

[15] James 1:13–15

[16] James 1:2–4

## CHAPTER 3

[1] Romans 4:12

[2] Romans 3:23

[3] I Timothy 1:15

[4] Matthew 7:5

[5] Matthew 7:24ff.

[6] McGoldrick, Monica & Randy Gerson (1985). *Genograms in Family Assessment*, 88–91. New York: W. W. Norton.

[7] Ibid., 90.

[8] Ibid., 90–91.

[9] Ibid., 7.

[10] Wolin, S. J. & S. Wolin, (1994). *The Resilient Self: How Survivors of Troubled Families Rise Above Adversity*, 87. New York: Villard Books.

[11] Proverbs 4:7–8

[12] Siebert, Al (1996). *The Survivor Personality*, 22. New York: Berkley.

[13] Frankl, V. E. (1962). *Man's Search for Meaning*, 14–15. New York: Simon & Schuster.

[14] Wolin, S. J. & S. Wolin, (1994). *The Resilient Self*, 109.

[15] Frankl, V. E. (1962). *Man's Search for Meaning*, 27.

[16] Wolin, S. J. & S. Wolin, (1994). *The Resilient Self*, 134.

[17] Proverbs 27:17

[18] Galatians 6:2

[19] Siebert, Al (1996). *The Survivor Personality*, 43. New York: Berkley.

[20] Luke 6:38

[21] Siebert, Al (1996). *The Survivor Personality*, 50ff.

[22] Ibid., 190–192.

[23] Phillippians 4:11

[24] Lankton, S. R. & C. H. Lankton (1983). *The Answer Within: A Clinical Framework of Ericksonian Hypnotherapy*, 291–311. New York: Brunner/Mazel.

[25] Siebert, Al (1996). *The Survivor Personality*, 57.

[26] Wolin, S. J. & S. Wolin (1994). *The Resilient Self*, 136.

[27] Siebert, Al (1996). *The Survivor Personality*, 91.

[28] Ibid., 229.

[29] Ibid., 245.

[30] Matthew 6:25–34

[31] Wolin, S. J. & S. Wolin (1994). *The Resilient Self*, 184.

[32] Proverbs 27:6

[33] Psalm 141:5

[34] Romans 8:39

[35] I Corinthians 13:8

[36] Frankl, V. E. (1962). *Man's Search for Meaning*, 66.

## CHAPTER 4

[1] Stuart, R. B. (1980). *Helping Couples Change*, 44. New York: Guilford Press.

[2] Ibid., 45.

[3] Brenner, David (1999). "Marriage loses in 'divorce culture.'" *New York Times* archive, July 16, 1999. Retrieved on March 5, 2006 from http://query.nytimes.com/gst/fullpage.html?res=9C01E2DE153FF 935A25754C0A96F958260.

[4] Martin, Paige D., Gerald Specter, Don Martin, & Maggie Martin. "Expressed attitudes of adolescents toward marriage and family life." *Adolescence*, 2003 Summer; 38(150):359–67. Retrieved March 24, 2006 from http://www.ncbi.nlm.nih.gov/entrez/query.fcgi?cmd=Retrieve&dlb=PubMed& list_uids=14560887&dopt=Abstract.

[5] Furstenberg, F. F. (1996). "The future of marriage." *American Demographics*, 18:34–37, 39–40.

[6] I Corinthians 6:18

[7] Martin, Paige D., Gerald Specter, Don Martin & Maggie Martin. "Expressed attitudes of adolescents toward marriage and family life," Summer; 38(150): 359–67.

[8] Sutton, CharlesEtta T. & Mary Anne Broken Nose (1996). "American Indian families: An overview." In M. McGoldrick, J. Giordano, J. K. Pierce (Eds.), *Ethnicity and Family Therapy*, 37–38. New York: Guilford Press.

[9] Black, Lascelles & Vanessa Jackson (1996). "Families of African origin: An overview." In M. McGoldrick, J. Giordano & J. K. Pierce (Eds.), *Ethnicity and Family Therapy*, 61. New York: Guilford Press.

[10] McAdams-Mahmoud, Vanessa (1996). "African American Muslim families." In M. McGoldrick, J. Giordano & J. K. Pierce (Eds.), *Ethnicity and Family Therapy*, 113–126. New York: Guilford Press.

[11] Shibusana, Tazuko (1996). "Japanese families." In M. McGoldrick, J. Giordano & J. K. Pierce (Eds.), *Ethnicity and Family Therapy*, 273–274. New York: Guilford Press.

[12] Abudabbeh, Nuha (1996). "Arab families." In M. McGoldrick, J. Giordano & J. K. Pierce (Eds.), *Ethnicity and Family Therapy*, 339–342. New York: Guilford Press.

[13] Tsemberis, Sam J. & Spyros D. Orfanos, (1996). "Greek families." In M. McGoldrick, J. Giordano J. K. Pierce (Eds.), *Ethnicity and Family Therapy*, 519–523. New York: Guilford Press.

[14] McGill, David W. & John K. Pearce, (1996). "American families with English ancestors from the colonial era: Anglo Americans." In M. McGoldrick, J. Giordano & J. K. Pierce (Eds.), *Ethnicity and Family Therapy*, 451–457. New York: Guilford Press.

[15] Bagarozzi, C. & S. A. Anderson (1989). *Personal, Marital and Family Myths: Theoretical Formulations and Clinical Strategies*, 51. New York: W. W. Norton.

[16] Rosen, Elliott J. & Susan F. Weltman (1996). "Jewish families: An overview." In M. McGoldrick, J. Giordano & J. K. Pierce (Eds.), *Ethnicity and Family Therapy*, 611–622. New York: Guilford Press.

[17] Matthew 4:7ff.

[18] Matthew 19:8–9

[19] Psalm 116:6

[20] Ecclesiastes 12:13

[21] I Corinthians 7:14

[22] I Corinthians 7:33

[23] Ephesians 5:22–33

[24] II Peter 1:4

[25] Patz, Aviva (2000). "A new quiz reveals that the newlywed years can predict the long-term outcome of almost every marriage." *Psychology Today*, April 23, 2000. Retrieved March 24, 2006 from http://www.divorceform.org/mel/apredicsuccess.html.

[26] Sprecher, Susan (1999). "I love you more today than yesterday: Romantic partners' perceptions of changes in love and related affect over time." *Journal of Personality and Social Psychology*, vol. 76, no. 1. Retrieved from http://divorceform.org/mel/aloveincrease.html.

[27] Blanc, Tara (1994). "Marriage mythology." *ASU Research Magazine*, Spring/Summer 1994. Retrieved from http://www.apa.org/journals/psp/Psp76146.html.

[28] Epstein, Norman B., Fuguo Chen & Irina Beyder-Kamjou (2005). "Satisfaction in Chinese and American couples." *Journal of Marital and Family Therapy*, January, 2005. Retrieved from http://www.findarticles.com/p/articles/mi_qa3658/is_200501/ai_n9520945.

[29] Matthew 5:1–12

[30] Achbar, Mark & Jennifer Abbott (2004). *The Corporation*. DVD. Produced by Zeitgeist Film.

## CHAPTER 5

[1] Matthew 13:3–8

[2] Matthew 8:23–27

[3] Nye, F. Ivan (1979). "Choice, exchange, and the family." In W. R. Burr, R. Hill, F. I. Nye & I. L. Reiss (Eds.), *Contemporary Theories About the Family*, vol. 2, 1–2. New York: Free Press.

[4] Ibid., 4–5.

[5] John 12:24–25

[6] Warren, Rick (2002). *The Purpose Driven Life: What on Earth Am I Here For?* 18. Grand Rapids, MI: Zondervan.

[7] Sternberg, Robert J. (2006). Retrieved March 24, 2006 from the homepage of Robert J. Sternberg at http://www.yale.edu/rjsternberg/.

[8] Ecclesiastes 9:9

[9] John 5:20

[10] I John 4:10 (NIV)

[11] Matthew 7:2 (NIV)

[12] I Samuel 16:7

[13] Romans 8:35–39

## CHAPTER 6

[1] Phillippians 4:8

[2] Romans 12:2

[3] Ephesians 4:22–24

[4] James 1:22–23

[5] I Corinthians 14:33

[6] Mark 12:30–31

[7] I John 4:19

[8] I Corinthians 13:2–8

[9] John 15:5

## CHAPTER 7

[1] Matthew 10:39

[2] Renaud, Trisha (2002). "Flaming pop-tarts spark Georgia suit." Retrieved December 1, 2006 from http://www.law.com/jsp/article.jsp?id=1032128880031.

[3] *Philadelphia Inquirer* (May 2, 2001). "Teen sues over bad coaching." Retrieved December 1, 2006 from http://www.calahouston.org/best01.html.

[4] *Toledo (Ohio) Blade* (May 22, 2002). "Inmate sues hospital where he raped a patient." Retrieved December 1, 2006 from http://www.calahouston.org/best02.html.

[5] *Fort Worth Star-Telegram* (November 21, 2002). "Lawyers claim Big Macs make kids fat." Retrieved December 1, 2006 from http://www.calahouston.org/best02.html.

[6] Matthew 5:39

[7] Huitt, W. (2004). "Maslow's hierarchy of needs." *Educational Psychology Interactive*. Valdosta, GA: Valdosta State University. Retrieved from http://chiron.valdosta.edu/whuitt/col/regsys/maslow.html.

[8] I John 4:10

9 Ephesians 4:22–4
10 Galatians 6:2
11 Phillippians 2:4
12 Matthew 20:28
13 Matthew 10:8
14 I Corinthians 5:6
15 Phillippians 3:12
16 Genesis 22:1–12

## CHAPTER 8

1 Gibbon, Peter H. (2002). "Making the case for heroes." *Harvard Education Letter*, July/August 2002. Retrieved December 1, 2006 from http://www.edletter.org/past/issues/2002–ja/heroes.shtml.
2 Ecclesiastes 4:11
3 Taflinger, Richard F. (1996). *You and Me, Babe: Sex and Advertising*. Retrieved December 1, 2006 from http://www.wsu.edu:8080/~taflinge/sex.html.
4 Spurgeon, Charles Hadden (somewhere between 1834–1892). *Gleanings Among the Sheaves*. Retrieved December 1, 2006 from http://www.worldofquotes.com/author/Charles-Hadden-Spurgeon/1/index.html.
5 Temple, William. Retrieved December 1, 2006 from http://www.quotegarden.com/humility.html.
6 I John 2:16
7 James 4:15–16
8 James 1:17
9 Colossians 3:10–14
10 Romans 12:16
11 Matthew 5:5
12 James 4:6
13 Ephesians 5:21
14 Romans 12:10
15 Philippians 2:3
16 James 1:19
17 Romans 15:7
18 Romans 15:1
19 Matthew 5:44
20 Romans 12:21
21 Matthew 18:4
22 Galatians 5:13
23 Phillippians 3:4
24 Romans 1:25
25 Galatians 5:22–23

## CHAPTER 9

1 Haley, Alex (2006). *The shadowland of dreams*. Retrieved March 24, 2006 from http://www.serve.com/davidchew/cgi-bin/truestory/story.cgi?fselect=story0032.
2 Luke 14:28–30
3 I Corinthians 13:6
4 Matthew 5:6
5 Matthew 6:33
6 James 1:18
7 John 1:1–2
8 Jeremiah 22:13–16
9 James 1:6–8
10 Psalm 55:22

[11] Psalm 37:5
[12] Matthew 18:21–22
[13] Matthew 22:16
[14] Jeremiah 7:9
[15] Romans 12:12
[16] John 8:32

## CHAPTER 10

[1] James 3:5
[2] I Corinthians 13:7
[3] Superior Broadcast Network (2006). *Heimo Korth and his family: Alone in Alaska's arctic wilderness*. Retrieved March 24, 2006 from http://www. Superiorbroadcast.org/Hiemokorth.htm.
[4] Hebrews 11:15–40
[5] Psalm 111:3
[6] Matthew 24:12–13
[7] Romans 8:25
[8] I John 4:8
[9] Romans 5:3–5
[10] James 1:4
[11] Romans 15:7
[12] Matthew 7:1–3
[13] Hebrews 12:28
[14] James 4:8
[15] Hebrews 13:8
[16] Hebrews 12:9–11
[17] II Corinthians 12:10

## CHAPTER 11

[1] Matthew 6:27
[2] Matthew 6:34
[3] Proverbs 27:1
[4] Derogotis, L. R. (1982). "Self-report measures of stress." In L. Goldberger & S. Breznitz (Eds.), *Handbook of Stress: Theoretical and Clinical Aspects*, 278. New York: Macmillan.
[5] McCubbin, H. I. & J. M. Patterson (1983). Family transitions: Adaptation to stress. In H. I. McCubbin & C. R. Figley (Eds.), *Stress and the Family: Coping with Normative Transitions*, 5–25. New York: Brunner/Mazel.
[6] II Corinthians 13:5
[7] Selye, H. (1982). "History and present status of the stress concept." In L. Goldberger & S. Breznitz (Eds.), *Handbook of Stress*, 10.
[8] Ibid.
[9] I Peter 2:9
[10] Ecclesiastes 3:11
[11] Romans 12:19
[12] Keirsey, David & Marilyn Bates (1984). *Please Understand Me: Character and Temperament Types*, 3. Del Mar, CA: Prometheus Nemesis Book Co.
[13] Ibid., 13–26.
[14] Thomas, Volker & Timothy Ozechowski (2000). "A test of the circumplex model of marital and family systems using the clinical rating scale." *Journal of Marital and Family Therapy*, October 2000. Retrieved March 24, 2006 from http://www.findarticles.com/p/articles/mi_qa3658/is_200010/ai_n8913038.
[15] Figley, C. R. (1983). "Catastrophes: An overview of family reactions." In C. R. Figley & H. I. McCubbin (Eds.), *Stress and the Family*, 3–20. New York: Brunner/Mazel.

[16] Ibid.

[17] Everstine, D. S. & L. Everstine (1983). *People in Crisis: Strategic Therapeutic Interventions*, 20, 45–47. New York: Brunner/Mazel.

[18] Melson, G. F. (1983). "Family adaptation to environmental demands." In H. I. McCubbin & C. R. Figley (Eds.), *Stress and the Family*, 154. New York: Brunner/Mazel.

[19] II Corinthians 4:16–18

## CHAPTER 12

[1] Matthew 5:9

[2] Hebrews 12:15

[3] Stuart, R. B. (1980). *Helping Couples Change*, 22. New York: Guilford Press.

[4] Acts 20:35

[5] de Shazer, Stève. *The miracle question*. Retrieved March 10, 2006 from http://www.brief-therapy.org/steve_miracle.htm.

[6] Stuart, R. B. (1980). *Helping Couples Change*, 198–208.

[7] Fisch, R., J. H. Weakland & L. Segal (1982). *The Tactics of Change: Doing Therapy Briefly*, 131, 159–162. San Francisco: Jessey-Bass.

[8] Lazarus, A. (1984). *In the Mind's Eye: The Power of Imagery for Personal Enrichment*, 17. New York: Guilford Press.

[9] Meichenbaum, D. (1985). *Stress Innoculation Training*, 76. New York: Pergamon Press.

[10] Fisch, R., J. H. Weakland & L. Segal (1982). *The Tactics of Change*, 131, 159–162.

[11] de Shazer, S. (1985). *Keys to Solution in Brief Therapy*, 34, 137–139. New York: W. W. Norton.

[12] Yapko, M. D. (1992). *Hypnosis and the Treatment of Depressions: Strategies for Change*, 129–130. New York: Brunner/Mazel.

[13] Lankton, S. R. & C. H. Lankton (1983). *The Answer Within: A Clinical Framework of Ericksonian Hypnotherapy*, 11–27. New York: Brunner/Mazel.

## CHAPTER 13

[1] James 3:2–8

[2] Proverbs 15:4

[3] Sieburg, E. (1985). *Family Communication: An Integrated Systems Approach*, 55. New York: Gardner Press.

[4] Matthew 18:21–22

[5] Miller, S., E. W. Nunnally & D. B. Wackman (1984). *Couple Communication I: Talking Together*, 38–41. Minneapolis: Interpersonal Communication Programs.

[6] Proverbs 25:28

[7] II Corinthians 5:14

[8] I Corinthians 13:5

[9] Ecclesiastes 7:9

[10] Proverbs 16:32

[11] Sieburg, E. (1985). *Family Communication* 56. New York: Gardner Press.

[12] Ibid.

## CHAPTER 14

[1] James 1:19

[2] Colossians 4:6

[3] Romans 12:3

[4] Burns, David D. (1980). *Feeling Good: The New Mood Therapy*, 64. New York: Signet.

[5] Goodman, G. & G. Esterly (1988). *The Talk Book: The Intimate Science of Communicating in Close Relationships*, 113–114. Emmaus, PA: Rodale Press.

[6] Matthew 13:13

[7] Gottman, J., C. Notarius, J. Gonso & H. Markman (1976). *A Couple's Guide to Communication*, 16–18. Champaign, IL: Research Press.

## CHAPTER 15

[1] Romans 2:5
[2] Ephesians 4:26
[3] I Corinthians 13:11
[4] Broderick, C. & J. Smith (1979). "The general systems approach to the family." In W. R. Burr, R. Hill, F. I. Nye & I. L. Reiss (Eds.), *Contemporary Theories About the Family: General Theories/ Theoretical Orientations*, 114–123. New York: Macmillan.
[5] Bagarozzi, D. A. & S. A. Anderson (1989). *Personal, Marital and Family Myths: Theoretical Formulations and Clinical Strategies*, 15–41. New York: W. W. Norton.
[6] Romans 12:2
[7] Hardy, K. V. & T. A. Laszloffy (1995). "The cultural genogram: Key to training culturally competent family therapists." *Journal of Marital and Family Therapy 21*, 239–250.
[8] McGoldrick, Monica & Randy Gerson (1985). *Genograms in Family Assessment*, 1–7. New York: W. W. Norton.
[9] Kuehl, B. P. (1995). The solution-oriented genogram: A collaborative approach. *Journal of Marital and Family Therapy 21*, 239–250.
[10] Marlatt, G. A. (1985). "Situational determinants of relapse and skill-training interventions." In G. A. Marlatt & J. R. Gordon (Eds.), *Relapse Prevention: Maintenance Strategies in the Treatment of Addictive Behaviors*, 74. New York: The Guilford Press.
[11] Anderson, C. M. & S. Stewart (1983). *Mastering Resistance: A Practical Guide to Family Therapy*, 165–206. New York: Guilford Press.
[12] Pillari, V. (1991). *Scapegoating in Families: Intergenerational Patterns of Physical and Emotional Abuse*, 1–38. New York: Brunner/Mazel.

## CHAPTER 16

[1] John 13:35

# INDEX

343

# ABOUT THE AUTHOR

JOHN T. ECKENWILER has been a licensed marriage and family therapist since 1985. He has a master's degree in marriage and family therapy from Abilene Christian University. John is a clinical member and approved supervisor with the American Association for Marriage and Family Therapy (AAMFT). He has worked with a wide range of clinical issues in many different settings, from hospitals to community mental health centers, and has been in private practice for most of those years. One of the formative experiences he had was while working with cancer patients in a general hospital. Seeing the different responses to life and death, John began to see the interconnection between spiritual outlook, general attitude, personal character, and marital/family relationships. He now integrates these into his work with couples. His work—and this book—is the result of this unique insight. John has been married since 1974 and has two grown children.